A CULTURAL HISTORY
OF FOOD

VOLUME 2

A Cultural History of Food

General Editors: Fabio Parasecoli and Peter Scholliers

Volume 1
A Cultural History of Food in Antiquity
Edited by Paul Erdkamp

Volume 2
A Cultural History of Food in the Medieval Age
Edited by Massimo Montanari

Volume 3
A Cultural History of Food in the Renaissance
Edited by Ken Albala

Volume 4
A Cultural History of Food in the Early Modern Age
Edited by Beat Kümin

Volume 5
A Cultural History of Food in the Age of Empire
Edited by Martin Bruegel

Volume 6
A Cultural History of Food in the Modern Age
Edited by Amy Bentley

A CULTURAL HISTORY
OF FOOD

IN THE
MEDIEVAL AGE

VOLUME 2

Edited by Massimo Montanari

Bloomsbury Academic
An imprint of Bloomsbury Publishing Plc

B L O O M S B U R Y
LONDON · OXFORD · NEW YORK · NEW DELHI · SYDNEY

Bloomsbury Academic
An imprint of Bloomsbury Publishing Plc

50 Bedford Square	1385 Broadway
London	New York
WC1B 3DP	NY 10018
UK	USA

www.bloomsbury.com

BLOOMSBURY and the Diana logo are trademarks of
Bloomsbury Publishing Plc

Hardback edition first published in 2012 by Berg Publishers,
an imprint of Bloomsbury Academic
Paperback edition first published in 2016 by Bloomsbury Academic

British Library Cataloguing-in-Publication Data
A catalogue record for this book is available from the British Library.

ISBN: HB:	978-0-8578-5024-9
HB set:	978-1-8478-8355-1
PB:	978-1-4742-6991-9
PB set:	978-1-4742-7075-5

Library of Congress Cataloging-in-Publication Data
A catalog record for this book is available from the Library of Congress.

Typeset by Apex CoVantage, LLC

CONTENTS

SERIES PREFACE

GENERAL EDITORS, FABIO PARASECOLI
AND PETER SCHOLLIERS

A Cultural History of Food presents an authoritative survey from ancient times to the present. This set of six volumes covers nearly 3,000 years of food and its physical, spiritual, social, and cultural dimensions. Volume editors and authors, representing different nationalities and cultural traditions, constitute the cutting edge in historical research on food and offer an overview of the field that reflects the state of the art of the discipline. While the volumes focus mostly on the West (Europe in its broadest sense and North America), they also draw in comparative material and each volume concludes with a brief final chapter on contemporaneous developments in food ideas and practices outside the West. These works will contribute to the expansion of the food history research in Asia, Africa, Oceania, and South America, which is already growing at an increasingly fast pace.

The six volumes, which follow the traditional approach to examining the past in Western cultures, divide the history of food as follows:

Volume 1: A Cultural History of Food in Antiquity (800 BCE–500 CE)
Volume 2: A Cultural History of Food in the Medieval Age (500–1300)
Volume 3: A Cultural History of Food in the Renaissance (1300–1600)
Volume 4: A Cultural History of Food in the Early Modern Age (1600–1800)
Volume 5: A Cultural History of Food in the Age of Empire (1800–1900)
Volume 6: A Cultural History of Food in the Modern Age (1920–2000)

This periodization does not necessarily reflect the realities and the historical dynamics of non-Western regions, but the relevance of cultural and material exchanges among different civilizations in each period is emphasized.
Each volume discusses the same themes in its chapters:

1. *Food Production*. These chapters examine agriculture, husbandry,
   fishing, hunting, and foraging at any given period, considering the
   environmental impact of technological and social innovations, and
   the adaptation to the climate and environment changes.
2. *Food Systems*. These chapters explore the whole range of the transportation, distribution, marketing, advertising, and retailing of food,
   emphasizing trade, commerce, and the international routes that have
   crisscrossed the world since antiquity.
3. *Food Security, Safety, and Crises*. We cannot have a complete picture
   of the history of food without discussing how societies dealt with
   moments of crisis and disruption of food production and distribution, such as wars, famines, shortages, and epidemics. These essays
   reflect on the cultural, institutional, economic, and social ways of
   coping with such crises.
4. *Food and Politics*. These chapters focus on the political aspects of
   public food consumption: food aspects of public ceremonies and
   feasts, the impact on public life, regulations, controls, and taxation
   over food and alcohol production, exchange, and consumption.
5. *Eating Out*. The communal and public aspects of eating constitute
   the main focus of these essays. Authors consider hospitality for
   guests, at home and in public spaces (banquets and celebrations),
   and discuss public places to eat and drink in urban and rural environments, including street food, marketplaces, and fairs.
6. *Professional Cooking, Kitchens, and Service Work*. These chapters look at the various roles involved in food preparation outside
   the family nucleus: slaves, cooks, servants, waiters, *maitre d'hotel*
   etc., investigating also the most relevant cooking techniques, technologies, and tools for each period, giving special consideration to
   innovations.
7. *Family and Domesticity*. The acquisition, shopping and storage,
   preparation, consumption, and disposal of food in a domestic setting

are among the most important aspects of food culture. These chapters analyze family habits in different periods of time, paying particular attention to gender roles and the material culture of the domestic kitchen.

8. *Body and Soul*. These chapters examine fundamental material aspects such as nutritional patterns, food constituents, and food-related diseases. Furthermore, spiritual and cultural aspects of thinking about and consuming food are highlighted, including religion, philosophy, as well as health and diet theories.

9. *Food Representations*. These essays analyze cultural and discursive reflections about food, which not only contributed to the way people conceive of food, but also to the social and geographical diffusion of techniques and behavior.

10. *World Developments*. These brief chapters overview developments, dynamics, products, food-related behaviors, social structures, and concepts in cultural environments that often found themselves at the margins of Western modernity.

Rather than embracing the encyclopedic model, the authors apply a broad multidisciplinary framework to examine the production, distribution, and consumption of food, as grounded in the cultural experiences of the six historical periods. This structure allows readers to obtain a broad overview of a period by reading a volume, or to follow a theme through history by reading the relevant chapter in each volume.

Highly illustrated, the full six-volume set combines to present the most authoritative and comprehensive survey available on food through history.

Introduction

MASSIMO MONTANARI

Translated by Leah Ashe

WHEN EUROPEAN (FOOD) CULTURE WAS BORN

The Middle Ages are a time of special importance in the history of European food culture, because of the simple fact that Europe was *born* during this period, a new entity that was cultural even before it was political. The transformation was a radical one, a veritable metamorphosis that created an entirely new set of geo-cultural identities. On the one hand, it reconstructed the Mediterranean, a factor that had earlier resolutely established the commonality and unity of the Greco-Roman world, by introducing new and important differences that distinguished the northern coast from the southern one. At the same time, it linked the northern part of that world to a new cultural horizon, one defined largely by the populations beyond its northern and eastern borders. Via this double operation of addition and subtraction, Europe took shape.

The Roman Empire, like Greek society before it, defined its cultural characteristics around the Mediterranean, the great *lake* that standardized (or at least bound together) customs and lifestyles, tastes and practices, celebrating a robust exchange of men, merchandise, and ideas from one province to the next, from one shore of *mare nostrum* (*our sea* in Latin) to the other. The sudden entry into that world of those the Romans called barbarians—comprising a mixture of ethnic groups, but for the most part all of German stock—signaled not only the end of the Roman Empire in the west, but also a crisis for its very model of civilization. The Romans, building on the vestiges of Greek traditions that they inherited, had built that model around ideas of the *city* and of *agriculture,* complementary concepts (agriculture understood as the way to feed those living in the city) that symbolized the desire of civilized man to free himself from his wild state by adopting artificial—that is, *man-made*—constructs in which to live, work, and produce that which did not exist in nature.[1] Bread, wine, and olive oil, the triad at the base of the Greek and Roman dietary models, symbolized an ideological construction that contrasted culture and nature as positive and negative values, respectively. Those with different lifestyles (that is, those who used means of production and had consumption habits not based on agriculture) were, for that reason alone, *barbarians.* Thus, Greek and Latin scribes were scandalized—or perhaps amused—at the central dietary role that Germanic peoples gave to meat and animal fat, milk and butter, wild fruits—in other words, to the resources of the forest, used for the wild grazing of animals, hunting, and gathering.[2] To be clear, such activities were important for everyone on an economic front, even for the Romans; but the Romans tended, in a way, to hide these aspects of their culture, to exclude them from the contexts of positive values and imagery.

Then, the unthinkable happened. The barbarians penetrated the borders of the Empire little by little, subjugating many of its provinces and becoming (in the fifth century) the new ruling order. Their culture and their customs took hold—as those of the winners invariably do—and challenged the values that defined what it meant to be Roman. It was a conflict that was a veritable ideological war[3]: the culture of bread and wine, of agriculture and the city, bitterly pitted itself (so strong was the symbolic value that these held for those nostalgic for the old regime) against the exaltation of meat and wild foods, against a culture that put the forest at the crux of daily matters rather than excluding it—as the older tradition had—from the predominant value system.

Nonetheless, with the passing of time, the conflict weakened and, though not disappearing entirely, gave way to a process of integration that changed both cultures. A progressive symbiosis between the two opposing models, a spectacular phenomenon of acculturation—to use the language

of anthropology—ultimately created new models of production and eating.[4] The culture of the new rulers took hold and spread, but it blended
with the enduring allure of the Roman culture, transmitted and promoted,
in turn, via the practice of Christianity, which, with regard to dietary models as well as in many other matters, evolved as the witness and heir to the
Roman culture. Bread, wine, and oil, invoked in the Christian liturgy as
fundamental instruments of worship (bread and wine for the celebration
of the Eucharist, oil for the celebration of other Sacraments), assumed a
symbolic force that re-asserted their ideological—and economic—centrality
with even greater decisiveness. This stood in sharp contrast to the centrality that meat had *also* begun to have in the symbolic and economic system
of the society that emerged from the period of the invasions. The result
was a new dietary model, neither Roman nor Germanic, but Roman *and*
Germanic—or, more accurately, Roman-*Christian* and Germanic.

Even ecclesiastic regulations regarding dietary behavior helped to standardize the new consumption models of the Europeans.[5] The Church required the faithful to abstain from meat and animal fats for quite a number
of days each year: during Lent (the forty-day period preceding Easter); on
certain weekdays (which differed according to local custom); on the vigils
of the main holy days; and at various other times throughout the year.
Altogether, more than one in every three days were days of fasting and
forced the faithful to turn to vegetable fats (olive oil and other substitute
oils) and other so-called lean or fasting foods (fish and vegetables, and
in some cases also eggs and dairy products). However, at the same time,
this implicitly confirmed the role of meat and animal products as the normal, daily foundation of the diet. It also strengthened the idea that holy
days and celebrations (Sundays, Saints' anniversaries, Christmas, Easter,
and so on) in fact *required* meat. Whether it is present or absent (often
substituted), meat is always the protagonist in the public banquets that in
medieval Europe constitute an essential element of social life and commu-
nication (see chapter 5 by Alban Gautier in this volume).

All this, while not eliminating the differences in traditions and tastes that
existed between one region of Continental Europe and the next, created a
certain uniformity with regard to food customs by forcing all Christians
to *alternate* the use of animal- and plant-based products at their home
tables. Consumption models that had, up to that point, been antithetical or

mutually exclusive now constituted part of a unitary system; a single, homogenous food culture. Bread and meat—food of the land and food from the animal world—waged a daily fight for supremacy, but ultimately, even with considerable tensions, managed to share the alimentary space and give to each component its moments of glory.

The symbiosis between different economies and cultures yielded a unique combination: an agro–forestal–pastoral production model that is likely the single most characteristic feature of European food consumption during the first millennium. *Terra et silva,* "cultivated lands and forests," appear inevitably as a pair in documents describing the assets of landowners and estates, no matter how large or small.[6] The systematic mixing of different landscapes and resources attests to a food regimen which was not always secure—hunger was a common affliction during these centuries, as Giuliano Pinto explains in this volume—but which nonetheless found its strength in variety. The fruits of the land (grains, legumes, vegetables) are frequently integrated with those offered by the *wild* (game, fish, animals raised in the forests and clearings).

Not everyone ate the same: abundance was a privilege of the few and, precisely because of this, eating in large quantities was one of the main signs of prestige and power—a fundamental symbol of *difference*—during the Early Middle Ages. This does not take away from the fact that all social classes enjoyed a broad spectrum of resources and, in particular, the regular inclusion in their diets of animal products (meat, fat, and dairy) as well as vegetable products. This is a point that merits emphasizing, because it is something quite atypical—truly anomalous—relative to all other periods in the history of food. European peasants of the period enjoyed a diet that was certainly better balanced than that of other periods, both earlier and later, characterized instead by the massive predominance of grains and the overwhelming scarcity of animal products. This did not eliminate the risks and difficulties of a time marked by severe natural and social scourges, but it did constitute a real help in meeting the challenge of daily survival.

During the centuries in which the outlines of European civilization were being defined, a new political-religious power took hold of the southern shores of the Mediterranean: Islam, the bearer of different cultural and food models that were, at least in part, in conflict with European ones. At the beginning of the seventh century, the Mediterranean was no longer a sort of internal lake, as it had been for centuries, but became instead a boundary sea.⁷ Afterwards, and in part as a result, European culture (including its food culture) began to assume a new identity, one leaning more toward the centre of the continent than toward the old *mare nostrum*.⁸

The religious, political, and military clash between Christian Europe and Islam easily found its dietary symbols. The religion of bread and wine could not help but strongly oppose itself to a world that had forbidden the very consumption of wine, and, though familiar with bread, used grains primarily to make flat breads, pasta, and couscous (and in any case, certainly did not endow bread with the sacred connotations that Christianity did). Another fundamental difference was the exclusion of pork—a primary resource in the European forest economy—from the Islamic table, and precisely at the moment that it was assuming an absolute centrality in the food customs of Christian Europe.

Paradoxically, on the northern shores of the Mediterranean the contrast with the new Islamic civilization allowed food and food-related values with very different geographic and cultural origins to become European—in fact, *above all else*, European. Bread and wine, old symbols of the Mediterranean civilization, transferred their identities to the Continent, so much so that even today a search for the culture of bread and wine will lead most obviously to Europe—not to the areas of the Fertile Crescent where it in fact began. The image of pork was reinforced, too: while once it had been the alimentary symbol of northern Europe, it became, during the Middle Ages, the meat *par excellence* of the Europeans, even in the Mediterranean regions: the cultures of *prosciutto* and *jamón*—cured hams—that developed in Italy and Spain constitute a perfect example of these dynamics.

The relationship between European and Islamic food cultures, however, was not simply one of opposition and reciprocal otherness. Despite the differences—which in fact served to better define a European identity—the boundary between Europe and Islam established itself from the beginning as a fertile area of exchange. Largely via Spain and Sicily, the two primary channels for interaction, the Arabs introduced new products and new flavors to Europe.⁹ It was the Arabs who brought to the Western world two elements that would come to play important roles in European food during the centuries to follow, altering, at least in part, the most basic flavors of its cuisines: citrus fruits (bitter oranges, lemons, citrons) and cane sugar.

The sweet-and-sour flavor that the Romans had attained by mixing honey with vinegar now assumed more delicate tones in the combination of citrus and sugar. Other products introduced by the Arabs included eggplants, artichokes, and spinach, and even the production of almonds increased. But there were imports that turned out to be even more important. One was rice, which spread throughout Sicily and Spain. The other was pasta, which the Romans had in fact used in a wide, flat form similar to *lasagna* but which became an authentic category of food in its full variety of forms (thick, thin, short, long, hollow, stuffed) only during the Middle Ages. The Middle Ages also brought—thanks to the contributions of the Arabs and Jews—the Middle Eastern technique of drying pasta, thus preserving it for long periods of time and making it possible to trade over long distances. The practice of drying pasta is documented in Europe from the beginning of the eleventh and twelfth centuries, and it is in Arab-influenced Sicily that we find the first industry dedicated to producing dry pasta for export.[10]

At least through the eleventh century—until the beginning of the Crusades—the Arabs continued to act as the critical bridge in linking Europe and the East in trade. They were also important in spreading and strengthening the role of spices, which, though not entirely new, would become one of the most characteristic features of medieval European cuisine.[11] Starting from the period of the Crusades, European merchants directly acquired their spices on the Asian markets, managing trade connections between East and West. However, these exchanges had existed for centuries thanks to the Arabic mediation, which represented a powerful factor in the development and the renewal of western European cuisine. At the same time the Roman model survived—faithful to its past but also stuck in time—in the areas dominated by the Byzantine Empire, which were more directly connected to the ancient culture and traditions.

Around the year 1000, as a consequence of all this, Europe had developed a common—but not uniform—food culture. The attempts of Charlemagne and his successors to politically and culturally standardize Europe (on the political aspects of medieval food history, see chapter 4 by Jean-Pierre Devroey in this volume) did not survive beyond the collapse of the Carolingian Empire at the end of the ninth century; and in any case, those attempts were limited largely toward ordering and coordinating a collection of diverse traditions rather than eradicating them entirely. The same complexity inherent in the new model of production and eating that blended the agrarian and forest economies created the possibility for countless local variants tied to specific environmental resources, territorial characteristics, technological know-how, traditional forms of knowledge, and, not least of all, taste. A Europe of wine, bordering the Mediterranean, still contrasted a Europe of beer in the center and north of the Continent (although the wine border reached more to the north than it does nowadays), and niches of cider consumers remained in certain traditionally Celtic zones such as Brittany and England. These regional characteristics have survived, to some extent, into the present day, as have other basic contrasts between Roman Europe and Germanic Europe. Bread, which had become the food par excellence of the Europeans during the Middle Ages, has thus played different roles in different regions. The Mediterranean countries have considered bread as a food of daily sustenance ever since the classical era, unequivocally part of every meal—so much so that in every house, as in every restaurant and canteen, it is still brought to the table along with dishes and silverware, much as part of the table setting. In northern parts of Europe, on the other hand, diners must ask for bread, just as they must ask for any other food. The notion of *companatico,* the foods eaten *along with bread*—that is, the idea that bread is the basis of the meal that everything else *goes with*—is not at all universal. Rather it is limited—even in language—to the countries and cultures most closely related with the Roman tradition. Similarly, Arab influences, though evident in the culinary traditions of Europe in its entirety, remain strongest in the Mediterranean countries that had established the closest relationships with Islam, or where they ruled for a long time; for example, the Sicilian and Spanish gastronomies emerge as those most strongly characterized (today, as in the Middle Ages) by a sweetness linked originally to the cultivation of cane sugar in these areas of Arab occupation.

The taste for meat—along with its level of consumption—also varied from one region of Europe to the next. Pigs, sheep, and cows were not appreciated everywhere in the same way, due, here too, to a complex confluence of factors. Part of the explanation is simply economic, linked to geography, soil, and climate: the oak forests where pigs were traditionally left to graze characterized much of the European landscape, but in certain zones of both northern and southern Europe, grassy pastures, where sheep and ox were raised (almost exclusively sheep, until the fourteenth and fifteenth centuries; then also ox), were predominant. Other reasons are more cultural than economic: the culture of the pig played a decisive role in the Germanic tradition (and even before that, for Celtic populations), while the sheep was the animal par excellence for Romans. Political and institutional events also contributed to regional customs: in Italy, for example, there is still today a pronounced preference for sheep's meat in the areas exempted from Germanic penetration during the Middle Ages (or that went through it later, or more marginally), while the pig rooted itself more firmly—perhaps building upon previous, autochthonous traditions—where the Germanic conquerors arrived and managed to bring and spread their own food culture.[12]

None of this takes away from the fact that the most significant event to happen in Europe during the Middle Ages was the construction of a common frame of reference, of a new food geography, inside of which differences were softened but not erased. Precisely this phenomenon—the construction of an identity made from a plurality of contributions that mixed without mutually eliminating each other and ultimately enriched the cultural heritage of each one—is the key to understanding the extraordinary variety within European gastronomic culture and its enormous capacity for invention and innovation. In this way, Europe developed during the first millennium what would become its most notable gastronomic characteristic, that taste for diversity, borne of a very real—and still persistent—diversity of taste.[13]

FROM CULTURAL DIFFERENCES
TO SOCIAL DISTINCTIONS

With the passing of time, intensified social contrasts emerged within the European food system, establishing profoundly different models of food consumption and behavior. This *social* characterization of the food system during the final centuries of the Middle Ages is perhaps the era's most evident trait in the eyes of the historian. In some ways, this characterization seems to have re-invoked older contrasts, such as that between meat and bread and between animal- and plant-based foods more generally. However, while in the past these contrasts differentiated two separate food civilizations (Roman and barbarian) they now assumed a very new meaning, with both sides of the contrast falling within the same social and cultural structure.[14]

The sharp demographic growth that began to mark European society beginning in the tenth and eleventh centuries brought, as an inevitable consequence, the expansion of cultivated lands and the destruction of forests. The productive system of the Middle Ages was, in fact, based upon the double foundation of the agrarian and the forest-pastoral economies. Yet this did not necessarily imply a true *integration* of these two systems: agriculture and herding co-existed everywhere but remained in physically separate spaces. Animals left their manure in the forests—wasting it, so to speak—and, primarily for this reason, as well as for the shortage of work animals and effective iron tools, the productivity of agricultural lands remained extremely low.[15] Given the space-extensive nature of agriculture, it fell inherently into competition with the pastoral sector of the economy: if one wanted to produce more grain, there was not any other choice but to expand the area dedicated to its cultivation and, in doing so, to eliminate pastures and forests. And since fields of grain—even with the outlandishly low levels of productivity that characterized the era—could produce more food than the forest could, the population growth of the period could not help but encourage agricultural development at the expense of the forest-pastoral economy (this phenomenon is explained in detail in chapter 1 by Alfio Cortonesi in this volume). From the food point of view, this meant that the diet of European peasants became ever more focused on grains—and ever more monotonous.[16]

Throughout Europe, north and south, the conquest of the land via an assault on the forest was the first response to hunger for a growing population's need for food. However, there were other reasons for deforestation. Often it was the upper class—noblemen, clerics, princes, and urban residents with rural landholdings—that advocated for cultivation of the land in order to increase the profitability of their holdings and to amass stocks (grains, mostly) that could be sold on the market. Sometimes peasants, connected as they were to the old ways, to the traditional economy of the forest and grazing, resisted these pressures. Nevertheless, the powerful got what they wanted, and most of all, precisely in those contexts where their interests met—and sometimes clashed sharply—with the hunger of the peasants.

It was an explosive coincidence of interests that, between the eleventh and thirteenth centuries, changed the physical face of the European landscape. Entire regions were marked by this pioneering epic (something of a *far west* in the heart of Europe), which for some time continued to bring newfound prosperity to the poor and newfound profits to the rich. Most frequently the advances were small ones, a cautious but continuous erosion of the old economic and dietary models.[17]

The erosion of the forest—or in some cases, its complete destruction—was not the only result of the general agronomization of the economy. In high hill and low mountain zones, where it would have been difficult to plant new terrains, the forest itself was transformed, domesticated, and put to use for cultivating crops. In many parts of Europe, especially in southern and central regions, this era saw the widest propagation of the chestnut, bred from wild species and planted, oftentimes, in place of old oak forests.[18] As an economic and dietary choice, this phenomenon was entirely analogous to the expansion of cultivated lands: the ways chestnuts were used mimicked the ways grains were used, and they were a perfect equivalent in the technical sense, if not in taste. During the height of the Middle Ages, many mountain zones developed a poor cuisine that used chestnut flour (along with flours made from legumes and the inferior grains) to produce polenta, flatbreads, fritters, and cakes—all kinds of preparations, both sweet and savory. The chestnut tree thus earned the moniker, then as now, of the bread tree.

The reduction in uncultivated land, driven by demographic growth and economic interests, might not have been sufficient to radically change the dietary regime of European peasants if it had not overlapped with a change in the social and legal orders, also profoundly linked to the transformation of the territory (along with many other matters, of course). While forests shrunk, they remained, in many cases, a persistent realty; and in some regions of Europe, they still are today. But everywhere, the traditional rights to use them—which peasants had enjoyed through ancient custom—became more and more restrictive.

As forest area decreased, the competition for its use grew.[19] Previously unknown tensions led to new privileges associated with the exercise of power: in different ways, more or less rigid according to the situation, the use of forest resources became a privilege restricted to the most powerful social groups. In countries with a centralized monarchic power, such as France or (even more so) England, control and use of the forest remained concentrated in the hands of the king and his aristocracy. Elsewhere, local powers claimed the best of the forest: lords, bishops, abbots, and even urban communities in regions of north-central Italy, where cities emerged as the cornerstones of political organization.

The multiplication of forest reserves set aside for the exclusive use of sovereigns, noblemen, clerics, and cities led to angst and protest in the peasant world. The limitations to hunting and pasturing rights threw the old social, economic, and dietary balance into crisis.[20] Only in marginal areas (the mountain and low-plain ones) did rural communities succeed in defending their rights of access. Elsewhere, the use of uncultivated spaces was subject to close regulation, tax payments, and recognition of land-owners' authority. Reasserting their rights to use the forests was one of the main motivations for peasants' protests against the abuses of the upper classes. Even legends such as Robin Hood reflect "the utopian image of a world in which one could freely hunt and eat meat."[21] Freedom of access to forest resources remained central among peasant demands into the following centuries, as, for example, during the revolt of 1381 in England.

The limitation or abolition of rights to uncultivated spaces was an event of decisive importance to the history of food. While during the early Middle Ages the table of the rich was perceived above all as a place of abundance (so much so that a powerful man identified himself foremost as a big eater), over time the divergence between rich and poor diets assumed an increasingly more qualitative nature. During the late Middle Ages (and subsequently in the Modern era), the diets of subordinate classes became ever-more vegetarian as meat was increasingly perceived as a *status symbol* of social privilege. *Difference,* even at a conceptual level, became the definitive element of the food culture.[22]

The agrarian growth that began between the tenth and eleventh centuries was accompanied by a renewed flourishing of the markets (which are explored in chapter 2 by Pere Benito in this volume). Significantly, at the local level: villages, castles, and monasteries became centers of renewed exchange activity, and nobles and clerics did not hesitate to turn a profit from the growing activity. On top of this network of rural markets, urban markets developed, too, earning protection and privilege from public authorities. In certain regions, such as Italy and Flanders, the development of cities was especially quick and intense. In north-central Italy, cities had an autonomous political organization (the *commune*) with the rural economy re-organized around it. A new form of urban imperialism was imposed upon the land, whose resources were appreciated primarily in relation to urban consumption and urban markets. A meticulous food policy founded upon legislation—but also upon economic and sometimes even military actions—aimed to guarantee the supply of food (*annona*), covering the entire production process, including stewardship of the agrarian landscape and the land's productivity; control of peasant labor and the processes of product transformation; and regulation of the market.[23] Popular consensus and public order depended, in large measure, on the success of this policy. In countries such as France or England with growing monarchic power, food policy and the norms protecting the markets were the prerogative of the king.

Notwithstanding the attention of public authorities, the supply of the urban market was discontinuous and not immune to periodic moments of crisis,[24] and times of famine could prove particularly dramatic in urban centers precisely because of their dependence on the market. While in normal times the markets guaranteed city dwellers a higher and more varied consumption relative to their rural counterparts, in times of greater hardship this could translate into conditions for town dwellers being even more precarious than those experienced by rural peasants; although rural peasants were left more or less without government assistance, they were in much closer proximity to the means and the places of production. For peasants, shortage meant that the land had not produced enough; but, except in very extraordinary cases, hunger could be beaten by scraping together a bit of grass and some roots from nearby fields, forests, and pastureland, or going off to hunt, perhaps illegally, whatever animal they could find. In contrast, in the city, shortage meant in the first place a sharp increase in prices, effectively making access to the market impossible for the poorest members of the population. Furthermore, a twofold, rather contradictory movement of men occurred during years of famine: rural peasants, in addition to searching for food in the fields and in the wild, came to urban markets in the hope of finding a supply of food there (though they ended up generally disappointed, sometimes simply turned away at the city gates); city dwellers unable to count on the market due to food shortage or steep prices, in turn, left the city to go in search of something to eat in the country. Chronicles from the high and late Middle Ages are filled with sad testimonies recounting many such episodes.

FOOD CULTURE: BETWEEN ECONOMY AND IDEOLOGY

European agrarian expansion slowed toward the end of the thirteenth century, but this did not necessarily indicate that an alimentary equilibrium had been reached. To the contrary, the situation was, in fact, becoming more dramatic than ever, as the cultivated space, having already expanded excessively, was pushing itself even upon marginal lands poorly suited to growing grains. The precarious balance between demographic growth and development in production fell apart, and toward the beginning of the 1300s, a series of brutal famines ravaged all of Europe. The repeated stresses on the food supply led to a population with diffuse malnutrition and physical weakness, readying the land for the plague epidemic to devastate the continent between 1347 and 1351. There is no direct causal link between the two phenomena: each has a life and a story of its own, and we know well that the bacteria causing the plague spread via rats. However, it is also clear that people's way of life (hygiene, housing, dietary regime) played an important role in improving or impairing their bodily defense to the infection process. A pandemic such as that which shattered Europe in the mid-fourteenth century "cannot be the result of a chance event; it was prepared for with difficult years that threw a too-numerous population into a precarious situation."[25]

After the tragedy of the plague, the food situation probably improved. Meat consumption increased, even among the lower social classes, due to the collapse of the agricultural economy and the return, in many cases, to various forms of exploiting the forests and fields of a territory that had once again become uncultivated. In certain regions, from northern France to Lombardy, farms for the first time delegated space to cultivating forage crops; and specialized farms dedicated to raising animals developed, especially in mid- and high-mountain regions (including most notably Swabia, Bavaria, Tyrol, Carinthia, Switzerland, and Alsace). All this meant a considerable stimulus for the meat trade over both short and long distances (as even

regions of Eastern Europe—Poland, Hungary, and the Balkan countries—
began to ship their livestock westward).[26] City markets were re-supplied
with greater abundance than before and prices dropped, while the dras-
tic decrease in population meant an increase in real wages—and this
made meat consumption attainable for a broader spectrum of consumers.
Fernand Braudel defined the Europe of this period—which would last into
the first half of the sixteenth century—as "carnivorous."[27]

Various studies have cited extremely high meat-consumption figures for
this period: up to 220 pounds per capita per year, according to Wilhelm
Abel, in fifteenth-century Germany.[28] It is an enormous quantity, equivalent
(if we take into consideration the number of fasting days obligated by the
ecclesiastic norms) to about 1 pound of meat per day over an effective consumption period of 200 to 220 days per year. Similar levels of consumption
would be cited for Poland, Sweden, England, and the Low Countries.[29] It is
likely an exaggerated figure, but in some cases such quantities were likely
accurate; the reach of such a phenomenon, however, would be limited by
at least two geographic and social variables: to countries in the north of
Europe (where meat consumption was, and still is, generally higher) and
to middle and upper social classes, or at least to those who lived in cities.
In Mediterranean regions, the dietary role of meat was not as significant,
but even here documentation from the fourteenth to the sixteenth centuries
attest to levels of consumption that were all but negligible: Louis Stouff has
calculated a per capita meat consumption of 145 pounds per year for the
family of the Bishop of Arles, and 57 pounds per year for the population of
Carpentras.[30] Similar figures have been cited for Sicily and other regions.[31]
The social context of reference thus seems to be the decisive factor in determining the scale of consumption; in any case, this was notably high if
compared to current figures. What is more, these calculations use market
purchases as their basis and fail to take into account the consumption of
meats produced domestically (pigs, sheep, chickens) that would have been,
in fact, anything but insignificant.

In rural areas the situation was entirely different. There were probably
no situations with a complete absence of animal proteins, as there have
been in more recent centuries (between the nineteenth and twentieth centuries, European peasants certainly ate worse than they did in the Middle

Ages). However, meat supply *was* more difficult to come by than in the city. According to Stouff, Provençal peasants of the 1400s ate meat twice per week. The urban–rural contrast thus remained—and would remain for quite some time—a critical point with regard to the social distribution of food. The animals most frequently destined for urban markets were cattle—able to be produced in ever greater numbers due to the expansion of pasturelands and the development of farms specialized in animal husbandry—since slaughtering a cow is almost never a family affair, in part, for the obvious matter of its extraordinary weight, and an operation made profitable only by the city's large number of consumers. Thus an opposition was drawn, even in terms of imagery, between pork, the symbol of a generally self-sufficient family economy, and beef, the symbol of new market dynamism; between the old economy of the forest and the new industry of cattle-raising; and between the country and the city.

While during the twelfth and thirteenth centuries salted pork was still a food for everyone (city dwellers and rural peasants alike), city dwellers who could afford it began to enjoy distinguishing themselves as *eaters of beef*—ox, steer, veal—the most expensive meat on the market, and thus the most exclusive. Those who could not afford it made do with mutton, an animal that would, for several reasons, find its moment of maximum expansion between the 1300s and 1400s. On the one hand, the transformation of the landscape had eliminated many cultivated spaces, but clearly had not restored the many forests that had been destroyed earlier; expansive natural prairies had grown in place of ancient forests, land more suited to sheep than to pigs. At the same time, the wool industry—a sector under rapid expansion during that period—depended precisely on these animals. Both of these circumstances made sheep a trendy animal in the urban society of the fourteenth and fifteenth centuries: even if the sheep was not a highly appreciated animal from a gastronomic perspective (its meat, if we read the dietetic texts of the period, is suitable only for people with poorly refined taste), it *was* a sign of distinction—even *emancipation*, perhaps— from the dietary lifestyle of the country, characterized, in turn, by another food, salted pork, that had become the veritable symbol of rural life. Thus, in addition to the desire to eat fresh meat, it was also a matter of image and a need to self-identify that the popular classes in European cities adopted

sheep's meat in knowing juxtaposition to pork, which after the 1300s became considerably less important in urban markets in Italy as in France and
England, all with more or less the same timelines and modalities.[32]

Finally, as far as the use of forests goes, the matter of hunting game and
pasturing animals had already played out by the fourteenth and fifteenth
centuries. The majority of uncultivated lands—excepting certain mountain-
ous zones—had been closed to public use. Wild grazing had given way to
in loco, stall-based breeding (with the only exception being the sheep). The
domestication of the pig inside peasant farmhouses was already widely
practiced in the 1400s, and certain medical treatises began to advise against
eating the meat of "confined animals, such as cattle and swine fattened
inside of stables."[33] Instead they recommended the meat of animals hunted
in the mountains, in the wild. But who could manage that anymore? The
traditional practices of herding and hunting were no longer viewed as rights,
but rather as *concessions* made (ever more rarely) by those who held those
rights in exclusivity: the king, the prince, the nobles, and the local powers.

Dietary discrimination—this dramatic class difference with regard to
food—does not appear simply as a matter of fact; in the Late Middle Ages,
this difference is in fact theorized, stipulated as necessary and natural. The
ideology of the dominant classes was particularly focused when it came
to defining the lifestyles of various social classes: ways of eating, dress-
ing, and lodging were meticulously codified in images and in the rules and
regulations that surrounded them. The ritual and choreographic aspects of
the convivial apparatus, as well as the hierarchical codification of kitchen
roles (examined in chapter 6 by Melitta Weiss Adamson), acquire growing relevance. Examples include the sumptuary laws,[34] intended to control behaviors and consumption practices so as to prevent ostentatious or
wasteful excesses, such as those associated, for example, with wedding
banquets, often designed to show off the public image of families, associations, and guilds. The laws were not motivated so much by morality as
by the desire for social and political control during a period marked by
intense social transformation. Thus, assuring and preserving the existing institutional order—by preventing certain consortia and professional groups
from assuming too much prestige and thus altering the present balance of
power—became very important as the bourgeoisie rose to status alongside
(or opposed to) the traditional nobility.[35] Regulating behavior and lifestyle

was a starting point for this operation of distinction: limitations were imposed only on some people and not on others; each person, each class, had his own particular standards to follow. Class differences were mostly about differentiating the dominant classes from other social groups such as the petty bourgeoisie, the working class, and the peasantry.

The founding premise is that one must eat "according to his nature,"[36] an idea that would be hard to disagree with, if by *nature* we understand the entire set of characteristics—physical, lifestyle habits, and so on—that define an individual. This was also precisely the fundamental notion of the Greek and Latin dietetic thought that European medicine was founded upon: how one eats should be decided on at an individual level, taking into account the age, sex, "humoral complexion,"[37] state of health, and types of activities of the individual, as well as the climate, season, and weather, each understood to have a specific effect on the person according to his particular nature. During the Middle Ages, the perspective began to change, with a predominantly *social* understanding of an individual's nature taking hold as the prevailing notion. A person's nature thus came to coincide more and more with his social status, his position in the hierarchy, his wealth, his power. And that nature—at least in the utopian vision of the dominant classes—was intrinsic, so to speak, to the person, a status defined once and for all, rigid and indestructible, just as the social order was—or at least as the upper classes hoped it was.

In late medieval Europe, the dominant classes did not seem to have any doubts in the matter: *nature* was power. Things were simpler this way, because social roles stipulated dietary behavior at the same time that precisely those dietary behaviors verified social roles. The foods most suitable for the belly of a gentleman were costly, elaborate, refined ones—precisely those that his power and wealth allowed him to regularly eat (and to display) at his own table. And those most suitable, on the other hand, for the belly of a peasant were common, even uncivilized ones. The poor—ever more numerous masses of the socially marginalized—would be happy with the scraps.

These ideas were conveyed not only in the fictional literature of the period (on which Bruno Andreolli focuses in chapter 9 of this volume) but also in its scientific—medical, botanical, and agricultural—texts.[38] For example, at the beginning of the fourteenth century, the Italian agronomist, Piero de' Crescenzi, advised that wheat was without question the best grain from which to make bread. Nonetheless, he recommended that those who work hard and expend large amounts of energy eat bread made with less refined grains such as sorghum, especially well-suited to the stomachs of peasants—as well as to pigs, oxen, and horses. Giacomo Albini, the physician serving the Savoy princes, threatened that pain and sickness would await those who ate foods unintended for their social status. The rich, he maintained, should stay away from heavy soups such as those made with legumes or innards, which were poorly nourishing and difficult to digest; similarly the poor should avoid foods that were too refined or of especially high quality, as their lowbrow stomachs would have difficulty assimilating them. It is a scientific justification of dietary privilege that was supported by many of the era's intellectuals, eager—as is often the case—to support the interests of the powerful. Philosophical thought, too, contributed to confirm the *necessity* of class differences about food (as Allen J. Grieco shows in his contribution to this volume).

However, we would be mistaken in interpreting so-called reality only through the perspective of this ideological construction. The powerful continuously celebrated their distinction, but this did not prevent the humble from enjoying culinary pleasures and developing their own foodways and preferences. It is always difficult to define the domestic dimension of food culture (the topic of chapter 7 by Gabriella Piccinni in this volume). This kind of endeavor always requires a close reading of the available documents to infer what they say and what they do *not* say. Literature, which tends to hide fact by subsuming information to ideology, is not less deceitful than archival documents that emphasize some aspects of reality (for instance, trade exchanges tend to leave more written traces) and hide those sectors of the food economy, such as direct provisioning, which during the Middle Ages, as in other periods, developed outside the market but nonetheless played a crucial role. At any rate, we do not deny that ideas are as real as facts. Food history is extremely intricate, connecting culture and power, economy and ideology, reality and the imaginary. This is also the reason for its intellectual appeal.

CHAPTER ONE

Food Production

ALFIO CORTONESI

Translated by Charles Hindley

POPULATION AND ENVIRONMENT IN
EARLY MEDIEVAL EUROPE

The impact on western Europe of the so-called barbarian migrations that took place between the end of the fourth century and the sixth century produced a substantial deterioration in the living conditions of the general population. Wars, rapine, and pillage, accompanied by famine and frequent and far-reaching epidemics, shattered the balance of the long-established social organization, sometimes irreversibly. Many once-flourishing cities emptied to the point of disappearing altogether; others suffered a very marked drop in population and occupied a considerably smaller area, often inside enormous surrounding walls, the evidence of the former sprawl. Numerous villages and hamlets suffered the same fate as urban settlements, often being absorbed into an environment where forest and wasteland or wilderness prevailed.

The decreased population level, scattered throughout vast areas of woodland and often isolated from each other, also prevented measures being taken to strengthen the banks of rivers and streams, and to maintain ditches and canals, with the result that bogs, marshes, and pools of water appeared everywhere, intermingling with the woodland, and giving rise to a changeable landscape, with the few remaining farmers unable to hold back the tide of change. The lack of human involvement meant that the spreading wastelands and waters eroded the ancient road network, which was already suffering from the consequences of inadequate maintenance from the fourth century onward.

The steep fall in population, which accompanied the passage from the late ancient world to the Middle Ages, and the demographic depression that followed it right up to the threshold of the year 1000, had a variety of causes. However, a clear and accurate explanation of these causes is hampered by the scarcity of relevant, early medieval documents. On the basis of recent research, however, we can see that in this period "marriages were...generally made early, infanticide and the limitation of births widespread, infant mortality very, very high,"[1] and that the average human life expectancy was pretty low. The wars and violence that were characteristic of the period of invasions, also occurring in various contexts afterwards, contributed to the high rate of mortality. Natural calamities (floods, particularly inclement weather, etc.), together with the famine and epidemics that they often gave rise to, added to the toll. For the period between the sixth and eighth centuries, twenty widespread plagues ravaged the population before there was any notable increase in plague-free years. In seventh-century Europe, the suggested population of less than thirty million inhabitants began to increase very slightly in the following century, probably after the improvement in living conditions during the Carolingian era. However, for many areas, the signs of recovery were cancelled out by a second wave of invasions, led by the Normans, the Saracens, and the Hungarians.

WOODS, MARSHES, AND CULTIVATED LANDS

The steep drop in the population that characterized the first centuries of the Middle Ages led to a huge increase in wasteland, to the detriment of cultivated land. The forests then grew very noticeably both in the Mediterranean area—where in the ancient world, the clearing of woodland for cultivation had been the most widespread—and in central and northern Europe, where woodland had always been a very important resource, but where it rapidly became a primary resource for survival. People made use of it in several ways. It was an excellent place for the rearing of animals and for hunting.

Especially where there were oaks, it was used for pigs to graze in, and their meat played an important dietary role. It is relevant that in contemporary documents the area of a forest was sometimes indicated by the number of pigs that could find enough food in them.[2] The wealth and variety of the game then living in European forests meant that hunting made quite a significant contribution to survival or subsistence among nobles and peasants alike, as all could practice hunting, without any curbs on the peasant population (a very different situation from that after the early Middle Ages).[3] Moreover, rivers and streams, marshes, and pools, to be found everywhere, often made fishing a very good source of food. The gathering of wild fruit, a more important activity than in later periods, completes the picture of the contribution that woodland and wasteland could make to the diet of the time.

Woodland was all the more precious because it provided ample supplies of wood for a wide variety of purposes: the building of houses (almost all of them made of wood), heating (also using charcoal), and the making of farming tools, boats, and utensils. The wood of oak, beech, chestnut, and other trees was skillfully employed, according to the properties of each.

The different types of forest did not simply derive from the kinds of trees present, but also from the ways in which those trees were exploited. Some woodlands were heavily exploited, dotted around with clearings for cereal farming, frequented by shepherds, wood cutters, and charcoal burners; others were nearly inviolate, only passed through by hunters, or serving as dwelling places for the occasional hermit (in addition to the elves, witches, and devils in the popular imagination at the time). Beyond the Rhine, as far as the Elbe and the Danube, before the year 1000, untouched forests were the most common, since, even in the ancient world, they had yet to be colonized.

The most important land types from among the arable and cultivated terrains, which began to expand only slightly from the eighth century onward, were sowable lands and vineyards. The former produced a huge variety of cereal. As the *polittici* or inventories of the Po valley show (we shall be returning to these in the next section), there had been a radical decline in wheat production in that area (the evidence for this is well documented) from Roman times, with wheat being superseded by a variety of other cereals, especially rye.[4] There seem to be two basic reasons for this: (1) the greater overall yield guaranteed by the so-called lesser cereals compared to wheat; and (2) the need to reduce, as much as possible, the effects of bad weather, through choosing cereal varieties that benefitted from brief growth cycles (millet, foxtail millet, sorghum, oats, and also a species of barley that required a spring sowing and was harvested in the summer). It was not until the eleventh and twelfth centuries that wheat regained its primacy among cereals, for reasons we shall be coming back to. Wine production also saw quite a significant increase before the year 1000, especially in the ninth and tenth centuries, above all, in the most suitable terrain. Olive production spread a little more widely in Mediterranean areas and, in Italy, taking advantage of a favorable micro-climate, it increased around Lake Garda and the other Italian lakes to the north of the Po valley.[5]

The low quality of the technical knowledge, combined with the sparse and inadequate tools available to farmers, did not allow for satisfactory levels of agricultural productivity in the early medieval period. This is particularly evident in the world of cereal production, where overall yield rarely exceeded three to one (three grains harvested for every one sown), and was sometimes lower than two to one. If we consider, in addition, that a part of the harvest had to be set aside for sowing in the following year, it is not hard to imagine that the amount produced was insufficient to guarantee subsistence for a family in itself. Nevertheless—as Massimo Montanari's research has suggested[6]—a composite diet not based on bread and, more generally, cereals but which was allied to foods deriving from rearing animals, hunting, fishing, and collecting wild fruit from trees and bushes, had a strong impact, allowing people to avoid the most dramatic of consequences, even from poor harvests.

THE MANORIAL SYSTEM OF PRODUCTION

From the eighth century, the *curtis* (*villa* in France and Germany, *manor* in England) was the main system in place to organize large areas of public property, both ecclesiastical and secular.[7] Thus, the manorial system of production developed that characterized most of western European farming under various names (*système domanial* in France, *Villikationverfassung* in Germany, and the *manorial system* in England). This system was founded on two characteristics. First, there was an administrative center consisting of the landowner's residence (with cellars and storerooms or storehouses for the preservation of products), artisans' workshops (to make farming equipment and to process wool and textiles), and the living quarters of serfs or *servi praebendarii*. And second, this system was based on the partition of manorial land into sectors. One sector was directly managed by the owner (in the documents this was generally termed the *dominicum,* the lord's), and another was indirectly managed (*massaricio*), being divided into *mansi* (from the Latin *manere,* to reside, to dwell in) or *sortes* (agrarian units of variable size). Over time, the indirectly managed parts grew to the detriment of the lord's sector (in Italy, from the second half of the ninth century), following population growth that required more land to be conceded to farmers' families in order for them to be able to survive.

The lord's lands tended, at least in part, to surround the landowner's residence, but they could be on irrationally organized territory, mixed up with the *massaricio,* and also with lands belonging to other courts, or to free peasants. They were worked by serfs, the *servi praebendarii*—whose name derived from the landowner's *praebenda,* which guaranteed their board and lodging—and by freely given service (*corvées;* in Latin *operae*) that the leaseholders of the *mansi* had to provide (for up to as much as three days a week), whether they were freemen or serfs (*servi casati*). It was specifically the *corvées* of the *massaricio* that linked the two sides of the *curtis,* thus emerging as the essential feature for the functioning of that productive system. At the beginning of the ninth century, the Parisian monastery of Saint-Germain-des-Prés exacted around 50,000 *operae* a year for the farming of 16,020 hectares (the data for 21 *villae* out of 25 overall); at the end of the same century, the Italian monastery of Santa Giulia di Brescia benefited from at least 60,000 *corvées.* The peasants who farmed the *mansi* owed the landowner a tax, in kind or in money, or sometimes in terms of craftmen's products of various kinds (poles, farming equipment, etc.), in addition to their services.

We owe most of our information on how the *curtis* functioned to an exceptionally interesting source that over the last few decades has especially attracted the attention of the historians of the early Middle Ages: the *polittici,* or the inventories of goods, people, and income compiled between the end of the eighth and the beginning of the eleventh centuries. These reveal the size and organization of some of the most important French and Italian properties (as we have seen, sometimes including a conspicuous number of courts), and also some that operated on a more modest scale. Recent republication of these documents[8] has encouraged their more detailed and accurate critical examination, with more firmly based results being gained than in the past.

The *curtis* seems to have originated between the Loire and the Rhine; its expansion roughly following the direction of the Carolingian conquests. In Italy, the *curtis* emerged with the arrival of the Franks (774), involving the northern and central regions down to the Lazio and Molise Apennines. In many of these regions it overlapped with, or was superimposed on the landowning organization of the Longobard period, characterized by pre-manorial forms of production destined to facilitate "the application of Frankish models."[9] In England, it is now clear that manorial structures began to spread before the Norman conquest (1066), in the tenth century, probably on foundations that were laid a couple of centuries before.

The spread of the *curtes* (in the eighth to tenth centuries) occurred at the same time as a slow but significant process of agrarian expansion that progressively reduced wasteland and marshes—a process that would continue more markedly in the following centuries. In certain areas an excess of farm products fostered a trading network that often went beyond the confines of individual properties.[10] The image, long cultivated by historians, of a self-contained manor with internal trading dynamics and no external trading flow, has to be substantially modified in the light of new knowledge, though we must continue to recognize that self-sufficiency was the principal aim of this production structure (never, however, within the individual manor, but of the *system* of manors that one landowner was the head of).

Since the first half of the nineteenth century, historians have debated the origins of the *curtis*,[11] and some have emphasized that the *curtis* was a continuation of the productive arrangements of the Roman *villa,* which was already characterized by bipartition into direct- and indirect-management structures. However, more recent studies tend to stress that only in the Frankish era did the manor's defining integration of the two parts (*dominico* and *massaricio*) take place, assured by the spread of the *corvées* that strictly linked them, and that because of this feature, a productive system arose of a decidedly original nature.

THE CRISIS AND TRANSFORMATION OF THE MANOR

Between the end of the tenth and the twelfth centuries, the manorial system gradually got into difficulties for a variety of reasons. One of them was certainly "the free circulation of *mansi*,"[12] no longer linked up to the lord's reserve, and the break up was also due to the increasing pressure of population growth: the time and place varied a good deal, of course. The destinies of the *pars dominica,* the object of usurpations, enfeoffments, and divisions among the heirs contributed noticeably to the crisis and metamorphosis of the *curtis.* Another factor was certainly—though in a European context generalizing is extremely difficult—the decline of the number and overall weight of the *corvées* that were not very productive due to the problematic commitment of those pressed into agricultural service on the lord's lands, and hence, whose labor was often commuted into monetary payments (commutations also took further precedence where the lord's lands were diminishing).

While the manorial system was disintegrating in the eleventh and twelfth centuries, the big landowners put strategies into place to limit the damage in order to take advantage of the favorable circumstances brought about by the population growth and the expansion of farmland. Secular and ecclesiastical holders of the *bannum* (the jurisdictional and noble powers) began to strengthen their control over their inferiors, by greater profiteering through adding fees and taxes, rationalizing their exploitation of the reserve, and by making the administration of property more effective and tighter (among the best known examples of this tactic are the abbots Sigeri of Saint-Denis and Meinhard of Marmoutier). There was some experimentation, introducing quite radically new features into methods of management; however, many novel approaches initially ran alongside the old manorial system. This was the case for the Cistercian monks, whose granges were characterized by exclusively dominical arrangements, and which hence excluded—according to the dictates of the rule—the presence of lands in concession.

The situation was evolving in significant ways for the smaller properties, too. Where tillage and deforestation sometimes gave rise to land that the peasants could keep as freeholders or as common land, the disintegration of the manorial system led to a greater number of people increasingly appearing to be owners of land themselves, as they were able to work on plots of land by then almost entirely free of service to a lord. In this way, family-run smallholdings multiplied.

It was in this context that a reduction in freely given service combined with the unsustainable cost of wage labor—some of the biggest landowners had begun to turn to the latter—opened up the way to a new type of tenancy, characteristically short- and medium-term tenancies, alongside a monetary payment. These tenancies began to outweigh indefinite censual concessions by landowners who had used cheap management tactics up to that point. Starting especially from the thirteenth century, the new kinds of tenancy—the expression of an increasingly dynamic agriculture involved in profits from the market—began to spread even at the level of small- and medium-size properties, resulting in a substantial change in farming contract arrangements, dominated up until that time by long-term or very long-term concessions or leases, called emphyteusis, and perennial rents. The course of new short-term agreements was associated, in many parts of Europe, with that process of landowning concentration by which the landowners, at several levels, intended to remedy the fragmentation of their lands under ownership. This happened especially in the presence of significant investments by town dwellers into, for example, Italian sharecropping or tenant farming. As well as this, the process of reorganization of plots of land and parceled-out land sometimes started with the farming plots resulting from the splitting up of either secular, or ecclesiastical lands.

POPULATION GROWTH

The population growth in western Europe between the tenth and early fourteenth centuries has recently generated a great deal of historical research.[13] When and why did the population begin to increase? Lacking sources for reconstructing population patterns, with the exception of a very few towns and, occasionally, other areas, scholars have always linked this population increase to the concrete phenomena of economic growth. Faced with the increase in cultivated terrain, without a concurrent, radical alteration in either agricultural methods or farming equipment, or a rise in cereal productivity, we must presume that there were a growing number of people at work and producing. Running parallel to this was the increase in the number of artisans' shops or workshops in towns, and this also leads us to conclude that the urban population was growing and that markets were busier. On the basis of these elementary considerations it may reasonably be asserted that the population growth in western Europe began in the period of institutional and economic reorganization that was planned and carried out across the Carolingian empire between the eighth and the ninth centuries. For the period following on from the year 1000, with further and even stronger economic growth, the undoubted, significant rise in the number of human beings is clearly backed up by sources, even though those sources are scarce and fragmentary. All this is not to say that there is purely a mechanical connection between population and economics, and, in fact, population studies have always posited that the economy is only one of the many variables influencing a rise or fall in the population level.

Though the evidence is not absolute, it has been estimated that for the European population in the twelfth and thirteenth centuries, there was an increase of around thirty million: from forty-two to seventy-three million inhabitants. On the basis of different calculations, an estimated European population of around a hundred million has been suggested for the beginning of the fourteenth century. These estimates do not go much beyond the approximate, but they certainly do give an idea of the scale of the leap in population size.

TOWARD THE CONQUEST OF NEW LAND

Population growth—involving both the towns and the countryside, determining profound transformations in the pattern of settlement—and the connected rise in the need for farming products, especially cereals, was accompanied, above all from the eleventh century, by a noticeable extension of cultivated land. Indeed, the modest improvements in techniques were unable to provide the increase in productivity that was needed to improve the harvests.

The expansion of agriculture meant that there were substantial changes in the production arrangements of nearly the entire European countryside.[14] From an economy strongly marked by the practice of hunting, rearing animals, fishing, and the exploitation of the many resources offered by woodland, the marshes, and uncultivated land in general, gradually production became ever more closely linked to working the land. Already by the middle centuries of the Middle Ages the area of cultivated land (*cultum*) had become the principle and absolutely essential source of subsistence in the towns and the countryside.

What saw by far the biggest growth were the areas of cereal production on which the survival of the population mainly depended. At the same time, wheat and other cereals acquired an increasing importance in people's diet.[15] Deforestation, reclamation, and tillage were often the work of individual farmers, whose domestic needs drove them into seeking new plots to put under the plough, not too far from their villages, on the edge of woodland or wasteland. Their efforts, although obscure, and with outcomes that were not immediately documented, have understandably left fairly weak traces in historical sources. Nonetheless, it was initiatives of this kind, especially in regions that had been settled long before, that after the year 1000 characterized the offensive against the woods and the untilled land. It was a different story for areas of recent settlement, whether these were large forests, pasturelands, heaths, or marshlands. The success of initiatives in these cases was linked to the presence of variously skilled farmers, to their abilities in carrying out reclamation projects in order to produce arable land, to the availability of quite considerable capital investment, and, finally, to the collaboration, or at any rate the agreement of those who enjoyed property rights, or rights of jurisdiction over the areas to be transformed.

Factors like those just outlined were clearly decisive in Germany between the twelfth and fourteenth centuries in the assault on the vast areas of forest east of the Elbe and the Saale, after which fairly stable and numerous settlements evolved in regions that up until then had been sparsely populated with only pastoral or woodland economies. Many villages were founded in the region due to the vast immigration of western German and Dutch peasants that was supported by the mediation of secular and ecclesiastical princes.

The wave of tillage in the eastern regions of Germany spread somewhat to the countries on its borders—Poland, Bohemia, and Hungary—where the local nobility welcomed the progress in farming and the immigration from central Europe. While this was happening in the east, to the west, in the oldest and most densely populated places in Germany, with marked alteration in settlement and productive patterns, new plots, and entire districts developed, eroding the areas of woodland. These developments were mainly as individual, unorganized initiatives; however, planned attacks on wasteland also occurred (for example, in Swabia, new villages were planned and founded into the fourteenth century).

In Flanders, it was at least from the years of Count Baldwin V (1035–1067) that the land that had been submerged by sea flooding began to be dried out via dams and canals; in the hinterland, at the same time, axes and spades were used to bring the areas of forest and moor between Ypres and Brugge under cultivation. The struggle against the sea's attacks was also undertaken in Holland and Zealand, where the economy of the *polders* was organized on the area that was reclaimed from the sea, and where conditions were created for the development of animal rearing. The experience these people acquired in the work of reclamation quickly attracted the attention of princes and aristocrats who had similar problems. The Dutch were, therefore, encouraged to settle along the German North Sea coast, and in the interior, between river basins needing effective draining.

Although some areas prior to the year 1000 (the basins of the Charente and the Saône, Maine, Normandy, Auvergne, etc.) had already undergone some deforestation and transformation into arable land of a certain importance, there is no doubt that in France, the wave of tillage and reclamation was at its height in the period between the middle of the eleventh and the end of the twelfth centuries.[16] Recent research has shown that in the sixty years from 1120 to 1180, in the Île-de-France, in Picardy, and in the Champagne region, the greatest increase in cultivated land occurred. In the same period, in the valley of the Loire, and especially in Anjou, dams (*turcies*) had to be built to protect crops from flooding due to overflowing rivers.

In the centuries either side of the year 1000, in the French countryside and in that of its nearest neighbors, it was mainly the initiatives of the numerous farmers, who individually and without additional support, in using their own labor and modest tools, worked to extend the arable areas. By the end of the eleventh century a new phase of great expansion began. What then became decisive in the drive toward reclamation and tillage were the princes and lords of the manor, and the bishops and abbots, who soon realized that profits could be made from the increase in cultivated land and in the rural population, and consequently they began to stimulate and direct the movement toward new settlements. Entire districts, up until that moment left to the forest and the marshland, were then placed under the plough, new *terroirs* were created on virgin territory, and villages of all shapes and sizes were conjured out of nothing. There was an evident change of pace in the rhythm of intervention.

A land of ancient settlements, in the centuries of great population growth, England certainly cannot be said to have seen a spectacular advance in land under cultivation. Toward the end of the eleventh century, on the other hand, according to the evidence from the extraordinary document, the *Domesday Book,* the occupation of clay land of good quality was nearly complete. Reclamations and tillage were certainly not lacking in the following centuries, but they were in the main on marginal lands, swamps, bogs, and marshlands, or peripheral districts on the borders of Scotland and Wales. From the thirteenth century, after persistent pressure from population growth, some sectors of the vast royal forests began to be exploited (Rockingham, Chippenham, Sherwood, etc.), which, up until that time, had been kept as hunting reserves.[17]

To the south, in the Iberian peninsula, settlement and the expansion of cultivated land was closely connected to the Catholic *Reconquista,* the gradual taking over of the peninsular from the Arabs—consequently, it followed a very particular dynamic and rhythm. In the northern and northeastern regions, the Catholics were the first to be involved in the advance of Christian kingdoms and in the consolidation of their positions, and the placing under the plough of the land passed mostly (more noticeably from the ninth century) via the individual initiative of appropriation (*presura*) and tillage (*escalio*). In Catalonia, by the middle of the tenth century, the cultivated lands had already nearly reached a limit in terms of possible expansion. Regarding the promotion of official settlement enterprises by the sovereign or members of the nobility, there is evidence that these were in place already by the year 800; afterward, enterprises like these follow closely on the heels of the stages of the Christian *Reconquista,* added to by the initiative and active participation of the knightly and monastic orders.

Taking Italy last, from the end of the ninth century deforestation and reclamation in the north, in the Po valley, was so widespread that it altered the environmental picture, creating important changes in the organization of production.[18] Here too, however, it was in the eleventh century (when collective initiatives increasingly took the place of individual efforts, and were promoted by monasteries, lords, and consortiums of farmers, and finally by rural councils and citizens) that the most outstanding results were achieved, in terms of providing proper banks for the rivers (the Po and its tributaries being especially prominent), in excavating canals and sewers, and in transforming woodland and marsh into agricultural land.[19] Well known, and among the earliest example of its kind, is the story of the marsh of over a thousand hectares that was conceded by Verona City Council to a consortium of citizens, who placed it under the plough towards the end of the twelfth century. We should also recall the work carried out in Lombardy, where reclamation and irrigation has recently been shown to have been linked. In the first decades of the thirteenth century the waterways of Milan, Brescia, and Muzza were built, soon to be an essential reference point both for the irrigation network and for navigation.

The creation of new agricultural areas in central and southern Italy was not on the same scale as those in northern districts. Reclamation and deforestation took place in the context of a dense network of settlements originating from ancient times, which, forming an environment more affected by human influence than anywhere else in Europe, limited the initiative of the tillers.

AGRICULTURAL WORK AND TECHNIQUES

The progress made by agriculture between the eleventh and thirteenth centuries was mainly of a quantitative kind; that is, it was linked to the increase in the area under cultivation. Tools and cultivation techniques improved much less so than has previously been thought—it was even asserted that for the middle centuries of the Middle Ages there had been a *revolution* in cultivation systems. Nevertheless, there were some significant innovations.[20] Essentially, they concern the most important production sector, that of cereals. First of all, there was increasingly widespread use of the moldboard plough, provided with a coulter and sometimes wheels. Although heavier and, hence, less easy to maneuver, this plough introduced the peasant to equipment that was certainly more effective than the simple, symmetrical plough traditionally used in the Mediterranean region, while also guaranteeing (thanks to the moldboard and to the asymmetrical ploughshare) the turning over of the clods of soil (and hence a deeper renewal of the land).

The emergence of the new kind of plough did not occur everywhere, nor, in the areas where it did appear, did it appear at the same time everywhere. In many regions its use did not exclude the use of less complex ploughs. It has, however, been proved that in the thirteenth century it was being used on the plains of northern Europe, from Flanders to Russia, and also in central Europe. In England, ploughs able to turn over clods of earth existed before the Norman Conquest. In the thirteenth century, the ploughs in use could be said to be of three different types: one with wheels (the wheeled plough), found above all in the south-east; a second one where, in place of wheels, there was a wooden or iron foot (the foot plough), which, keeping itself above the terrain, enabled the depth of the plowing to be controlled quite easily, as did the wheeled plow; and a third type, light and easily managed (the swing plough), whose work had to be entirely governed by the farmer. As far as Italy is concerned, the symmetrical plough, which goes back to pre-Roman times, continued to be used in the regions on the Tyrrhenian side of the peninsular, in the South, and on the islands, whereas in the Po valley, and high up on the Adriatic side, the *più* or *plovo* prevailed: a heavy plough that was asymmetrical with wheels.

Adaptation to the requirements of more robust ploughs and the need for greater speed, given the increase in the land under cultivation, meant important changes for whatever was used to pull the plough along. These involved the kind of animal used, how they were attached to the plough, and the iron fittings. In Mediterranean countries the ox continued to be the draught animal par excellence, although at least in Italy there is evidence that cows were used, and where the land was heavy and badly drained, buffaloes were used. On the cereal-producing land in the Po valley, in the later Middle Ages, horses were also used, confirming that the region was a kind of link between central European and Mediterranean agriculture. It should be added that the heavier weight of the ploughs from the eleventh and twelfth centuries onward made it necessary to yoke together more than one pair of animals, thus accentuating the distance between those who could hardly even afford a light plough, and those who were able to benefit fully from technical progress.

Unlike the south, in central-northern Europe, especially from the twelfth century, there was a slow, if partial replacement of draught oxen with horses, prevalent in the thirteenth century in the richer agricultural areas (e.g., the

Île-de-France, Picardy, Flanders, and the Lorraine region). The higher price of the horse, as well as its high maintenance costs, and the fact that it was more prone to sickness than the ox, was probably felt to be compensated for by the speed of the animal and by the success enjoyed with the cultivation of the oat, a cereal suited to the horse's diet, in a cold but temperate climate.

In the middle centuries of this period, whether horses or oxen were the draught animals, the new teams made a big difference. The introduction of the shoulder collar (rigid and padded) enabled the horse's energy to be exploited to the full. It replaced one made of soft leather, which when hung round the neck, made breathing difficult, because it tended to press on the tracheal artery. As for the ox, the team's improvement consisted in no longer making the yoke weigh down on the withers when fixing the yolk with a belt around the neck, but fixing the belt on the forehead, securing it to the horns. There is proof of iron shoeing of the horses used for plowing at least from the eleventh century. For oxen, the custom of shoeing them took much longer to emerge, yet it could have helped save costs in the long run. It is a fact, nonetheless, that even at the end of the fourteenth century, not more than a quarter of English landowners who shod their horses took the trouble to shoe their oxen as well.

In medieval agricultural practice the plough certainly played an essential role, though this should not lead us to underestimate the contribution of tools such as the spade, hoes, sickles, harrows, and so on, which farmers used as well as the plough (and sometimes without the plough). The use of these tools reflected the improvement in agricultural technology that took place between the eleventh and thirteenth centuries. The rise in iron production, the result of progress in mining techniques, and a more widespread recourse to the metal, allowed both for a greater number of tools and for an increase in their effectiveness and durability.

THE PRODUCTIVITY OF THE SOIL

If the technological innovations, however much they should not be over-estimated, must to some extent have contributed to an increase in production, appreciable results also seem to have derived from new forms of organization of the land and systems of agricultural work. We are, above all, referring here to the diffusion of those more rational and shorter cycles of cultivation that substituted for, if only in part, the rotation proper, to produce a more extensive agriculture.[21] Specifically, from the middle of the twelfth century, there was an increasing emergence of a triennial crop rotation, and a concurrent fall in the areas run along traditional biennial lines. By the terms *biennial, triennial rotation,* and so on, we mean the well-known working of the land so as to protect its productive capacity, involving regular cycles for sowing, and then allowing the land to rest. Biennial rotation, already known in ancient times—which had been largely supplanted in the early Middle Ages by more rudimental systems of cultivation—was based on the burning off of the original vegetation and on the long-term alternation of arable and pasture land, where half of the land was left as fallow land every year, while in the other half cereals were grown (wheat or any kind of lesser cereal, generally winter cereal). Unlike this, triennial crop rotation involved only a third of the land being left fallow, whereas, of the other two-thirds, one was for the sowing of winter cereals (wheat, rye, winter barley, etc.), and the other was for spring crops, which might be cereals (oat, spring barley, millet, foxtail millet, sorghum, etc.) or legumes. The winter cereals, more valuable and more demanding of the soil, were usually grown in the fallow land from the previous year; the plants for the spring sowing were alternated with the winter crops. Of course, the crop rotations could be applied (without having to carry out any division) to the plots of land in their entirety, spread out in either biennial or triennial periods of time. From what we have just shown, it can be inferred that the adoption of the triennial cycle offered quite significant advantages compared to the biennial system, not only because it allowed two harvests per plot every three years, but also because it encouraged, where the land was divided up proportionally, a balanced distribution of the year's agricultural tasks (plowing, sowing, and reaping). And thanks to the spring and winter crops that could to some extent balance each other out, it reduced the risk that the harvest ran into unfavorable weather. It should be added that very early on, especially on more fertile lands (and not unusually through necessity, arising from a marked increase in the population) the custom emerged of sowing on fallow land (on all or in part) spring cereals, and more particularly, legumes. The latter, given their well-known property of providing the soil with nitrogen, not only did nothing to impoverish the land, but actually served to encourage its productive capacity.

In France triennial crop rotation, for which there is evidence (however generally imperfect) from the Carolingian era, became more commonplace from the thirteenth century, when it was practiced in Normandy as well as in the fertile lands of the Île-de-France. Shortly afterwards it appeared in the south, too, together with biennial rotation. In England the first evidence of triennial rotation goes back to around the middle of the twelfth century. The thirteenth century provides much more evidence of the triennial system, but it by no means signifies the shelving of the biennial cycle: for example, in early fourteenth-century Lincolnshire, the latter clearly prevails, and the same thing happens in a large number of counties of southern England (Berkshire, Wiltshire, Dorset, Somerset, etc.). The early warmth of Mediterranean springs combined with the dryness of its summers meant that southern Europe was unable to enjoy spring cereal production to the same extent as was observed in the districts of the central-northern region. As a result, the triennial cycle was obviously adopted to a more limited degree and biennial rotation predominated.

It is clear that the full valorization of crop-rotation cycles of various kinds (from the thirteenth century there is also a four-year cycle, generally founded on the sowing of legumes) could not be realized unless it was systematically applied, which, realistically speaking, could almost only occur in the central-northern regions of Europe, characterized by the collective organization of agrarian areas. If the requirement for the regeneration of the soil, especially of the poorest quality, often drove the farmer to introduce prolonged periods of rest between the completion of one crop cycle and the start of another, it was often the case that a pressing need for cereals induced him to force the rhythms of production, sacrificing the fallow period to further sowing, leaving to one side any kind of rationally planned crop rotation. And the effects of such behavior were all the more serious when, both as a result of a still modest development in stall rearing, and of the difficulties that pastoral practice brought about in terms of the gradual erosion of uncultivated land, the availability of manure remained generally inadequate (moreover, it was utilized, when there was any, almost exclusively for vegetable plots and for the other areas of intensive agriculture).

CHAPTER TWO

Food Systems

PERE BENITO

Translated by Leah Ashe

AN AUTARKIC EARLY MIDDLE AGES?

The early Middle Ages have been described as a period that was dominated by the autarkic responses of a primarily rural peasant population, with minimal regional specialization and limited trade and exchange. The inertia of the systems of production prior to the eighth century—with low-yielding grain harvests, low productivity, and overwhelming rents—and the inadequacy of the structures of exchange, created an essentially static agrarian economy with little growth.

However, a systematic reading of legal and narrative sources from the eighth through to the tenth centuries leads us toward a reality that, in fact, breaks with much of the historiographic tradition. For example, the capitularies of Charlemagne in 794 and 805 document grain policies resembling those seen from the thirteenth century onward, with the creation of stocks, the sale of grain at controlled prices, and the establishment of maximum prices for bread and grain. Such measures attest to the importance of the grain trade and a certain uniformity of prices throughout the Carolingian Empire.[1]

The existence of controlled border crossings (*clusae*) in the Pyrenees and the Alps, and the tolls (*telonea*) situated along the length of Empire's main rivers—the Seine, the Rhine, the Loire, and, to a lesser degree, the Rhone—and on the Mediterranean and Atlantic coasts attests to the importance of long-distance trade of a wide variety of merchandise, with salt, grain, and wine among the most significant. Ships transported foodstuffs from the high seas to the interior of France by way of the Seine and its tributaries. The large monasteries of Paris had their own merchants and trading networks crisscrossing their dominions. From 710 on, the Fair of St. Denis attracted Anglo-Saxon merchants and, a generation later, Frisian ones. At the beginning of the tenth century, the great French wine fair expanded to welcome traders from even greater distances, including Lombardy, Provence, and Spain. The Alps did not hinder the arrival of merchandise from Italy and beyond. Beginning in the latter half of the ninth century, the Danube acted as an important link between East and West, while the northern estuary of the Rhine allowed the Frisians, strategically situated on the North Sea coast, to control maritime transport routes to England and Scandinavia.[2]

Just as the expansion of Islam during the seventh and eighth centuries failed to cause the end of trade in the Mediterranean, neither did the disintegration of the Carolingian Empire or the Viking invasions of the late ninth century mean the end of booming, long-distance, river- and sea-based trade in northwestern Europe. Beginning in the twelfth century, however, the proliferation of written sources allows for a broader, much more precise image of the old and new trade phenomena to emerge: an extraordinary flowering of urban markets throughout the entire Western world, growing regional specialization of agricultural and livestock production, and an expansion of the long-distance trade of primary foodstuffs such as grains, wine, fish, salt, and Eastern spices.

THE TRIUMPH OF BREAD: URBAN SUPPLY
AND INTERNATIONAL TRADE

Following a long, gradual decrease in meat consumption in favor of plant-based products, bread became the basic dietary component for much of the European population around the year 1000.[3] Numerous factors contributed to bread's success as a dietary staple, including, most notably, its nutritional advantages (high carbohydrate content and easy digestion), the adaptability of the crops that could be used in bread production to a wide variety of climates and soils, and the ease of preservation and transport of the finished product. Although breads continued to be made from barley, rye, oats, and millet, the most valued breads were produced from fine, white wheat flours. Wheat bread gradually lost its luxury status, and in some parts of Europe it became a staple for a large portion of the population—from the end of the thirteenth century onward, for example, people in Italian cities were able to eat it even during years of scarcity, and in southern Italy it became the staple food of peasants.[4]

Beginning in the middle of the twelfth century, the majority of western cities and towns had a protected grain market and provisioning areas that usually guaranteed the supply of high-quality grain. However, the rapid urbanization and industrialization that was seen in some parts of Europe between the twelfth and fourteenth centuries, along with the specialization in other regions of the surplus production of grain, accentuated the contrast between urban centers that were self-sufficient and those that were not. In the Italian Peninsula, for example, the plains of the Po, whose grain production was sufficiently large enough to ensure the supply of the region's cities (with the exception of Venice and Bergamo, and to some extent, also Bologna), contrasted with Tuscany, a densely urbanized region that suffered a structural imbalance between wheat supply and demand. The most extreme case occurred in the city of Florence, whose county, complained the merchant Domenico Lenzi, could not manage to supply the city for more than five months a year; in order to cover the rest of its needs, Florence needed to buy grain on the regional market, and, during years of shortage, turn to international trade routes.[5]

To avoid the structural or temporary shortage of grain, the large consumption centers in the western Mediterranean were forced to turn to importing overseas wheat that came not only from nearby regions, but also from distant markets. Thus an active, powerful maritime trade emerged that, beginning in the twelfth century, joined together the vast regions that specialized in grain production (Castile, the Ebro Valley, the Camargue, Sicily, Sardinia, southern Italy, and northern Africa) with the large consumption centers in northern Italy, Occitania, and the Crown of Aragon.[6]

Since grain demand was strongly inelastic,[7] a city's supply zone varied according to its internal needs, as determined essentially by its population;

by the cyclic and intra-cyclic fluctuation of grain prices; by the political control of its surrounding territories; and by the trade relationships established between a city and its redistribution centers and grain-production zones. Normally a city's supply radius shrunk in years of abundance and low prices, and expanded in years of famine and during the months of highest demand in the annual agricultural cycle. Venice, for example, was able to supply itself with grain from the Adriatic from June to November, and from the Black Sea in March and April. Genoa imported its wheat from the Pontic regions, especially those in southern Russia and the Crimea.[8] From the thirteenth century onward, Barcelona, Valencia, and Mallorca depended, during average years, both on a surplus from the Ebro Valley and on imports of Sicilian wheat, to which it might also add shipments from Tuscany, Lazio, Provence, Languedoc, Castile, and northern Africa. However, during the famines of 1333 and 1376, wheat shipments also arrived from Rhodes, Asia Minor, Lisbon, Harfleur, Brugge, England, Burgundy, Zealand, and Germany.[9] Toulouse typically supplied itself with wheat from the Languedoc region and managed to export grain; however, in leaner times this town was forced to import grain from Sicily, England, and Burgundy.[10]

The Atlantic countries combined their grain-deficient cities and regions such as London, Paris, Gascony, and Bordeaux—the latter area being specialized in the production of wine—with surplus-producing areas such as the Banks of the Somme and the Seine, or the plains of Hainaut and Artois, the veritable breadbaskets of northern Europe. On the other hand, beginning in the thirteenth century, the developed regions of Flanders, Brabant, Holland, and the Banks of the Rhine needed to import grain and other products in order to satisfy the food demands of their urban centers.[11] Wheat from north-central France arrived in Paris by way of the Oise, in Flanders by way of the Scheldt, and in Rouen and overseas by way of the Somme. Around 1200, England exported the grain it harvested in East Anglia and in the lands of the Bishop of Canterbury to Norway and Flanders.[12]

As a result of the Germanic colonization of the Slavic territories east of the Elba, new, more extensive grain-producing zones opened up in eastern Germany, Poland, Prussia, and Livonia. Thus, beginning at the end of the thirteenth century, Baltic rye began to flow westward, contributing significantly to the food supply of the Flemish, displacing the English grain that had previously flowed into the Scandinavian markets. Hanseatic merchants and the Teutonic Order later controlled the maritime grain trade in the North and Baltic Seas in the fourteenth and fifteenth centuries.[13]

Throughout Europe, the international grain trade was extraordinarily supple: in periods of famine, it expanded in proportion to the severity of the crisis. When famines reached a certain level of intensity, the two primary trade areas—the western Mediterranean and the North Sea—became connected: a strong increase in demand in northern Europe affected grain prices in Mediterranean Europe and vice versa. This, combined with the rapid circulation of news, and of rumors within the urban markets, explained the rapid diffusion of famines throughout the continent.

It is not surprising, then, that states' grain policies had—along with the establishment of grain prices and the increase in grain production and supply—the control of trade as a primary goal. Beginning at the end of the twelfth century, sovereigns began to simultaneously use, in a complementary fashion, trade prohibitions, and grain export licenses as a way to both combat famines and as a source of fiscal income. During the continent-wide famine of 1235, for example, Frederick II, the Duke of Austria, banned the land- and sea-based export of grain to northern regions following Jewish-led advice; and if we are to believe the *Annals of Salzburg*, the measure achieved its goal: just a short while afterwards, Swabian wheat, and wine from Italy and France, abounded in the city and in its entire province.[14]

The role of the grain merchant was thus contradictory: he imported grain to help assuage the effects of famine on cities that were not self-sufficient, but at the same time he transferred the price increase to regions of grain export. In the mid-fourteenth century, the chronicler, Fernán Sánchez of Valladolid, considered trade to be one of the primary causes of shortages in Castile, and the cities, united in the *Cortes* (the Castilian parliament), petitioned the King to veto the exports. Meanwhile, the councils of Catalan cities entrusted independent merchants with the mission of importing large shipments of grain from overseas, precisely in order to free their fellow citizens from the scourge of hunger.[15]

THE ORIGINS OF A MUNICIPAL WHEAT POLICY

Beginning in the thirteenth century, urban authorities throughout the entire Western world began to put policies into effect, with different rhythms and timelines in different cities and regions, which sought to guarantee the grain supply, influence grain prices, protect consumers against fraud with regard to the weight and quality of bread, and limit the de-structuring effects of famines. Municipal governments had sufficient authority, resources, and financial means to regulate and govern the local market, increase the food supply, and limit price inflation. They also had larger moral and ideological motivations such as working toward the common good of the entire community, and avoiding the risk of popular uprisings subverting the social order.[16]

Guaranteeing the food supply of a city became the guiding principal of municipal economic policy, upon which the oligarchies established their capacity to govern the city. Throughout the thirteenth century, Siena, Pistoia, Florence, Lübeck, and Cologne, among other cities, each turned to the imposition of taxes to stimulate the grain supply, and they chose magistrates with the competencies necessary to closely follow their administration.[17] The urban magistrates acted, first and foremost, preemptively, authorizing and incentivizing imports of grain, and favoring regulatory stocks sold at a taxed price that was lower than that of the free market.[18] The Catalan councils carried out intensive diplomatic activity aimed at soliciting the permission of the authorities of other territories in the Crown of Aragon and overseas to export grain. To incentivize and facilitate such imports, they granted local merchants warranties for the safety of their people and goods, tax exemptions, debt and fine cancellations, and subsidies.[19]

The municipalities concurrently made use of their coercive abilities to prohibit exports and to force producers and intermediaries to sell their reserves on the local market. With this goal in mind, they conducted surveys, periodically inventoried current grain supplies, and carried out inquiries regarding private grain reserves. Prohibitions on removing grain from the city, though frequently implemented, were usually ineffective because they were aimed more at obtaining tax profits from the sale of licenses than at effectively limiting the export of grain. In the Low Countries, governments established legal measures that channeled the food traffic toward certain cities and obligated merchants to sell their merchandise while in transit.[20] In 1251 Venice forced all ships transporting food in the Adriatic to unload in the city before being able to re-export their goods.[21] The maritime cities of the Mediterranean turned to much more expeditious methods such as the confiscation of grain shipments from foreign merchants transiting through their jurisdictional waters. Intercepting foreign shipments and then forcibly rerouting them toward the shore was another very old policy that was repeated during each crisis period. In 1328, Barcelona, in fact, legalized this forceful measure via the *Vi vel gratis* privilege, granted by King Alfonso the Kind.[22]

The second major battle horse of city governments was the control of grain prices and bread quality. During the frequent grain crises, municipal authorities reflected the decrease in grain supply in the weight and composition of bread rather than in terms of its price, which they tried to maintain at a constant level. Such a policy stemmed from an old practice with legal precedents dating to the ordinances proclaimed in Nuremberg (at the beginning of the thirteenth century), Liège (1252), Lübeck (1255), England (1266–1267),[23] and Marseille (1273),[24] which established the weight of bread according to grain prices and bakers' costs. This system was most likely already in use during the decline of the Roman Empire, and was certainly in use during the Carolingian Empire, when the shortage of low-value currency forced the need to establish a fixed bread price corresponding to the smallest coin in circulation.[25] Maintaining a constant bread price obligated local authorities to enforce meticulous control over daily grain prices, as well as over the work of bread makers and bakers. Selling bread at less than the established weight constituted fraud, punishable with a heavy fine, along with seizure of the fraudulent loaves.

FROM THE MILL TO THE TABLE: INTRA-CITY GRAIN CIRCUITS

From the moment they arrived in the city until their delivery to the consumer in the form of bread, grains travelled a lengthy route. The circuit normally began in the wheat-market square (*alhóndiga, alfòndec, halle*), a functional space fitted with a handful of minimalist structures and used as a grain market. The wheat market was often surrounded by silos and

warehouses, where shipments were initially deposited to be properly inventoried and taxed. The normal users of these facilities were import merchants and intermediaries, who sold their goods to retailers, or transformed
them into secondary products.

The retail sale of grains and grain products fell to innkeepers, shopkeepers, flour merchants, bread makers, and bakers—a collection of closely
related professions selling similar products. While bread makers and bakers dedicated themselves to the sale of bread, shopkeepers specialized in
the re-distribution of grain, flour merchants primarily dealt in flour, and
innkeepers dispatched wheat, as well as bread acquired previously from
the bakers. Each phase of the intra-city grain circuit represented additional
costs that were added cumulatively to the initial price of the incoming grain
shipments.

This was the normal route that grains took in their urban circuit, but
not the only one: importers could also sell all or part of their shipments directly to consumers.[26] On the other hand, when authorities fixed maximum
bread prices during times of scarcity, black markets developed, in which
grains were sold at prices much higher than on the official circuits.[27]

Due to the population growth of the eleventh through to the fourteenth
centuries, the number of mills multiplied dramatically throughout Europe.
England alone calculated that it had more than 6,000 mills in 1086 and
more than 12,000 around the year 1300.[28] The majority of these mills
were hydraulic, situated strategically along the flowing waters of rivers and
tributaries, and far from urban centers, but every city had at least one mill
within the city walls that it could use in case of siege.[29] The miller transformed wheat into flour of equivalent weight, receiving a part of the milled
grain as his salary from those who used his facility.

For most of the Middle Ages, the common practice in both cities and in
rural areas was for each family to prepare its own bread dough, and then
bring it to be baked at a common oven, a dangerous piece of equipment
that only the baker *(formarius)* was authorized to use, maintain, and repair.
The baker baked the dough that customers delivered to his oven, retaining
a certain percentage of the loaves baked as his salary, which he then sold for
profit. Until the end of the twelfth century, this trade was undistinguished
from that of the bread maker *(pistor)*, who not only baked and sold bread,
but also prepared its dough. It was easy to confuse the baker with the bread

maker, since the baker also sold bread—that of his customers, both private and professional, who left some of their loaves as payments, or that bread prepared by the baker himself during times of increased demand.

In fact, conflicts between the two trades were recorded as early as the twelfth century. In several royal cities in France between 1150 and 1200, the bread makers petitioned the king to guarantee them exclusive exercise of the profession in return for regular payments and acceptance of super-vision by the king's administrators. Shortly afterwards they obtained au-thorization to build their own ovens. At the beginning of the thirteenth century, English bread makers, as well as the majority of bread makers in German cities, had their own ovens. However, the appearance of private ovens did not mark an end for the public ovens, which did not disappear completely, or for the bakeries, where bakers sold a great variety of breads and pastries.[30]

During the final centuries of the Middle Ages, however, the bread mak-ers increasingly tended to prevail over the bakers.[31] In Mediterranean cities, the custom of entrusting the production of daily bread to a bread maker, who would then be paid periodically with quantities of grain, or of buy-ing bread directly from the bakeries, took hold after the Black Death. This change in habits, which seems to have stemmed from a desire to consume higher-quality bread, led municipal administrations to construct new ovens, and strengthened the economic and social ascent of the bread makers.[32]

THE RENOWN OF FRENCH WINES

It is clear that throughout the Middle Ages—though without being able to establish a more precise evolutionary timeline—wine was consumed in great quantity,[33] not only in the Mediterranean but also in northern Europe, both in the wine-producing regions (such as those in France and the Germanic Empire) and in nonproduction zones (such as in England and the Low Countries). The social hierarchy was reflected not so much in the quantity of wine consumed, but in its quality and origin.

Wine production was gradually concentrated in certain regions that were highly specialized in growing grapes, some since Roman times. In France, the viniculture map in large part resulted from the advantages of fluvial and maritime transport toward the consumer countries of northern

Europe, as well as from the dominant taste for lighter wines. Among the seventy wines cited by the Norman cleric, Henry d'Andeli, in his poem "The Battle of the Wines," composed shortly after the death of Philip II Augustus (1224), were those of Île-de-France, Laon, Soissons, Champagne, Auxerre, and Beaune.[34] Laon was an important wine market during this period due to its proximity to the Flemish cities, while the wines *of France,* produced in Île-de-France, supplied a growing city, with its court and university, and were exported in great quantities by way of the Seine.

The English wine market, supplied initially from Île-de-France and the Rhine Valley, stimulated the growth of vineyards in Poitou (Aunis and Saintonge), which were able to export wine via La Rochelle during the twelfth century. However, with the Capetian conquest of this territory in 1224, the job of satisfying English demand shifted to Gascony and its primary port, Bordeaux. At the beginning of the fourteenth century, Poitou, La Rochelle, and Gascony supplied the majority of wine on the international trade circuits, with certain specialization: while the wines of Poitou and La Rochelle were sold primarily in France and the Low Countries, the rosés of Gascony found their market in England.[35] Consequently, in the Plantagenet lands, trade integration developed between the islands and the continent: England was one of the primary importers of Gasconese wine, and it, in turn, supplied Gascony with grain, using its own production during abundant years, and using Baltic grain that it re-exported during years of shortage.[36]

The wines of the Rhine were among the principal products of Frisian trade during the sixth and seventh centuries.[37] These wines were also among the primary products imported by England via the merchants of Cologne toward the end of the eleventh and twelfth centuries.[38] At the same time, during the Middle Ages, an important trade of sweet wines existed from the Iberian Peninsula (*Muscatel, Malvasía,* or *vernage* from Alacant or Malaga, *osey* and *Bastardo* from Portugal) and the Eastern Mediterranean (Greece and Crete) toward northern Europe.[39] In general, in the Mediterranean regions where the production and consumption of wine were more or less balanced, wine was not traded over long distances until the end of the Middle Ages.

The fifteenth century brought an end to the golden age of the wine trade, which, in much of central Europe, suffered under the harsh competition of cider, hydromel or mead, and beer. Beer, obtained since the ninth century by fermenting barley or oats and flavoring it with hops, firmly established itself at the end of the Middle Ages, after being perfected by Flemish monks and Hanseatic merchants, in Holland and in northern and central Germany, leaving wine dominant in the southern zones, especially in the Rhine, Mosel, and Alsace.[40]

THE SPECIALTIES OF AL-ANDALUS

The cultivation of olives, the third element of the Mediterranean trilogy, extended generally throughout the western Mediterranean beginning in the twelfth and thirteenth centuries; however, only a few regions specialized in the surplus production of olive oil for export. In the Norman–Swabian epoch, the olive was widely planted throughout Sicily, Campania, Calabria, and especially in Puglia, whose oils, obtained from several olive varieties that were already in use from the classical period, were the most highly appreciated in markets both throughout the Italian Peninsula and further abroad.[41]

The other large zone of Mediterranean Europe that produced and traded oil was Seville. Arab geographers and historians were unanimous in praising oil from the Seville region, produced and exported in large quantity throughout the entire Mediterranean region during the Omeya and Taifal periods. In the twelfth century, al-Idrisi confirmed the wide market reach of oil from the region of Aljarafe (Sharaf), near Seville, which was exported "to the farthest points of East and West, by land and by sea."[42] In the same vein, toward the end of the twelfth century, Zurhi specified that the oil of Sharaf was exported to the lands of the Rum, the Maghreb, Ifriqiya, Misr, and Alexandria, and also to all the kingdoms of Christian Spain.[43] The reputation of Sevillian oil was maintained after the Christian conquest, and in the thirteenth century Genoese chroniclers described Seville as the leading oil producer in Europe.[44]

Al-Andalus also excelled as a producer and exporter of figs, grapes, Zante currants, wines, and—in general—dried fruits and nuts.[45]

THE ORIGINS OF CARNIVOROUS EUROPE

The Black Death has been recognized as the point when meat consumption, until that point a symbol of status, became widespread among the lower classes of urban medieval society. The increase in meat supply in western markets, coming largely from regions of Eastern Europe such as Poland, Hungary, and the Balkans, as well as the increase in the purchasing power of wage earners after the mass death, led to a dramatic decrease in the price of meat and an increase in the number of consumers who had access to it, thus beginning the period that Braudel termed *Carnivorous Europe* (lasting from the mid-fourteenth through to the late-fifteenth centuries).[46]

Sources from the fourteenth century highlight the increased levels of meat consumption in all of western Europe, though those levels were noticeably higher in the north than in the Mediterranean. Moreover, meat consumption varied between rural and urban areas with regard both to the quantity and the types of meat consumed: kid, calf, top-quality lamb, and, in general, all meats that could be sold at relatively profitable prices went to urban slaughterhouses, while pigs, oxen, older sheep, and cows—animals of lesser value—were consumed directly by those who raised them.[47] At the same time, during the fourteenth century, the consumption of sheep and lamb meat culturally distinguished the diet of the main urban classes from the diet of rural dwellers, which was characterized instead by salted pork, the veritable icon of rural life.[48]

It is doubtful, however, that the establishment of these dietary models was the consequence of the new situation that followed the mid-fourteenth-century demographic crisis rather than simply being the continuation, or evolution of an earlier pattern. During the early Middle Ages, meat played an important role in the diet of the rural population[49] and, after decreasing with the expansion of grain cultivation in the eleventh through to the thirteenth centuries, it began to regain its market share in major western cities. From the end of the thirteenth century onward, governments routinely intervened in the meat market in order to assure an adequate supply for their cities,[50] granting privileges, and extending tax exemptions to butchers and livestock merchants. Certain cities showed themselves to have especially high meat-consumption levels—in Florence, for example, the figure was 75 pounds of meat per person per year, according to data presented by Matteo Villani in 1338.[51] The high- and mid-altitude mountain regions of Switzerland and Alsace, from Swabia to Bavaria, and from Tyrol to Carinthia, had specialized for centuries in cattle and sheep rearing, and they traded the meat they produced over varying distances. At the same time, the twelfth and thirteenth centuries saw vast regions in both the north and south of Europe specialize in raising livestock.

Sheep breeding developed throughout all of Europe to some extent, from the North and Baltic Seas, all the way to the Mediterranean. In France it became widely practiced, especially from Normandy south to the Languedoc region. The Iberian Peninsula witnessed the introduction of new sheep varieties, as so-called Berber sheep accompanied the Islamic expansion of the eighth and ninth centuries. The development of Merino sheep had important consequences, particularly after the Battle of Las Navas de Tolosa (1212), which freed up much of the *Meseta* in the middle of the Iberian Peninsula for the Kingdom of Castile. Christian hegemony created favorable conditions for the collective migration of millions of livestock in an annual transhumance from the south to the north of the Peninsula and vice versa. For centuries, the trade of fine Merino wool, leather, meat, skins, and fleeces from animals that had died, or that had been sacrificed during the transhumance, were a source of wealth for the Castilian economy.[52]

The English economy was also deeply marked by the extraordinary development of sheepherding, favored for its use of closed pastures. Cistercian monasteries selected subspecies that were well adapted for wool production in order to satisfy the needs of the strong Flemish textile industry, which reached its peak during the fourteenth and fifteenth centuries.

At the same time, the countries of northern and central Europe saw considerable growth in cattle rearing and in the number of different breeds. During the late Middle Ages, Denmark, Poland, and Hungary became the primary beef providers for German cities. The Hungarian livestock trade shipped products via the Rhine to be unloaded in Aix-la-Chapelle and Mainz, reaching Venice via Slovenia and Friuli.[53]

Butter and cheese also became important items of international trade. Holland, Scandinavia, southern Poland, and, to a lesser extent, England all specialized in the production of butter, which was then exported to other countries. During the twelfth and thirteenth centuries, the English ports of Ipswich, Boston, and Lynn exported tons of butter and cheese to the continent that were produced by the cattle-raising farms owned by the counts of Lancaster in Lancashire and Yorkshire.[54] Scandinavian butter gained ground in southern Europe, replacing lard, suet, and vegetable oils.

As the Middle Ages unfolded in the new Carnivorous Europe, butchery evolved as one of the most tightly regulated trades: on top of the strict requirements for honesty enforced by municipal authorities upon all economic activities of the period, hygienic regulations were also imposed. Though most purchases took place in neighborhood food shops, in Occitan and in Italian cities, slaughterhouses were confined, for hygienic reasons, to the outskirts of urban centers, in some cases located outside the walled enclosure of the city centers and close to the route by which live cattle arrived in the city.[55] On the other hand, in other cities—for example, in France and in towns bordering the Baltic—butcher shops were centrally located, close to the main market.

In all cases, butchers were obligated to slaughter animals only after they had passed a rigorous sanitary inspection, carried out in a designated, closed space, preferably near a flow of water. Large animals were sacrificed there and later drained, gutted, and beheaded. Though this was the rule, some butchers preferred to slaughter their animals in the middle of the street, in front of their houses. Sacrificed animals were ultimately transported to the butcher shops, where they would be sectioned and sold as cuts of meat.[56]

Butcher shops could adopt one of two models. The most frequent was the market, an exchange where each butcher had a stand, or a shop of fixed size that he would set up in a place that he had bought or rented at times when sales were authorized. The second model consisted of small, open facilities, each fitted with cutting tables, meat cleavers, knives, hooks, and containers for waste products and innards.[57] In large cities, two specialized markets existed separately in order to avoid transactional fraud: the *bocaria,* where vendors sold male and female goat and sheep meat; and the *macellus,* where vendors sold other meats. The sale of sick, wounded, or dead animals had to be carried out outside of the *bocaria.*[58]

Meanwhile, butchers brought the innards of recently sacrificed animals to a common site *(casquería)* and prepared them for sale there.[59]

THE SUCCESS OF HERRING

As the number of days of penitence grew, fish acquired great importance in the European diet. The supply of fish, however, was much more rigid than that of meat. The main problem was transport; fish proteins are extremely perishable and easily become toxic with the passage of time. But the perfection of preservation methods brought salted fish within easy reach of the popular classes, while more privileged groups remained faithful to fresh salt- or fresh-water fish, which retained their status as expensive foods.[60]

Beginning in the mid-twelfth century, its special preparation technique distinguished herring—"that small fish which can be easily salted and thus conserved for great lengths of time," as described by Lambert of Saint Omer around 1125—from other salted fish.[61] The combination of salt with smoke, in addition to preserving the herring, changed its color and lent it a delicate flavor and aroma. The fish was maintained in brine for eight to ten days, de-salted for one to two days in fresh water, drained, and, once dry, left to smoke for between eight and eighteen hours above beech or oak wood. The use of this smoking technique ultimately permitted the large-scale trade of herring from the North and Baltic Seas.[62]

Though in the early centuries of the Middle Ages fishermen from Brittany and Normandy probably brought whale and seal meat to market, and the Frisians exported large quantities of herring fished in the waters of the Rhine in the northwest of Europe, neither of these ever achieved the importance that the salted and smoked herring did beginning in the twelfth century. In England, the biggest herring fisheries were situated off the coasts of Norfolk and South Lincolnshire. The red herring of Yarmouth in fact became an important element in England's food supply. The Rhine estuary was another center of the fishing industry throughout the Middle Ages. In France, herring fishing took hold beginning in the eleventh century in the ports of the Channel. Fishermen from Calais, Dieppe, Fécamp, and above all, Boulogne supplied much of the kingdom with millions of herring per year; still, however, they occupied a clear second place in comparison with the Baltic ports.

Indeed, during most of the Middle Ages, and certainly from the thirteenth century onward, the most important fisheries in Europe, as well as the center of the salting industry and of the herring trade, were the Baltic fisheries of Scania, off the south coast of what is now Sweden. Its period of greatest prosperity spanned the thirteenth and fourteenth centuries, and still, in 1537, they processed and salted more than 90,000 tons of fish.[63]

Both sea- and fresh-water catches, once unloaded, were placed in baskets, crates, and lightweight barrels, wrapped in seaweed or grass, periodically refreshed, and brought directly to the places of sale. Salted fish,
especially herring, were sold separately in the market. Fish sales in Paris
were left in the hands of fishermen who worked in fresh, salt, and so-
called royal waters, where they caught pike, barbell, eel, and carp from
their boats anchored in the Seine and the Marne.

THE WHITE GOLD OF THE MIDDLE AGES:
PRODUCTION AND TRADE

Conserving food was, thus, very much a necessity. The most frequently
used preservative during the Middle Ages was salt, the same essential mineral seasoning found on every table. The presence of salt-preserved foods
in the regular diet of the popular classes was considerable: peasants an-
nually salted ham, bacon, pork butt, and entire animals. Salt was also indispensable for the preparation of sausages and cheeses, and to preserve
fish.[64] Grey, brown, or black salts deposited at the bottom of salt marshes
were good for producing cheeses, but salting fish required white salts. The
boom in the herring-preservation industry and the broad social diffusion of
using salt as a preservative led to high demand for high-quality salt across
Europe.

Some of the salt used to satisfy this demand came from the salt marshes
of the Atlantic coast, from Guérande in Brittany, to Setubal in Portugal,
and from the Languedoc coast (Aigues-Mortes, and the *étangs*, or salt
lakes south of Narbonne). Sea salt could be obtained with very little investment simply through the evaporation of water. At the same time, great
quantities of rock salt were extracted from mines in the south of Germany
and Austria, such as those at Hallein near Salzburg, the salt mountain of
Cardona in Catalonia, the saltworks of Franche-Comté, and the mines of
Lorraine.[65]

Salt was therefore a strategic product whose supply was geographically
distributed non-uniformly throughout the continent. This led to a lucrative long-distance trade by both land and sea, already attested to in the
year 700, when merchants from Comacchio on the Adriatic coast travelled
inland up the Po to sell their salt.[66] From the twelfth century onward, the

salt marshes in the Bay of Bourgneuf on the Atlantic coasts supplied salt to England, the Low Countries, and the cities of the Hansa, with Brugge as the main distribution center.

Attracted by the profitability of salt production and trade, public bodies, which converted salt into an important source of tax income, rivaled private-sector initiatives.[67] The kings of France monopolized the sale of salt—which had to be bought in the royal saltworks—and imposed a high duty (up to 30% of the final sale).[68] Venice built a veritable empire around salt: early on, the Venetians began to import the fine salt of Istria, Dalmatia, and Albania, as well as coarse salt from Ibiza and from the salt lakes of Cyprus. As salt passed through its ports, Venice imposed high taxes, that transformed salt into luxury merchandise.[69]

Where low temperatures and low sunlight hours considerably limited high levels of salt production, the most commonly used preservative was smoke. Meat and fish from the Baltic and North Sea shores, and from high mountain towns, were routinely hung to smoke in kitchen chimneys.

PLANTS FROM THE EAST

From the eleventh century onward, spices enjoyed great prestige in the Western world. Privileged classes appreciated them for their organoleptic qualities, since they improved the flavor and aroma of foods, ranging from the tasty meats enjoyed during banquets to the legumes and vegetables that made up fasting-day meals. Spices were also esteemed for their antiseptic properties, their use in preserving certain foods and extending their availability throughout the year, and for the therapeutic and tonic virtues attributed to them by contemporary medicine, in particular that of the Salerno School.[70]

The spices available in European city markets beginning in the twelfth century were plentiful and varied. Among the most common were plant-based resins: aloe, the bitter resin extracted from the leaf of the same plant, produced on the island of Socotra (in the Indian Ocean south of Arabia), consumed as a purgative; camphor, the resin of a tree that grew in Sumatra and Borneo, used against rheumatisms and heart diseases; scammony, the whitish sap from the root of a plant originating in Syria and Asia Minor, also used as a purgative; and cane sugar, used to fight chest illnesses. There were also plants and parts of plants: galangal root from China and India that was used as a stimulant; rhubarb root, also of Chinese origin, used as a diuretic and laxative; ginger, from India and Arabia, either fresh or crystallized, used as a seasoning due to its aromatic properties, and as a medicine; cinnamon bark, grown in China, Indochina, and Sri Lanka, appreciated as a cooking aromatic; and saffron, the dried stigmas of a type of crocus flower cultivated in Sicily, Italy, and Spain, and used to make medicines and cosmetics, as seasoning, and as a dye for high-quality textiles such as silk. Standing out among the fruits were: cloves, the dry bud of a plant growing in the Moluccas, east of Borneo, appreciated in both pharmacy and cooking; nutmeg, the seed of a fruit growing on trees on the islands of Ambon and Célèbes (Sulawesi) in Indonesia, used as an aromatic; and pepper, the dried berry of a climbing plant grown in India and Sri Lanka, both white pepper, when its skin was removed, and black pepper, used as a seasoning.[71]

With the exception of saffron, whose cultivation was notably developed in Catalonia, these were rare, curious plants that had arrived from afar, mostly from the Orient. The supply of spices in the west grew throughout the twelfth century as Christian fleets cornered Muslim ships in the Mediterranean, and as Italian, Occitan, and Catalan merchants, protected by the Crusades, began to arrive in the ports of Syria and Palestine. To respond to the demand for spices, large import groups emerged in the maritime cities of the northwestern Mediterranean. Spices were brought from the markets of the Near East by a near monopoly of Italian merchants, mostly Venetians, who benefited from relatively fast transit, experience in the market, permanent agents, and good credit terms.[72] Beginning in the fourteenth century, two other well-differentiated professions prospered on the coattails of the spice merchants: spice vendors and pharmacists. The first sold spices, tapers, and candles on the retail market, while the second sold medicines, preserves, sauces, and jams.[73]

Spices radically changed the taste of food for the well-off, so much so that they became a key symbol of privileged status. Spices' versatility and range of use beyond the culinary, in addition to their symbolism and link to exotic origins, lent to their mysterious and sacred value, and explained the high demand for them—and led to one of the most lucrative trades of medieval and modern times.

Spices, livestock, and some food products were traded among the dense network of weekly markets and annual fairs established in the twelfth through the fourteenth centuries that were held regularly in cities and towns throughout the Western world. As we have seen, the demand for some of these food products—most importantly bread, but also wine and meat—led to a system of long-distance trade by land, river, and sea that linked areas of production with cities and other regions of consumption. The regulation of the food trade reached an unmatched level between the mid-thirteenth century and the end of the fourteenth century, coinciding with the implementation of provisioning policies and the imposition of taxes by cities and states.

Nonetheless, even given the importance achieved by these structures, we should not forget that some food never became part of the trade circuits. Indeed, on one hand, the peasant population, settled on hereditary tenures, continued to produce a portion of what they consumed. At the same time, for people living in rural areas and in small towns, uncultivated lands and forests never stopped being an important, alternative source of food that helped them to lessen the impact of hunger. Grasses, roots, wild fruits, some types of wild animals, and certain fresh-water fish naturally became part of the medieval diet even outside periods of famine.[74] Thus, throughout the Middle Ages, a significant proportion of total food sidestepped the trade structures—and, therefore, also the regulation and taxation imposed upon them.

CHAPTER THREE

Food Security

GIULIANO PINTO

Charles Hindley

HUNGER: A DISQUIETING PRESENCE

Libera nos Domine a fame, a bello, a peste. Famines, wars, epidemics: in this Latin invocation, these are the three scourges of the apocalypse that strike at the European peoples more or less throughout the Middle Ages and beyond. We are not dealing with separate phenomena; the three are linked by a network of connections of cause and effect, which are summarized in Figure 3.1.[1]

Hunger, mainly due to poor harvests brought about by bad weather or wars, forced whole populations to move in search of food, and led to an increase in the death rate and to outbreaks of epidemics, which, in turn, affected food production. It was a vicious circle, all too familiar to people in the Middle Ages.[2] Hunger, wrote a witness of the great famines and epidemics of sixth-century Italy, Procopius of Caesarea, is the worst of all evils: "When hunger arrives, it shows that other evils can be withstood, and, when it appears, it sweeps into oblivion every other evil, and makes all deaths, except the one caused by itself, smile on mankind."[3] He had seen the effects of hunger at first hand—"I have seen it with my own eyes,"[4] with its many victims:

They all became gaunt and pale, because their flesh, through under-nourishment, as it were fed upon itself, and the excess of bile, having

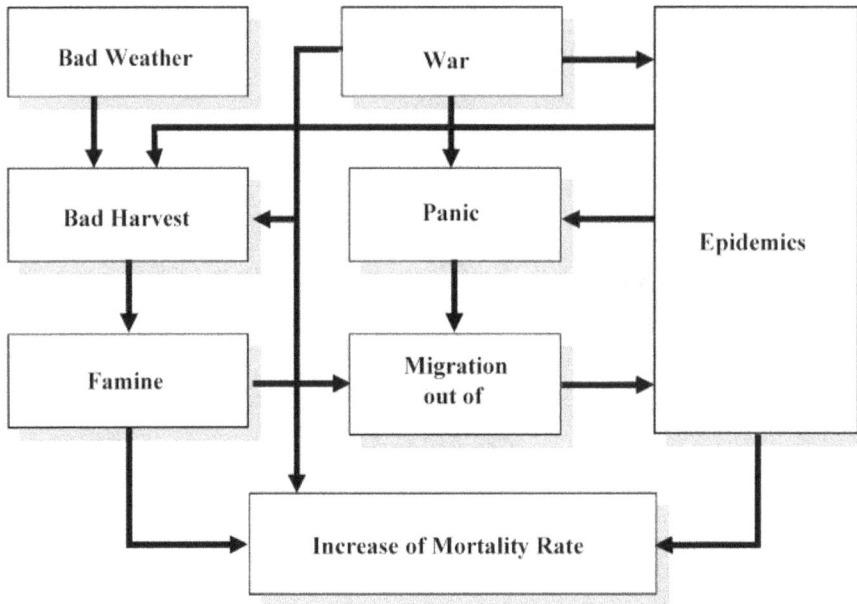

FIGURE 3.1: The cause and effect relationships between famines, wars and epidemics.

got the upper hand, left a yellowish film on it [...] The skin, all dried up, looked more like pigs' hide, and gave the impression of being attached to the bones, while dark complexions changed to black.[5]

When we speak of *hunger* during the European Middle Ages, we mean a general scarcity of food, but mainly (though not only) a scarcity of cereals and a lack of bread. For a very long time, European and Mediterranean civilizations were based on the production of wheat. The so-called barbarian peoples, according to Roman writers, knew nothing of bread. They lived on various kinds of meat, milk, cheeses, and wild fruits, together with oat soups and barley cakes, yet once they had settled within the borders of the Roman Empire and converted to Christianity, they too became consumers of bread.[6]

Consequently, bread provided basic and, indeed, essential nourishment. One could often do without the various accompaniments that went with bread—as well as wine and the other alcoholic drinks, which in the Middle Ages provided both pleasure and calories—but one could not do without bread. Bread-producing lands, or farming methods such as *reducere terram ad panem,* were expressions that were quite commonly used to indicate fields ploughed for cereals, or for the cultivation of new land.

In the early Middle Ages, vast, empty spaces encouraged the growth of a woodland and pastoral economy that was based on the Germanic model, and meant that the gathering of wild fruit and the rearing of animals was integrated with agricultural production, which lessened the effects of bad harvests.[7] But what wild fruit, fungi, edible roots, and game could offer in times of necessity was not enough to protect people when the harvest failed. From this perspective the differences between the early and later Middle Ages were maybe less marked than one might think. Of course, at the end of the thirteenth and beginning of the fourteenth centuries we find some heavily populated areas, some fairly dense networks of towns (e.g., Flanders and central-northern Italy), and even before then we see farms divided up among several peasant families; but an overall evaluation leads us inescapably to the conclusion that in the later Middle Ages, pasture and woodland more or less continued to be dominant across the greater part of Europe. Population figures at the height of medieval development show that for England there were maybe six million people, with a density of five or six people per square mile; in Italy, one of the more populous countries, there were just over twelve million inhabitants. In France, the average density was about eight people per square mile, and this figure dropped to around four people per square mile in Germany. The population was more sparsely scattered the further one went into central and eastern Europe and Scandinavia.[8] In addition, if we are to believe the surviving narrative sources, episodes of cannibalism and death from hunger appear more frequently in pre-twelfth-century sources. On examining current evidence, famine then took a rapidly increasing hold of the region; famine probably occurred more often, but perhaps with less devastating effects, due to the creation of a rationing system, and a more efficient trading network.

Bread did not mean the same thing for every social class. White bread made from wheat flour was for the upper classes, although in certain areas of central Europe the darker rye, or spelt bread was commonly eaten. The less well-off classes and peasants often ate bread mixed with flour from inferior cereals (barley, millet, foxtail millet, and sorghum). These were also used in the preparation of the broths, soups, and porridges of the poor. In difficult times the cereals were ground, without taking off the bran.

At the higher altitudes of southern Europe, especially from the beginning of the second millennium, the answer to food problems, which had been made more acute by population growth, lay in the planting of chestnut trees. The flour from the grinding of dried chestnuts was used as a substitute for that of cereals. Yet it was a poor substitute, which the local people themselves complained about, envying the peasants of the plains who could eat bread made from wheat all year round.[9]

However it was made, what worried people the most was the *inopia panis*—the *maxima penuria panis* to which chroniclers allude. In times of famine, when there were no cereals to be had, substitute products were created in order to produce something that resembled bread. It was quite usual in difficult periods for pulses (beans, vetches, or chickpeas) and acorns to be used in order to make bread; but in extreme circumstances this went much further. Gregory of Tours (538–594) describes a severe famine across Gaul in the years 585–587, where grape seeds, the inflorescence of hazel trees, and the roots of ferns, dried and reduced to powder and mixed with a small proportion of cereal flour, were used to make bread.[10] Raoul Glaber wrote that in Burgundy (1033), "many dug out of the ground a white dust similar to clay that they mixed in with the little flour or bran they had; they thus baked a bread they calculated would help them escape death. These efforts served to give them at least the hope of being able to survive, because in reality the benefits were nil."[11] Three centuries later in Florence, during the famine of 1346–1347, millers and bakers were arrested for adding chalk and sand to flour; one baker went as far as to make bread from a very carefully kneaded mixture of bran, chalk, and sawdust, adding a plentiful amount of fennel to cover up the unpleasant smell and taste.[12] Expedient measures of this kind, even if they filled the bellies of the unlucky victims, had devastating effects on their health.

Consequently, there was bread made with imagination and cunning, using everything that might resemble flour; and then there was bread that, during times of famine, was reduced in weight. During times of famine, the authorities often resorted to the stratagem of selling an individual loaf of bread at the same price, but reducing its weight as the price of wheat rose.[13]

The Middle Ages saw local famines, regional famines, and what are termed general famines, the latter being those that hit one or more of the larger countries of Europe. The first type is certainly the one we know the least about, because there was often no chronicler to write about what happened. It is a fact that for many centuries we owe our knowledge exclusively to the existence of descriptions in narrative sources: the systematic collection of this evidence is still the one indispensable tool we have to aid in our understanding of the frequency and intensity of famines.[14] For example, was the food situation in Germany between the tenth and thirteenth centuries in actual fact worse than in other parts of Europe, or is it that we have gained this impression due to the plentiful supply of narrative sources for that area, and their very thorough examination by Fritz Curschmann?[15] It is not until the late thirteenth century that we have access to other sources (especially documents in the public domain) that provide useful evidence; otherwise we need to carry out extensive, detailed research on private or personal documents, from the eleventh century onward, to find any reference to difficult situations due to poor harvests.[16]

The situation concerning the sources certainly leads to errors in reconstruction. Were there more famines or more sources providing evidence of them? Were the desperate accounts we read about based in reality or did their authors exaggerate? Some famines, further back in time, are indissolubly linked to the pages of a chronicler or a historian: those of the sixth century to Procopius of Caesarea (c. 500–c. 562) and Gregory of Tours; that of the 1031–1033 famine to Raoul Glaber; and that of the 1197 famine to Reineri of Liège.[17] The great famines of the first half of the fourteenth century (1315–1317 and 1346–1347) are written about by quite a few more chroniclers at a time when the sources multiplied and the focus on the scourge intensified.

Writers, especially in more ancient times, rarely had the chance to compare their own accounts with those of others. What they saw seemed entirely exceptional to them. Not infrequently, the descriptions of the effects of famine resemble each other: people are forced to eat the roots and bark of trees, animal carrion, dogs and cats; sometimes corpses were eaten, including those of criminals hauled down from the gallows, or people went as far as to kill other human beings to feed on their flesh.[18] On several occasions, cases of this kind certainly occurred, but we may ask whether we are dealing with stereotypes: maybe the description of a great hunger *has to be* colored by episodes of this kind.

The main causes of famine lay in the weakness of farming (its very low productivity in terms of cereal cultivation, which rose only slightly between the early and later Middle Ages); in the difficulties, only slightly reduced in the last centuries of the Middle Ages, in trading grain over medium to long distances; in the weakness of the political institutions that had to regulate procurement or supply; and in the slowness and unreliability of systems of information. Sometimes it was enough for rumor, whether true or false, to cause an increase in prices and the concealment of corn, or vice versa. Matteo Villani, the mid-fourteenth-century Florentine chronicler, vividly highlights the phenomenon:

> The great purchases of grain from across the sea may provoke considerable losses of public money, and it is by no means certain the corn will arrive; but it serves to give hope to the populace and to get the granaries open for the citizens. On the other hand, you can achieve nothing with the use of force: those who have great reserves of corn keep them hidden, and its scarcity means hunger for the many.[19]

From the twelfth to thirteenth centuries, coinciding with the development of the market economy, famines were affected by speculators, who took advantage of the great oscillations in cereal prices. It might not be appropriate to talk of *induced*[20] famines, but there were certainly cases of price increases that were artfully provoked by speculators in times of difficulty (rich landowners, merchants, millers, bakers, etc.). Speculators faced considerable risks during times of famine, as their stockpiles could simply be seized, they could be assaulted by the hungry masses, and they were often forced to sell their grain at politically directed prices, yet when the harvests were good, speculators had no room in which to maneuver.

Famine was almost always sparked off by bad harvests due to bad weather. Excessively heavy or prolonged periods of rain that prevented sowing or rotted the grain, were especially to blame, with drought rarely leading to famine. Drought could stop mills from working and mean no flour at the local level, due to the drying up of streams and smaller rivers in some of the drier areas of the Mediterranean.[21] Sometimes, in central to eastern Europe, the frosts of late spring would endanger the harvests.[22] However, the main culprit was rain. That there was a worsening of climatic conditions in the last two or three centuries of the Middle Ages[23] has been proved by scientific analysis (pollen analysis, dendrology, etc.), and confirmed by the written evidence. The accounts of the thirteenth-century English chronicler, Matthew Paris, with a wealth of information on bad weather, rains, and good and bad harvests, has been aptly termed a *weather report*.[24]

Wars were another cause—armies on the march lived off the land—mainly at the local or regional level. Procopius of Caesarea (councilor and secretary of the Byzantine general Belisarius), describing the great famine of 538, points out how in Emilia and in Etruria harvests were lost because of the war between the Goth and Byzantium forces; part of the population sought food and refuge in the Picene (Marche region), but there, too, food was hard to find.[25] Gregory of Tours describes Frankish soldiers roaming around in search of food, devastating everything in their path.[26] In the fourteenth century, mercenary troops terrorized the Italian countryside.

Sometimes insects and animals would also damage harvests, or their preservation. The chroniclers tell of invasions of grasshoppers between the sixth and twelfth centuries in various parts of Europe, and rats were frequently accused of infesting grain deposits.[27] Storage in years of good harvests was often hopelessly ineffective: public deposits, granaries, or grain pits did not stop wheat from rotting in the course of a year, and it then had to be sold at a much lower price.[28]

Diseases, especially epidemics, affected the work in the fields. A peasant family losing an adult worker would no longer be able to manage its land. Famines themselves increased mortality. Even when hunger was not the immediate cause of death, the weakened population, after fairly long periods of undernourishment or poor nourishment, was more likely to catch infectious diseases or fall ill, though the plague would hit rich and poor alike.[29]

A famine often lasted for more than a year because of continued bad weather, but other factors would contribute as well. Serious famine would affect the next harvest because the less wealthy peasant families—in other words, most families—would find it hard to set aside the usual quantity of seed rather than eat it, and hunger then reduced people's capacity to work in the fields. The animals then suffered from hunger because humans would compete with them for nourishment (oats, sorghum, spelt, barley).

For the entire Middle Ages, then, famine was a sword of Damocles hanging over the heads of European society; fear of hunger marked people's lives and determined their behavior, with invocations to God to keep hunger at bay (such as the one that begins this chapter), and an exceptional diffusion of stories of miracles concerning food and bread. The biblical episode of the manna from heaven falling into the desert was very widely known, and this was even more the case with the miracle of Christ's multiplication of the loaves, often portrayed in bas-reliefs and pictures; and the miracle returns in many hagiographical texts, though on a more modest scale, attributed to a large number of saints. People's fear of hunger is likewise behind the myth of the land of Cockaigne that spread widely from the thirteenth century onward: people dreamt of a country where the most delicious foods were to hand, and where hard labor would not be needed to enjoy them.[30]

TOWARD A CHRONOLOGY OF THE CRISES

Historians have traditionally divided the Middle Ages (up until the mid-fourteenth century) into three periods that are related to problems of agricultural production, the burden of a growing population, and crises of subsistence: these periods are the early Middle Ages (until the end of the tenth century); the period of population expansion lasting until towards the end of the thirteenth century; and the years of the great food crises, roughly between 1280 and 1348. Then, the great depopulation crisis brought about by the Black Death, and by later waves of epidemics, created a new cereal supply-and-demand dynamic, while, in the meantime, storage systems underwent further development.

There is evidence of crises of subsistence in the later years of the Roman Empire, despite the survival of much of the imperial food system, which had functioned so excellently for so long.[31] The situation worsened roughly between the middle of the fifth and middle of the sixth centuries. In Italy, the region providing the best evidence for that period, there were at least fifty years of hunger and famine; one in every two. As well as bad weather, war was the main cause: the invasion of the Ostrogoths, the war between the Goths and Byzantium (535–553), the descent of the Longobards (568), and the long war between the Longobards and the Byzantines. There was no real let-up for around 150 years. The wars contributed to outbreaks of famine, yet famine was also the cause of war: the devastation ruined harvests and armed, hungry populations sought food elsewhere. The Germanic peoples, once settled in the areas they had conquered, did not immediately give up their nomadic habits and propensity to sack.[32]

Even in regions where war was not so commonplace, there were occurrences of serious hunger. Gregory of Tours goes into a wealth of detail about the hunger in Gaul in the years 585–587; Bede (c. 672–735), about that of 680 in Britain.[33] In a time when there were no longer any public authorities—only the bishops exercised some degree of power in the towns—it was almost impossible to find a remedy for the crises of the harvest, or to have recourse to trade, or exchange of some kind with less unfortunate areas.

Epidemics of pestilence, which shook the Mediterranean and southern Europe between the middle of the sixth and seventh centuries,[34] badly affected agricultural production. Paul the Deacon (c. 720–c. 798) describes the effects of a pestilence that struck Italy in the second half of the sixth century, where, "the harvest awaited the reaper intact, in the vineyards there was no the vintage, no grape harvest."[35] Leprosy, spreading throughout Europe more or less at the same time, though not killing its victims, reduced the number of people available for agricultural labor.[36]

The increased stability of the newly formed kingdoms and fewer wars, an improved organization of the great landed properties along the *curtis* system, the first faint signs of a food system, the growth of a network of markets, and the disappearance of pestilence epidemics, certainly had a positive effect on agricultural production and on the circulation of commodities—yet all this did not stop the repeated reappearance of serious famine in Europe and the Mediterranean region. Narrative sources such as annals provide a type of calendar of hunger: leaving aside local and regional famines (the latter richly documented) the years 792–793, 805–806, 821–822, 868, 896, 940, and 992 were marked by very serious famine on a continental scale.[37]

Between the beginning of the eleventh and the end of the thirteenth centuries, the European population grew considerably, together with the expansion of areas under cultivation, an increase in the number of settlements, and the considerable growth of the urban population. Outbreaks of war were less frequent over much of Europe: the Normans and Hungarians settled down and set up kingdoms; and conflict with Muslims was concentrated in the Iberian Peninsula and the Eastern Mediterranean. New agricultural techniques meant higher productivity of the land. Nevertheless, despite this progress, famines did not decrease; on the contrary, they sometimes seemed still more cruel and of the general type. In this case, too, the evidence is clear. Taking only regional famines or those that spread right across the continent into consideration for this period, famine years, on average, occurred once every two to three years. Especially evident among the latter were the years 1004–1006, 1031–1033 (the terrible famine described by Raoul Glaber), 1044–1046, 1090–1099, 1124–1126, 1150–1151, 1195–1198, 1233–1235, 1252, 1257–1259, 1271–1272, and 1281–1282.[38] However, this picture is certainly incomplete.

The six or seven decades from 1280 to the mid-fourteenth century have been indicated as a period distinguished by a further resurgence of famine, within a specific set of conditions that historians commonly refer to as the *crisis* of the fourteenth century. The years of hunger were more frequent. The people of the time were aware of this to some extent: Domenico Lenzi, a Florentine grain merchant, decided to make a note of price variations for cereals on the Florence market and wrote down the events linked to famines, realizing the latter were getting worse.[39] The towns, having grown so rapidly, became the sounding board for hunger.

Although there were many famine years in the various European regions, the focus here is on the two great crises of 1315–1317 and 1346–1347. The former struck hard in central-northern Europe and the latter mainly struck Mediterranean Europe.

The great hunger of 1315–1317, set off by very heavy and continuous rains over a period of three years, was a scourge for most of Europe: France, Flanders, England, Germany, Austria, Poland, and so on.[40]

Not only in many cases did the seed rot or the grain not ripen properly, but the abundance of rains caused flooding that left lower-lying lands uncultivateable. Cereal prices then rose enormously, even by as much as eleven or twelve times, compared to previous years. Hunger drove many of the peasantry to abandon the fields and seek food in the towns, where many fell, exhausted, in the streets. Every kind of bread substitute was tried. People sacrificed domestic animals and even those that were used for work. Perhaps there were episodes of cannibalism (if not stereotyped, as previously mentioned). Malnutrition and recourse to foul or filthy food brought on fevers, infections, and dysentery, with an inevitable increase in the death rate. At Ypres between May and October 1316, 2,794 bodies (around 10% of the population) were buried at the expense of the town; in Brugge, between May and September, 1,938 (around 4% of the inhabitants) died.[41]

The famine of 1346–1347 was also brought about by continuous rains from the autumn of 1345 until the end of spring 1346, and it struck Mediterranean areas (Italy, Provence, Languedoc, and most of the Iberian Peninsula), but also Burgundy, Aquitaine, and even England.[42] The harvests of 1346 in the areas most badly affected were a quarter or even a sixth of the usual in quantity: in other words, they yielded seed or little more. Consequently, prices rose. Some chroniclers called the famine the worst they had ever seen: for example, among others, Giovanni Villani (c. 1270–1348) recounted that wheat could not be found in Florence, not even by those with plenty of money.[43] In Valencia, the year 1347 was long remembered as "the year of the great hunger."[44] However, the worst suffering lay with the countryside dwellers, who abandoned their villages and their lands in many areas in an attempt to find food in nearby towns.

The causes of this resurgence have been the subject of a great deal of debate, which we need not go into in great detail. The worsening of the climate has been stressed; the excessive exploitation of marginal lands; the imbalance between urban and rural populations, or rather between those who worked the land and others involved in other kinds of work; the excessive burden of the increased population in certain areas; production weighing too heavily on a subjected peasantry; and the development of trade in the countryside (of food and raw materials), which enriched a few and endangered the *ménages* of many.

From this rapid summary it is evident that famine struck throughout the Middle Ages; there were no happy interludes, as some have suggested for the mid-eleventh to the mid-thirteenth centuries. It is also quite possible that the apparent scarcity of crises in the seventh and eighth centuries is due to the scarcity of written sources that cover the period.

There was certainly a turning point with the increased effectiveness of public authorities starting, very approximately, from the first decades of the twelfth century,[45] and the creation of an extensive cereal market, whose network extended to medium and even long distances, covering the entire Mediterranean area—where trade was facilitated by sea transport—and a good deal of the rest of Europe. It was no coincidence that among the larger European cities the one that suffered the least was Venice, which had no dependent territories, but did have intensive trade relations with cereal-producing areas (the Veneto hinterland, the Marche, Puglia, and the eastern Mediterranean).[46] During the famine of 1315–1317, Brugge, which had direct access to the sea and had a particularly strong merchant class, suffered less from the consequences of the crisis compared to Ypres, whose economy was based exclusively on manufacturing, and was further from the North Sea coast.

A comparison between the various periods we have divided the Middle Ages into, and between the various parts of the Western world, is possible only on a statistical basis. However, we are impeded in terms of comparison both by the lack of direct evidence as we go further back in time, and by our difficulty in measuring the extent of the seriousness of the crises. Everything depends on the presence or otherwise of chroniclers and on the reliability of their descriptions. Often an eyewitness would be led to exaggerate the dimensions of the crisis; expressions such as "the greatest hunger here for a very long time" are common, and derive from an inability to gain a critical perspective over the medium to long term.

Useful comparisons could be made by considering the trends in wheat prices and their oscillation in times of crisis; but indications of this kind are fairly unusual before the thirteenth century. One of the first to provide them is Raoul Glaber, who recounts how, during the great hunger of 1031–1033, the price of corn, already high in some areas, rose in other areas that were more exposed to the famine by three times as much as in the less affected areas.[47] Then, from the mid-thirteenth century, the written evidence is so much more plentiful that it allows us to reconstruct the cereal prices even for particular European countries.[48] The great oscillations, in both the medium term and for the crisis years, confirm the gradual worsening of the situation in the hundred years or so before the Black Death.

SOCIAL AND ECONOMIC EFFECTS OF FAMINE

The years of bad harvests with rising cereal prices were particularly bad for the poorer classes of both the countryside and town. In the countryside, the situation varied a great deal. The rich peasants—holders of substantial and fertile property, who made use of laborers from outside the family—produced grain not just, or not so much, for their own consumption as for the market; they were therefore capable of managing their reserves, putting them on the market when prices were higher. For them, famine could be an occasion for good business—to make a killing, in fact. However, we are only talking about a minority of the peasant population.

For the small peasant landholders, things went differently. Their small plots of land—in some cases not even very fertile, especially in higher altitude Mediterranean areas—did not enable them to set a surplus aside, even in the years of good harvests as what little surplus there might be ended up on the market to help pay for other requirements of the family. With bad harvests—by no means infrequent, as we have seen—not only was any surplus lacking, but the bare minimum to feed the family and have the seed for the next sowing was also lacking. Bad harvests meant getting into debt, all the more heavily if bad harvests came one after the other. The peasantry thus fell victim to speculators, and to obtain loans in money or food they signed away future harvests, or even the land they held, the evidence for which has come down to us from several European countries.[49]

As far as the dependent peasantry went—the great majority of the rural world—once they had paid the rent, very little remained of their harvest, and their difficulties in finding enough food for consumption and to set aside seed for the next sowing multiplied. For these people too, perhaps their only chance was a loan. The landowner would be approached for loans, but obtaining these in cereal or in money could have dire consequences. The contractual relationship with the landowner would alter to the latter's advantage. This clearly shows in the analysis of contracts in Italy in the period of the great fourteenth-century famines (1315–1348), when the obligations burdening the dependent peasantry multiplied and weighed them down all the more.[50]

For the great landowners, the fall in rent was compensated for by the rise in prices. In addition, the ample reserves they built up gave them the chance to take political advantage of the situation, obtaining the plaudits of the masses through handing out wheat at bargain prices when it was wise to do so.[51] Merchants and speculators gained the most from these difficult times. We have mentioned the profitable loans conceded in times of crisis; the other method was to corner and hoard away cereal at harvest time and release it onto the market when prices reached their peak.

In the towns, famine drove broad strata of wage earners towards poverty, with them joining the poverty-stricken masses who normally lived on charity, or from begging: widows, old people, disabled people, or those whose ability to work was compromised in some way. Faced with unchanging daily wages, remaining rigidly fixed at their low levels, the increase in cereal prices by four to five times, and often more, forced people to drastically reduce their consumption, eliminating everything that was not strictly necessary; for example, wine and other alcoholic drinks, meat, or new clothes. Pawning things offered one way out, but often this was not enough. For many, the situation would become appalling, and only the intervention of public authorities and charitable organizations could provide some relief. Thus, in Florence in the spring of 1347, the *Commune* distributed some 94,000 ration cards (one for every mouth) to allow people to access the bread baked in the public bakeries. At that point in time the town had around 85,000 to 90,000 inhabitants: evidently, a very high percentage of the citizens applied for the ration cards, and likewise, many of the inhabitants of the city's surrounding areas.[52]

Another result of the famine was the increase in criminal elements: theft and looting for necessity are documented, smuggling or poaching of every kind, assaults on the convoys carrying grain, and riots in the cities provoked by lack of wheat.[53] Considerably rarer, on the other hand, was the occurrence of revolts or rebellions caused directly by hunger.[54]

Finally, famine radically affected people's mindsets.

Expectations concerning the next harvest kept entire populations and their rulers on tenterhooks. An old Florentine custom was for the officials dealing with the food supply to climb up to the top of a high tower every year on February 3 to examine the surrounding countryside. From the amount of greenery they could see they would regulate the purchase of grain.[55] Anxiety over the coming of famine is vividly illustrated in a well-known episode narrated by Salimbene di Parma (1221–1290) about the year 1286: a teacher from Reggio Emilia, inspired by a devil who had informed him of an imminent famine, stored in a trunk pieces of bread picked up here and there and bags of pressed flour; dying in his home after being suffocated by the same devil, he was found by his neighbors lying by putrid sacks of flour and trunks full of bread that had gone rotten.[56]

The time spent in expectation of the grain meant to be arriving from afar generated hope, but also tremendous disappointment when its arrival was delayed. The fear and rage of the hungry people turned them in general against merchants, millers, bakers, and above all against the ruling authorities, who were well aware of how dangerous famines were for the town.[57] To all this was added the anguish of those who saw in the scourge of hunger divine punishment for sin.[58]

CHAPTER FOUR

Food and Politics

JEAN-PIERRE DEVROEY

Anne McBride

In Antiquity and the Middle Ages, the majority of the population living in the countryside ate only the food that they themselves produced. In cities, however, food took on other economic and political dimensions because food came from the *outside,* which, particularly during periods of famine, could cause enormous food shortages and social unrest. If the so-called great hunger shook the very foundations of power in its legitimacy and fed popular emotions (e.g., mobility crisis or riots), everyday malnutrition and the lasting consequences of nutritional deficiencies were of no concern to the elites. Yet, the divergence in diets was obvious both physically, in the varying statures of people, and politically, in the opposition between the *popolo grasso* (fat people) and *popolo minuto* (thin people), the higher and lower part of the citizenship, as they were called in Italy at the time.

FEEDING THE POOR; FACING FAMINE

In Antiquity there was little evidence of systematic governmental interventions in the day-to-day food procurement for the residents of cities, with the exception of the imperial capitals, Rome, and later Constantinople, where the grain supply became, from Augustus onward, an imperial monopoly.

Elsewhere, in most cities, food procurement in times of scarcity mostly depended upon the actions of the urban magistrates, the *aediles,* to prevent food crises from turning into riots. At other times, supplying food to city dwellers took place either through domestic circuits, inside the large aristocratic households (whose *pater familias,* because of his status, had to feed all family members, free and enslaved, and his family and business relations), or through the market, for free salarymen, or, more occasionally, through individuals' philanthropy during civil and religious celebrations. The only new factor in this social and political system resulted from Christian charity, which progressively became an alternative to other forms of food distribution for indigents.[1] The distribution of food and clothing was a path to salvation resulting from the believer's desire to fulfill the moral obligations of the Christian doctrine. This generosity remained episodic, however, with no real political or economic impact. During periods of violent crisis, such as in 792–793, Charlemagne asked each powerful person, both ecclesiastical and secular, to feed "four starving poor until the next harvest."

In the Middle Ages, food aid to the hungry took place in three separate social spaces:

1. The aid given to those who depended on a lord occurred within the structure of the aristocratic household or within the framework of the *seigneurie* (the lord's land). The ninth-century capitularies frequently reminded the powerful to look after their *familia* (dependents). They evoked the strength of the ties between a master (*dominus*) and his household. After the famine of 1095, the Abbey of Gembloux bought properties from small lords who were ruined, having accumulated debts from usurers to feed their peasants.

2. The wandering poor, associated with beggars, were stigmatized. In 806 the capitulary of Nijmegen asked the king's subjects to both feed their own poor and not feed the wanderers, unless it was in exchange for work. Those that hunger forced to the roads found temporary relief in monasteries (at the door of abbeys or in hospices), following the model of evangelical hospitality. They received a meal, bread, and a small amount of money to pursue their journey. The number of those seeking assistance at monasteries was often greater than one

hundred, or even several hundred a day. These first two types of assistance rely primarily on direct consumption, through the intermediary of producers or owners who controlled their production.

3. All collective and anonymous aid (whether temporary or long term) was institutionalized by either secular (princes, urban authorities) or religious (bishops) authorities. In the early Middle Ages, this aid was organized by the bishop, who was traditionally in charge of the care of the Christian poor (elderly, widows, and orphans). However, the charities of episcopal cities, whose number rose in the last quarter of the seventh century, acted mainly on behalf of small, closed clienteles of people receiving permanent assistance, who were regularly listed in the churches' registers (*matricula*). This aid became formalized with the Carolingians (in the eighth and ninth centuries), and then in the cities (starting in the eleventh century).

In Merovingian sources, famine is described as a natural disaster. Beginning in the middle of the eighth century, contemporaries link the penury of hunger (*inopia famis*) with mankind's misbehaviors and sins. The reigns of Pepin III and Charlemagne were shaken by three famines of a rare intensity and geographic reach, in 763–764, 793–794, and 805–806. Once abundance returned in 765, Pepin III attributed the tribulations of the kingdom "to *our* sins" (including his subjects and himself). To give thanks to the divine mercy, the king asked the bishops to organize fasts and litanies and made, for the first time, paying the tithe mandatory for all, "whether they want it or not." In 805, during the famine, Charlemagne made the decision not to wait for the order to ask for divine mercy in situations of famine, diseases and epidemics, natural disasters, or any other tribulation. In 793–794, the first allegations of cannibalism in the Middle Ages appeared (they will surface again in the context of the famines that took place from the beginning of the eleventh century onward). These rumors seemingly echoed a disastrous political and religious climate. The famine of 793 followed the rebellion, drowned in blood, of Charlemagne's own son, Pepin the Hunchback. During the same period, chroniclers mention the general uprising of the Saxons and the victories of the Saracens of Spain over the Franks. The *Moselle Annals* and a 794 capitulary, in which Charlemagne reiterates the obligation of paying the tithe, tell of

demonic manifestations: in the spring, fields, swamps, and woods had supposedly been overwhelmed by a most abundant grain crop, but the hulls
were empty, devoured by demons. *The Anglo-Saxon Chronicle* reported
that the 793 famine was preceded by "dreadful fore-warnings over the
land of the Northumbrians, terrifying the people most woefully: these were
immense sheets of light rushing through the air, and whirlwinds, and fiery,
dragons flying across the firmament." Then, pagans (Scandinavian pirates)
destroyed monasteries and massacred their monks. While looking for their
model of sacred royalty in the Ancient Testament, the Carolingians also imported a conception of the world that incorporated the king "into the God-
given, and thus 'natural' order of the world…The 'good king' is thus the
linchpin of a world view that regarded the ordering of human society as an
integral part of the wider ordering of the entire cosmos."[2] Food shortages
(and other scourges, such as epidemics, earthquakes, or bad weather) were
interpreted as signs of divine punishment. But this cosmogony was able
to draw on other non-Christian traditions in which the sovereign shares
the fecundating powers of nature: if he discredits himself by misbehaving,
sterility sets in. This narrative scheme appears in the story of King Lugaid
Mac Con: after rendering an unfair judgment, the grass stopped growing
on the earth, the leaves on trees stopped growing, as did the grains on the
wheat, until the Irish chased him from the kingdom.[3]

It took widespread and repeated famines, along with the new ideological dimension that state and society adopted after 750, to see the general
concept of a politic of hunger that was initiated by Charlemagne reappear,
and, after a long eclipse, be progressively reinstated by princes and cities
in the twelfth century. Hunger was a factor in social and political disorder
that the authorities tried to cast aside by means of preventive measures and
food-purveying regulatory policies. The ideological context of the 794 and
806 capitularies promulgated by Charlemagne is that of the construction of
a state and of a Christian moral order, achieved through the general ordering of the kingdom and the reformation (*correctio*) of the different strata of
Frankish society. This struggle against disorder was translated into general
measures: the standardization and the control of weights and measures in
order to fight counterfeit goods and usury; and the instauration of a strong
and stable currency, the silver denier, to stabilize prices, and to standardize
exchanges. With urgency, the king reminded the *domini* of their obligation

to protect their dependents against hunger, but he also put in place measures that forbade exports and that limited fluctuation in high-cost times by setting a maximum price for the harvest, regardless of its quality. During times of famine, the royal stocks had to be sold at half of that maximum price. The 794 capitulary also set the weight of bread received for a fixed price: twenty-four pounds of wheat bread for one denier. Three centuries later, in 1124, the regulation of bread was still in the hands of the Count of Flanders. Later, in the second half of the twelfth century, the Flemish cities set their own fines and thus regulated the sale of bread, ensuring the regular inspection of loaves and determining the weight of bread based on the fluctuating price of cereals. The Carolingian legislation also announced the medieval policy of fighting intermediaries and fighting attempts to raise the stock price of cereals. Despite the maximum set in 794, Charlemagne had to double these values during the 805–806 famine. After recalling the definitions of usury, cupidity, greed, undue profit, and interest, he declared that those who bought cereals without necessity, to sell them at twice or three times the price, were guilty of usury (*turpe lucrum*).

If the later capitularies still contained dispositions that aimed at regulating the circulation of food, such as the obligation to sell on public markets, the interdiction to not sell after dark other than to travelers, or the control of the currency and of weights and measures, none of these later edicts deployed as energetic a policy to prevent the effects of famine, and to control the supply of food, as Charlemagne's had. According to the ninth-century biographer, Archbishop Hincmar of Reims, Saint Remigius († c. 533) stocked cereals for lean years. Starting in the eleventh century, the biographies of numerous, particularly Germanic bishops, attest to the same measures. According to Heribert, the Archbishop of Cologne, in his c. 1050 biography, his earnings were dedicated to the rebuilding of destroyed churches and to the poor: when a famine began in Gaul and in Germany in 1005, and a multitude of poor arrived in Cologne, he gave them food and clothes, and ordered the clerics of the other cities in his diocese to distribute money so that the faithful could purchase food. Once the famine was over, the archbishop helped those who had fled return to their holdings. During the large-scale famine of 1042–1048, Wazo, the Bishop of Liège, purchased wheat wherever possible, stored it in his granaries, and distributed food and money. To prevent the Church of Liège's tenants from having to sell

their oxen, he gave them each two deniers. Such behavior is also noted by
Sigebert of Gembloux, who depicted Abbot Olbert (1012–1048) as both a
good manager of his abbey's patrimony (*dispensator et prudens*) and a new
Joseph, using divine providence to fill his granaries in times of abundance,
and distributing the surplus to the poor in times of shortage. Around 1100,
chronicler Hugh of Flavigny, who repeated Raoul Glaber's frightening tales
of the 1032 famine, highlighted the actions of Richard of Saint-Vanne,
one of the leading reformers of Benedictine monasticism in northwest
Europe. He sold the treasures from his church to buy goods and distributed the stocks of his monastery to the poor, writing to "kings, princes,
and pontiffs" to encourage them to follow his example. Around 1095, a
canon from Speyer, Sextus Amarcius, expressed this new relation to poverty when writing in his *De sobrietate et elemosinis faciendis,* "how poorly
he fasts, the one who does not provide anything to the indigent." In 1124
it was in one of the principalities where Richard of Saint-Vanne had been
called a century earlier to reform monasteries, Flanders, that the prince deployed a hunger policy comparable to the measures Charlemagne and the
Ottonian bishops of the eleventh century had put in place. While the poor
came from the countryside to beg around wealthier residences and in cities, Count Charles the Good made his officers distribute food and clothes
everywhere that he owned properties: in one day, they distributed 7,800
loaves of bread in Ypres. He forbade the production of beer (which takes
grains away from the cereal market), invited merchants to buy grain outside the county, and ordered bakers to make smaller breads (for half a denier) so that the poor could afford them. Biographers also depict the prince
(who would be beatified upon his assassination in 1127) as a good lord,
offering his tenants the remission of their debts, and a far-sighted manager,
recommending sowing one measure of beans and peas for two measures of
cereals, "since this type of vegetable grows faster (...) and produces fruits
that the poor can eat." Lastly, every day until he died, the Count fed one
poor person.[4] In the middle of the eleventh century, Capetian propaganda
had already introduced the model of Christ, servant of the poor, in dining
formalities to raise royal stature. According to Helgaud of Fleury († 1045),
the Pious Robert had cured cases of scrofula during meals ritually served to
poor people. These interventions for the starving poor appeared, of course,
in the biographies of Saint Louis at the end of the thirteenth century. But

in those examples, interventions by the monarch to regulate supplies were never mentioned. Rather, episodic, charitable acts, which have a mostly symbolic significance, took place: Saint Louis served thirteen poor people himself every Wednesday, Friday, and Saturday during Lent and Advent. During those same periods, he had meals, bread, and money distributed to thirteen other poor people. He also liked to serve at the table of the monks and nuns (who voluntarily chose poverty) from his favored monasteries.[5] From the middle of the twelfth century, the duty to plan for and fight hunger had been solidly rooted in political philosophy, but it had mostly become the concern and work of urban magistrates.

THE MARKET

Between the middle of the fourteenth century and the first years of the fifteenth century, several cities in northern France took the initiative of collecting and putting in writing a set of regulations of economic law and policing of the trades. Each volume opened with food-related products and trades, as if urban magistrates gave food top billing among the preoccupations related to governing their city. This notion already appeared in the middle of the thirteenth century in the *Book of Ordinances (Livre des Bans)* in the Flemish city of Saint-Omer.[6] These volumes, as do the charts and regulations promulgated from the twelfth century onward, testify to a truly homogeneous regulatory policy of the food market by the occidental urban elites. The principles were the same everywhere: to ensure a sufficient and regular supply to not rouse the masses, without negatively affecting the interests of the merchants and producers; to protect the consumer against fraud pertaining to the quantity and quality of the goods; and to fight against hoarders and monopolists, in order to avoid excessive price hikes. To achieve this, cities required transactions to be publicized, they strictly regulated the place and time of exchanges, and imposed the control of weights and measures and of the quality of the products.[7] The bulk of the food trade, oriented to the cities, had to go through markets and, since the early twelfth century, through specialized buildings such as halls. To prevent hoarding, it was forbidden to purchase products within a certain radius around the city or to accost vendors on the street. In London at the start of the twelfth century, a code of citizens' liberties provided merchants with a pass, and specified the interdiction to forestall: "Within the space of three miles beyond the city on all sides nobody should detain or impede another, nor yet trade with him, if he wishes to come to the city under the city's protection. But when he has reached city, then, both poor and rich alike may trade with him."[8]

Similar rules framed, temporally and spatially, the trade of foodstuffs in cities. Essentials, such as cereals, could only be sold at the markets where their quality could be verified. The foods could not be sold in bags, but rather had to be on display. Once the sale began, the price could not be increased until the market finished. The baker had to *sign* his bread, as did the weaver his cloth. For some products, such as wine, a crier had to announce prices and qualities, which further improved the transparency of transactions. As a matter of fact, these had to take place in public, aloud, and in full view of the other buyers. Markets' opening and closing times were set by the city and often announced with a bell. Regulations gave absolute priority to local consumers, who were the only ones who could purchase foodstuffs between the opening of the market and the early afternoon. Only then could resellers, wholesalers, and food professionals—bakers, millers, brewers, butchers, innkeepers, and so on—proceed with their own shopping. To not leave the markets devoid of goods, the quantities that each person could buy were limited, often related to the needs of each household. Public opinion and legislators were outwardly hostile to food peddlers (*regrattiers*), wholesalers, or even to the main food-related occupations, such as butchers and bakers, all of whom were suspected of artificially raising prices and short-circuiting the market by buying directly from producers. Even the guilds were closely watched until the fourteenth century, when they obtained power and attempted to remove the constraints on their activities. A large number of officers, princely or urban, were in charge of both qualitative and quantitative control of products, and were tasked with taxing and checking merchandise and sanctioning offenders.[9] In Chester in 1086, whoever brewed poor-quality ale was "either put in an unpleasant apparatus described as the '*dung seat*' or made to pay a fine of 4 *denarii*."[10] Urban authorities were in charge of controlling the correct weight of bread; according to Jean d'Outremeuse, the chronicler from Liège, cheating bakers had their fists cut off in 1203.[11] Other clauses were inspired by the fear of monopolies and hoarding. The regulations around food trades forbade the formation of a collective operation, or the practice of two related, or complementary professions.

Civil and religious principles fundamental to the Middle Ages, such as the concept of loyalty, the doctrine of fair price, and the tendency clerics had to consider mercantile activities as fraudulence and any price speculation as a form of usury and greed, motivated this "moralization" of the markets. It has perplexed many historians, who had trouble understanding that patrician social strata (comprising important merchants and property owners, who dominated urban magistracies until the end of the thirteenth century) sought, against their material interests, to ensure that food markets functioned in a way that prioritized supply over profit and that aimed at keeping prices as low as possible. These policies were the price to pay to maintain peace within a city and legitimize a body of authority whose foundations were still influenced by the ideology of the House (*oikos*). Beginning in the fourteenth century, these urban laws saw their legitimacy reinforced by the new political concepts of the public good or common benefit, spread by secular jurists. They were executed at the next level by princes, whose actions were measured in relation to the commonwealth. The strict supervision of food markets had, of course, favored taxation by the prince and by urban authorities in charge of transit, weighing, sale, and consumption of foodstuffs. These taxes were among the first to appear in cities; almost everywhere, they represented the largest source of the city's income. The population referred to them pejoratively as *malatosta* in Latin (*ongeld* in Dutch, and *maltôte* in French): literally, poorly removed.

Small and medium cities could obtain food by exploiting agricultural lands from within their enceinte (particularly for the production of fruits and vegetables) and by politically dominating their rural hinterland, a zone within which their citizens actually controlled part of the fields and livestock operations. For its supply of bread-appropriate grains, a medium-sized city needed to be within a 6- to 12-mile radius of about 150 villages.[12] In most instances, the city (*chef-lieu*) was the mandatory marketplace for grains harvested within the territory it controlled; it could limit exports and even forbid them during shortages. During serious crises, the most powerful cities held nothing back to guarantee their food procurement, to the detriment of smaller cities, peasants, and property owners, including their own citizens.[13] With more than 20,000 inhabitants, the medieval city had to either use coercion to monopolize the import of cereals in one region (the staple solution), or gain control of a larger region by dominating a hierarchic network of other small and medium cities (in the urban republics of north-central Italy). The staple system allowed cities within the large transportation axes to channel trade to their advantage by forcing foreign merchants to stop to be taxed and to unload and sell their goods. In Italy, the most powerful cities imposed commercial treaties on their neighbors that guaranteed them priority or a purchasing quota for grains. Venice was one of the first cities to establish these monopoly policies in the early thirteenth century. In 1251 it required every ship carrying foodstuffs and livestock on the Adriatic Sea to unload it in Venice before being able to, possibly, re-export it.[14] Contemporary chroniclers were sensitive to the un-balanced supply levels that made constant exports, especially of grains, indispensable. At the beginning of the fourteenth century, Dino Compagni (1255–1324) asserted that Florence could only sustain its food needs using its neighboring resources for five months out of the year.[15] Around 1300, the economic structure of all of northern Italy relied on manufactured goods and services being traded for foodstuffs from other regions around the Mediterranean Sea, particularly Apulia, Sicily, and Tunisia. In 1311 Genovese ships carried 45,000 tons of grains from Apulia to Florence.[16] Dutch cities, which also had high levels of urbanization before 1300, ob-tained their grains (particularly the wheat that was sought after by the wealthy) from the fertile agricultural lands of Picardy, Hainaut, Artois, and Normandy, and of England. In England, the interdiction to export was used as a form of retaliation at the beginning of the thirteenth century; the export of cereals later became (starting in 1207) gradually framed by a system of royal licensing.[17] The Hansa also became an important supply source: Flanders was under a blockade of grains from the Wendish cities beginning in 1284.[18] Positive measures, such as the de-taxation of foreign-ers and passes, completed these types of competitive warfare between cit-ies. Magistrates improved urban potential by having canals dug out, as in Ghent (in the twelfth century) and in Ypres (1251). Beginning in the twelfth and thirteenth centuries, Italian cities purchased grains in the name of the city and transported them on communal boats.

If riots that were directly tied to hunger seem to have been extremely rare in the Middle Ages (Samuel Cohn estimates them to be fewer than 1%

of recorded cases in the most urbanized areas of medieval Europe, Italy, Flanders, and northern France),[19] securing the food supply was a central political element in the struggle for power between patricians and leaders of the people. In the thirteenth century, one no longer died as a result of local food shortages; thanks to the intensification of trade networks, "people no longer flee to look for bread—bread comes to them." But price increases kept bread out of the reach of the poorest population strata. The word *carestia* (costliness) is used as a synonym of scarcity (*inopia*), even of famine (*fames*).[20] Any rumor related to supply levels or to a threat of costliness caused prices to increase and could be embarrassing to the powers that were in place, who reacted promptly: In a completely patrician-based regime, in 1243, the urban authorities of Perugia forbade the export of the *contado*'s grains, wine, and livestock. In periods of famine, in 1269, 1279–1280, and so on, the rural and urban markets of Perugia were closed, and the sale of grains was limited to the city's central square.[21] Beginning in the twelfth century, everywhere in Europe, the fear of going without and, above all, of no longer being able to buy bread, or of allowing spoiled, or low-quality goods to circulate, led to the redeployment of constraining measures and market oversight. One of the ways to check the work of bakers was to set the weight and quality of bread loaves produced from a given volume of grains, as was already the case during Charlemagne's reign. During the first half of the eleventh century, Liège already had a connecting system in place linking the weight and volume of bread and wine. To fight against speculators during the 1042 famine, Bishop Wazo stocked and introduced onto the market the quantities of grains that he had purchased. His successors tried, but apparently in vain, to set a maximum price for grains: in 1118, the price of a bushel of wheat, set at five *sous,* had nearly doubled. Charlemagne had also been unable to prevent the prices of cereals doubling between 794 and 805. These policies were often destined to fail. Maximum prices were only set in times of extreme urgency and for a short period, such as in 1301 and 1315 in the kingdom of England. It was not a normal way to confront supply issues. Authorities were more likely to allow the price of grains to fluctuate, possibly intervening when it was low with massive sales in lean periods and by limiting hoarding opportunities. In Liège, a series of food-related ordinances tightly regulated the production and commercialization of foodstuffs during the thirteenth century, by establishing (in 1252) a scale of legal bread weight for rye and spelt, based upon cereal prices within a very large range: between one and seven and a half. In 1232 the city's authorities committed to having the goods sold "at fair weight, fair price, and fair measure." The prices recorded between 1194 and 1225 by the Benedictine Abbot, Renier of Saint-Jacques, show that their author closely observed the climatic conditions that, in his mind, primarily controlled the market. For Renier, a fair price existed at between two and four *sous*. Lower prices caused the market to collapse, while the upper limit was the threshold of costliness beyond which the price of bread could be more devastating to the population than the plague.[22] These scales were generally used in assizes that were also in charge of the taxation of bread consumption (and often beer or wine too). The oldest text of a bread assize in England appears in a compendium assembled between 1206 and 1216 for the Guildhall of London.[23] In the Low Countries, the first testimonials appeared in charters granted by Philip of Alsace between 1168 and 1177, authorizing Flemish cities "to place bans on bread and on wine and on all other goods," with the agreement of the count, and negotiating an equal split of assize fees between the count, on one side, and the chatelain and the city, on the other. In Germany, the oldest assizes were certified in Lübeck in 1255.[24] As Abbot Galiani wrote in 1770 in his *Dialogue sur le commerce des blés,* bread and grain must be "objects of administration" rather than "commerce."[25]

CONSUMPTION AND TABLE MANNERS

The dining table was an essential place of power building in the Middle Ages. Commensality (the ordering of diners at the table) acted as an element that created social distance and established reciprocal relationships at the hierarchical (vertical) and solidary (horizontal) levels: "Esteem demands marks of esteem, and there can be no social rank without orders of greetings and seating."[26] Widely distributed, food was a symbol of social rank. Its abundance, the quality and quantity of guests, the service, the charm and setting of the meal (with tableware, entertainment, etc.) made tangible an essential aristocratic quality: generosity. In 1200 Gilles of Paris wrote the *Carolinum,* a mirror of princes, for the young Louis V. In it, he offered as a model the moderate eater (*temperans*) as Einhard depicted Charlemagne:

"leading a measured lifestyle, except when it was appropriate for the royal palace to shine in abundant luxury." The king, even if he were a saint, had to be a good host; that is, he needed to eat with pleasure (*hilariter*) and not skimp on either the quality, or quantity of dishes. If Saint Louis modeled his daily diet on the codes of the Christian meal—eating what was less good (small rather than large fish), depreciating what was good (adding cold water to sauces), and eating and drinking in moderation—he would know how to entertain like a king. During the banquet in the honor of Henry III of England's visit to Paris, meat was served on a fish day. According to the Benedictine chronicler Matthew Paris, "The never-ending variety of dishes was resplendent, the abundance of beverages delicious, the quality of service enjoyable, the arrangement of guests well organized, the bounty of gifts superabundant."[27] One of Liutprand of Cremone's anecdotes concerning Guy of Spoleto's (?–894) candidacy to the throne in 888 of West Francia appears as a counterpoint of similar codes. The bishop of Metz was getting ready to welcome the contender and had had "much food [prepared], according to the Franks' customs"; Guy's snide squire answered that a third of it would suffice. They all chose Eudes as king, since "he was not worthy of ruling over us, the one who had prepared a vile meal of ten silver coins!"[28] Practices evolve according to parameters such as the status and lifestyle of the sovereign (Otton III [980–1002], for example, chose to be served and to eat alone at the table), or the spread and complexity of the kingdom. In the Anglo-Saxon kingdoms of the seventh through to the ninth centuries, and in the first princely courts of the ninth and tenth centuries, the aristocratic suites were small enough to create intimate ties based on commensality. It was, of course, impossible beyond a critical size: in 1135, under Henry I of England (1068–1135), the king's household comprised approximately 150 people, clerics and laymen, to which must be added the households of the other members of the royal family.[29]

The table brought together both passing guests and regulars. In doing so, it referred to two essential values: hospitality and feeding the household. According to Einhard, if he was moderate at the table, Charlemagne was prodigal with strangers, "to the point that their charge was costly not just for the palace, but for the kingdom." The king was not affected because "in exchange for these immense nuisances, this attention provided him with a reputation for generosity and good standing." The hospitality relation was also strengthened by its reciprocal nature. The king and the court were regularly invited to feast with the Greats. This reciprocal model appeared at all levels of society as obligations of hospitality, gift-giving, and reciprocity. Peasants owed rights (lodging, *feorm*) and presents (*xenia*) of hospitality (hens, eggs, wine and honey, cakes, etc.) as fees. In return, the great religious holidays were cause for banquets (during which the *xenia* were sometimes consumed) that the lords offered their peasants. According to Paul the Deacon's account of the life of Gregory the Great († 604), the *xenia* of the tenants of St. Peter's in Rome were distributed to the poor. The more delicate products that arrived in the pontifical warehouses were given to the Greats.[30]

Food, thus, occupied a central place in the construction of the social bond—what Marc Bloch evoked when speaking of the "taste of home-made bread" of the vassalage (after the old English *hlaford*/lord, literally, the donor of bread).[31] We must pay attention to the degree of violence that can be expressed through these culinary transactions. The relation between the *pater familias* and the members of the household represented the archetype of the bond between the one who shares and distributes food and those who were fed (*nutriti*). This function (which is obvious in the familial circle), transposed to the political realm, indicates patriarchal authority. That authority was ambiguous, since the family of the Antiquity included blood relatives, guests and friends, legally free customers, and slaves. Between the indigent and the one who protected him, the relation settled at the domination realm. The act of feeding (and clothing) creates a relation of submission and degrades the one receiving assistance. When the sovereign shared his meal with his soldiers, commensality, to the contrary, established a relation that used food to connote the sharing of danger when fighting. Context was thus essential: following a sovereign meant that one no longer needed to obtain one's own food, but that one received daily rations and more than enough food and drink (and in many cases, the necessary equipment, clothing, weapons, and horses). In 1066 in Hastings, men who had feasted at Harold's side died, paying, in their minds at least, for their mead.[32] These episodes of brutal fraternity were also combined in hunting. One of the strongest practices of social cohesion and formation of the elites, the king had to master hunting, which he learned as a child, by being the *best*.

The institution of the meal was thus a social reality that crossed through all societies, but with variations in intensity and complexity in the *grammar of food* that structured it within time and space.[33] If, in the tenth century, a treasure chest was enough to showcase the power of a Byzantine bishop (who ate simply and was often his own cook), it was not the case for the Franks, according to Liutprand of Cremone, for whom power had to be expressed through abundance, the profusion of servants, and all forms of material magnificence.[34] Literary sources such as the *Beowulf* suffice to demonstrate the central place that the *culture of the hall* occupied in the social practices of the Anglo-Saxon elites. The banquet hall was the "center of the heroic world and a place of harmony and abundance, where communities of warriors were defined and invigorated."[35] It was impossible to find a profane Romano-Germanic text that expresses as fully the centrality of the *convivium*. These practices were not exclusively centered on Germanic and Scandinavian models. After Christianization, they acculturated and mutually benefitted from the Christian models, such as Christ's promise to his disciples that they would eat and drink at his table in the Kingdom of Heaven. Anglo-Saxon and Frank kings rapidly adopted the main Christian holidays as occasions for the banquets during which they would wear their crowns.

Eating together and hosting banquets for one another signified entry into *one* society and the creation of ties between equals. According to Icelandic sources, the heritage banquet celebrated the sovereign taking his functions among his subjects. The presence, or lack thereof, of a leader is what gave the meal its hierarchical (the subordination of the guests to the one who sits at the head of the table) or egalitarian meaning. To signify equality among King Arthur's entourage, Arthurian novels have created the image of the round table, with no head seat and no long sides. Other groups naturally had an egalitarian nature. Appearing as rural associations in the Frank countryside in the ninth century or as merchant organizations from the tenth century onward in the Low Countries, guilds constituted a fraternal grouping—a brotherhood of equals or quasi equals. At the beginning of the eleventh century, the statutes of Saint-Omer guaranteed commercial privileges to the merchants who were members of the guild and who organized mutual assistance. They structured the life of the organization around the collective consumption of an alcoholic beverage (20 articles out of 28 pertain to these collective *potationes*). The guild examined internal conflicts and offered moments and rites of reconciliation (such as breaking bread and drinking together). The shared banquet represented a central element of celebration and of cohesion for the guild, because conviviality created relations that were close to family ones, as did the funeral banquets that had brought relatives together for the anniversaries of a deceased since the Antiquity. According to Galbert of Brugge (?–1134), the assassins of Charles the Good, Count of Flanders, used this ritual in reverse when they gathered to eat around his tomb, so that no one could avenge his death. The same symbolic system turned the refusal of drinking or eating with someone else into an insult and a sign of a rupture of the peace, while it was impossible, according to jurist Albert of Ghent in the thirteenth century, to accuse or try somebody if one had drank or eaten with him after the implied facts had come to one's attention. In the eleventh century, Adele, grand dame in Gelderland, brought the ire of God upon her country, which was flooded, after refusing to prepare the peace-signifying meal that was requested of her to reconcile her adversaries.[36] During banquets, medieval rituals sublimed sharing by having guests eating on the same trencher, drinking in the same cup, and using the same bowl.

THE EATERS

Man is what he eats, and at the same time, he eats who he is, or *what he would like to be*. In the Arthurian novels, two culinary triads—bread/meat/wine, gruel/vegetables/water—metaphorically oppose the knight and the hermit.[37] The villain of the fables differs from the rest of society by his physical appearance, his manners, and his feelings. But what mostly isolates him from others is his way of eating: he enjoys cheeses, eggs, and milk gruels, prefers boiled meat to a roast, eats everything without sauce, drinks water and milk, even at the inn (when even servants drink wine). He does not wash his hands, sits on the ground, and eats everything as one.[38] In the *Song of William*, Dame Guibourc, after having served the young Girart, her husband's nephew, recognized through his appetite the qualities of his lineage: "By God! Beautiful sire! This one is undoubtedly from your lineage [seeing the way he eats and drinks]. What a tough war he must fight against his neighbor."[39] While he slipped incognito among the guests of a banquet thrown by Charlemagne, the son of the defeated king of the Lombards, Adelchis, was recognized because of his carnal behavior. He asked for all the bones that were removed from the royal table, broke them, and sucked the marrow, "like a famished lion devouring its prey," then he threw the fragments under the table and made an enormous pyramid out of them, before leaving. When Charlemagne, getting up, discovered this sight, he asked around; one of the guests answered that he saw, seated there, "a very strong warrior, who broke all these deer, bear, and ox bones like someone else would have broken stalks of hemp."[40] The Christianization of manners had only slowly eroded these aristocratic codes. Saint Louis provides an example. As a young man, Brunon (youngest son of the King of Germans, Henry the Fowler, future Archbishop of Cologne, and Duke of Lotharingia at the end of the tenth century), was as cheerful as the others at his banquets. After a joyful carousal that lasted until its participants fell asleep, the pious duke spent the rest of the night praying. He did not take part in the *ebrietas* of his guests, but he partook in the collective fun.[41] It was only in the middle of the twelfth century that the aristocratic culture of culinary excesses became stigmatized as a sin of mouth (*gula*) and that temperance was progressively transposed from individual virtue to the social norm. In 1159 John of Salisbury borrowed from Boethius, in his *Policraticus*, the idea that Epicureanism leads to the individual and political degeneration of princes. For the *Lament on the Battle of Poitiers,* the defeat of the French cavalry in 1356 was due to warriors being weakened by their gluttony. These new standards of behavior were mostly introduced by thirteenth-century legislators in the first sumptuary laws of Italian cities. Before the fifteenth century, culinary excess consisted primarily of organizing banquets for many, and mostly too many, people, more rarely of limiting the quantities of food consumed. But for the nobles, excess still did not exist.[42]

CHAPTER FIVE

Eating Out in the Early and High Middle Ages

ALBAN GAUTIER

Did most people eat at home in the early and high Middle Ages? Such an opinion would, of course, be considered as evident in view of the fact that the vast majority of the population lived in peasant communities, where food was primarily produced and consumed on the farm. In fact, that question is both difficult to answer and, maybe, not even appropriate. Difficult because the sources, which are few for the first centuries of the Middle Ages, and which are also difficult to interpret, are not always clear as to where, and exactly when, food and drink were consumed: all kinds of communal consumption existed then, from feasts, to taverns, through to open and compulsory hospitality, and it would be a pointless exercise to try to calculate the proportion of food that was actually consumed by farming families within the precincts of their farms. The question is also not necessarily appropriate, because the notions of eating at home and eating out are not necessarily valid notions for the study of that period: a warrior eating alongside his comrades-in-arms in his lord's hall could perfectly well feel at home, even if his family lived miles away from the place where he was having his meal; a king staying overnight in one of his numerous estates could well imagine himself eating out, as being received by the steward of the place with a splendid dinner, all the important people of the area being gathered to share in the occasion of meeting him, and the fact that the place was actually his home would not have mattered that much. In thirteenth-century towns, people would often buy prepared food and eat it either in the street or at home, but in both cases the food would have been a takeaway and not prepared within the family circle. Our familiar boundaries are then blurred when we begin to think about the early and central Middle Ages: notions of public and private feasting, for instance, do not necessarily match the reality of the time, as feasting could have both public and private aspects, should it actually take place in the king's hall or in a farmer's home.

That said, it is of course possible to study the occasions when medieval men and women had the possibility of eating and drinking outside of their familial and familiar setting. Four aspects will be considered here in turn, whilst bearing in mind the fact that we do know much more about lords and princes than about peasants and common people, especially in the early centuries. The first aspect will be the feeding of kings, lords, and their men: in a period of itinerant kingship, rulers and their agents were always on the move, seldom staying in the same place for a long time, and they had to be fed on their way, both from royal estates and from other places such as noblemen's houses and monasteries. Our second area will consider the feeding of all kinds of travelers. Monastic hospitality was not the only kind of hospitality that existed in that period, but it dominates the record. Feasting is considered in a third section, both as an occasion of communal merriment and as a serious activity with heavy social meaning. Finally, we will briefly explore the question of inns and taverns, and all places where food and drink could be bought and consumed on the premises. None of those cases, except maybe the last one, exactly fits with our notion of eating out, but they were the occasions in which early and late medieval people would have had a meal outside of their ordinary setting.

FEEDING LORDS AND THEIR MEN

Kings, queens, and princes are the first category we will consider here. Kingship in the medieval west was mostly itinerant in nature: rulers and their agents were endlessly on the move, visiting the different regions and localities of their dominions. In those cases, kings and lords would stay and eat on their own estates, as well as on those of their subjects, men, clients, and vassals, where they would be guested. The word *guesting,* often used to describe this kind of compulsory hospitality, is akin to the Latin *gistum*—itself adapted from a Germanic word—and it has equivalents in several European languages: *gastung* in German and *droit de gîte* in French.[1] It refers to the possibility for medieval and early modern authorities to demand hospitality for themselves and their agents, regardless of the size and nature of the area governed by a ruler: the situation can be observed in the very small Irish polities of the eight to twelfth centuries as much as in the immense Carolingian Empire.

Irish kings, who generally ruled over very small populations—the Irish clans or *túatha* would have numbered only a few thousand individuals—but also lords protecting clients, and landlords leasing livestock to peasants, were entitled to be guested. Those obligations were often strictly defined by law or custom, and generally differed according to the status of the guest: the *Crith Gablach,* an eighth-century law tract, very precisely defines every individual's right and obligation, from the *ócaire* (young freeman) to the *rí* (tribal king), and shows that a commoner could only expect barley bread, whereas a nobleman should receive wheat bread, butter, meat, and ale. Moreover, lords could only exact guesting from their clients during the *aimser chue,* the winter season between Christmas and Lent; a king, on the other hand, could demand it at any time for himself, or for his agents.[2]

The best known case of compulsory hospitality can be found in the Carolingian Empire and its successor states, particularly Ottonian Germany. Charlemagne (768–814) and his descendants were itinerant kings who would journey over long distances. Even if, in his later years, Charlemagne spent most of his time in his palace in Aachen, he would nevertheless cover an average of 280 miles per annum, and in his early years it would have been much more: in 800–801, admittedly an exceptional year that included a journey to Italy (but none to Saxony), he traveled nearly 3,100 miles in approximately a year and a half.[3] We know from charters and annals that, when traveling in those years, he stayed in various locations: in his own palaces, of course (Thionville, Aachen), but also with bishops (in Paris, Pavia, or Ravenna), in monasteries (those of St Omer or St Riquier on the northwestern coast of his kingdom), or with lay lords (e.g., the Duke of Spoleto in Italy). Those locations would seem very different at first glance: what is there in common between staying overnight at a monastery and having a feast in one's own palace? In fact, the way food issues were handled would have been very similar: church property, both in royal monasteries and in bishoprics, was considered by Carolingian kings as part of their resources, and their grandees were their men, the people they could rely on, both in war and in peace. Most of the bishoprics, all of the great monasteries, and a great many lay grandees were expected to furnish the king with *fodrum* and *gistum,* that is fodder for horses, food for the king and his entourage, and shelter for all the company.[4]

When the king arrived, everything would have been organized to welcome him, beginning with the buildings. We know that Charlemagne had many of his palaces refurbished, with the building of impressive feasting halls out of stone in Aachen, Frankfurt, and Paderborn, and his son, Louis the Pious (814–840), did the same in Ingelheim;[5] but Archbishop Leidrad of Lyons († c. 821) also had a house built for him next to the archiepiscopal palace, with two floors and space to relax, "so that, if you happened to come to our region, you could be received there."[6] A royal entry would be held, followed by a religious service (generally a mass), a meal (called *convivium* in most of the Latin sources), and a drinking session (the word generally used is *potatio*).[7] Notker of St Gall's *Life of Charlemagne,* a work of the later ninth century, largely fanciful as far as political facts and chronology are concerned, but very useful if we are to understand Carolingian mentalities and their conceptions of kingship, gives an example of the close links that existed between the king's guesting and his manner of eating at home. One day, says Notker, Charlemagne was having dinner at a bishop's residence. Since it was on a Friday, no meat was served, but instead of the expected fish, the guests were served cheese. Notker explains that, because no previous arrangements had been made concerning the king's stay, the bishop had not been able to serve fish, but Charlemagne, of course, accepted that with patience.[8] This suggests that, normally, things would have been planned and prestigious and abundant fare would have been provided; when the king arrived at short notice, things could be more difficult—rulers less patient and less virtuous than Notker's Charlemagne would have felt offended.

Several hagiographic texts echo the panic that could seize a saintly abbot or abbess when, learning that a king, a bishop, or any other authority was arriving, they realized that they did not have enough food—or worse, enough drink—to offer them and their itinerant court. The anonymous *Life of Dunstan,* Archbishop of Canterbury († 988), tells how a saintly woman named Æthelflæd had been warned that King Æthelstan of Wessex (924–939) wanted to stay at her home in Glastonbury, next to the monastery of which Dunstan was abbot; messengers from the king had actually arrived the day before to check that everything was ready to receive him. But as Æthelstan was approaching with a large retinue, Æthelflæd realized that she did not have enough mead to offer to him and his men: indeed, she only had a small quantity of it, "only the height of a palm." She then prayed to the Virgin and, when the king arrived at lunchtime, just after having heard the mass, she served all the mead she had for the first toast. A miracle then happened, for the vessel would not empty for the whole duration of the banquet, "and all day the butlers, as is customary at royal feasts, served drinks in horns, cups, and a quantity of other vessels."[9] This story is interesting for three reasons. First, it shows how kings would warn their subjects of their arrival, making sure that they would be received properly, especially since they normally journeyed with a large number of retainers. The second interesting aspect is the miracle itself: Christ and his apostles had multiplied bread and fish, but generally not inebriating drinks. There was of course the miracle at Cana, but this very particular miracle, only mentioned in John's gospel, was generally interpreted in a purely allegorical way. We must remember that Christian authors such as Isidore of Seville, or Alcuin of York, tended to treat scriptural images of inebriation in a firmly spiritual sense, even warning their audiences not to see them as an apology of physical drunkenness. Medieval Christianity, on the other hand, is full of such miracles, which see the multiplication of wine, mead, or ale. Those drinks were absolutely necessary for a proper feast, and medieval Christian kings needed them. The presence of mead in the story is only due to the fact that the text was written in a Northern European country: in France, Spain, or Italy, wine would have been multiplied in just the same way. Thirdly, the author insists on the fact that everything went ahead smoothly, "as was customary at royal feasts": for early medieval kings, a good meal out would have been just like home—meaning that a successful feast, whether it was organized in a royal palace or elsewhere, should always be abundant, delivering the king's retinue what they wanted and needed (here, mead), and expressing the ruler's superiority and his capacity to provide food and drink to his men, to his guests, and, symbolically, to the whole population.

Kings and lords would then have had many of their meals in places that they did not own. Guesting the king was a heavy charge indeed, especially when it meant guesting the whole court. But, at the same time, it could be a very efficient way of approaching the king—for good or less good reasons, as the historian Paul the Deacon suggests when he tells the story of a Lombard nobleman, Rothari, who planned (and failed) to kill King Liutprand (712–744) during a feast that he had prepared for him in his house in Pavia.[10] But even with the best intentions, guesting could be worth the costs, since it gave hosts a privileged access to the sovereign—*Königsnähe* (proximity to the king), as German historians call it—and hence the possibility to further their own political agenda. *Voluntary* guesting, if such a phrase can be used, was very honorable indeed, because it could assume the shape of an honorable and spontaneous invitation, as it provided hosts with an occasion to demonstrate their worthiness and generosity,[11] and because it was an opportunity to approach the king in person. Goscelin of St Bertin, a Flemish hagiograph who wrote in late eleventh-century England, tells how Wenflæd, the aunt of St Wulfhild, invited King Edgar of England (957–975), who was in love with her niece, to feast at her residence at Wherwell.[12] She may well have thought that guesting the king was a reasonable expense, and indeed a good investment, if it brought a royal bridegroom into her family.

In fact, it could be much more interesting, in political terms, to guest one's king or one's lord than to pay them some anonymous food render—even if it was indeed costly, because a ruler never journeyed alone and always went with a numerous retinue. Notker's story of Charlemagne, which continues with a description of the Emperor's meal, shows that very well. The bishop, who was entertaining Charlemagne with creamy cheese, remarked that the Emperor was only eating the white part of the cheese, leaving aside the skin that he thought was not edible. He then told the king that he was throwing away the best part and advised him to taste the skin. Charlemagne actually loved it and asked the bishop to have two cartloads of cheese sent to him at Aachen each year. The bishop, from host to the king, had been turned into provider of the royal palace. To the king, it meant the same: in both cases the bishopric was participating in his own feeding and revenue. However, the bishop then had to come to Aachen in person three years later to see the king and get from him a grant of land: his *Königsnähe* had been impaired.

That kind of evolution, from guesting the king to providing for his palace, seems to have been an important evolution from the ninth century onward: with the growth of kingdoms, of royal administration, and of the size of royal courts, kings were less and less guested by their subjects, especially by the more modest ones. Only the highest in the realm could now dream of inviting the king: such a burden had actually become a privilege, even if it had become a very costly one. As to the majority, their obligations were either transformed into renders in money or in kind, or diverted to the entertainment, lodging, and feeding of lesser political agents: messengers of the post, tax gatherers, and above all, troops.[13] Guesting had become a means of billeting: an obligation as heavy as was the duty to feed and entertain authorities, but far less interesting for the host.

CATERING FOR TRAVELERS AND PILGRIMS

This mention of billeting soldiers and agents of rulers brings us to the question of the means by which all kinds of travelers could be catered for when they were on the road. Contrary to a battered image, the Middle Ages were not a time of immobility. Kings, as we have just said, were always on the move, as well as their agents, but so were clerics, aristocrats, merchants, and even numerous peasants. The central Middle Ages saw the rise of pilgrimages, which sometimes took Christians over very long distances, to Rome, Santiago de Compostela, or Jerusalem.[14] Even in the early centuries, traveling was common and much practiced. However, as we will see later on, inns and taverns were not very frequent, and travelers generally had to resort to different kinds of hospitality: institutionalized in the case of officials and more spontaneous in the case of simple travelers.

The early medieval state inherited some institutions from the late Roman Empire, which enabled rulers to send their agents on errands along the routes of their kingdoms. The *cursus publicus* remained largely operative in the first centuries of the Middle Ages, and state officials were given the right to require food and shelter from several places on the road. In the Frankish kingdom, ambassadors or *missi domininci* normally traveled with a *tractoria,* a letter which enabled them to take food and shelter on the road: one of them, issued by an eighth-century mayor of the palace, amounted to *un véritable passeport.*[15] A good example of a *tractoria* can be found in a text from the time of Emperor Louis the Pious, which asks local authorities to provide imperial messengers with "twenty loaves of bread, two young animals, piglet or lamb, two chickens, ten eggs, one *modius* of drink, salt, and vegetables from the garden."[16] This short list shows that the food that traveling officials expected on their way was typical of elite consumption: fowl and young animals are prominent, together with more common foodstuffs such as bread and vegetables. Early medieval grandees, like many modern-day tourists, did not necessarily appreciate exotic food and drink, and preferred more familiar fare. In the northernmost parts of Europe, ale and mead were foremost on elite tables, whereas wine was much more frequent in Gaul and in southern Europe: from the eighth century at least, the Franks considered ale unworthy of a *potens,* and Frankish magnates expected to be offered wine even when they journeyed to other countries. An episode consigned in the Redon cartulary tells how Juhel Béranger, Count of Rennes in Britanny (c. 930–970), was anxious to get some wine to offer to the envoys of the Count of Anjou—a Frank—when he only had mead and ale: a miracle was needed to find a large vat of wine.[17] Noble travelers could then expect to receive food and drink according to their status—which meant, according to their taste.

This was true of important travelers, members of an elite group who traveled with official sanction from a king or a prince. What about more simple travelers, merchants, or pilgrims? The first possibility was for them to stop at any house on the road and ask for hospitality. This kind of archaic hospitality was supposedly much practiced in ancient times, and Tacitus, in the second century AD, had described it as a typical feature of the Germans.[18] However, when we look precisely at early Germanic law-codes such as the Salic law or the Law of the Burgundians, we see that such open and free hospitality was not as frequent as an idealized vision of the barbarians—such as is Tacitus—would have it.[19] Very often indeed, travelers would have brought their food with them, and this could even happen in the case of officials traveling on duty: in 804, Abbot Fulrad of St Quentin, traveling as a messenger of Charlemagne, took food with him on the road.[20] If shelter was generally given to any traveler, food and drink were not necessarily part of the hospitality package, and the precise nature of the hospitality which might or might not be provided depended on the guest's position within a larger hierarchy: did they travel with recommendation? Were they noble or common people? Did they travel on official errands? Moreover, strict limitations were set upon the duration of a guest's stay and the quantities of food and drink they could get from their host. We have already explained how Irish law tracts set the limits of what a compulsory guest could demand, but we may also include that numerous sources insist on the fact that guests could not stay in their hosts' house, eating their bread and drinking their wine, for more than three days and three nights.[21]

If travelers did not resort to that kind of archaic hospitality, they could be welcomed in specialized institutions. In sixth- and seventh-century Gaul and Italy, many cities saw the building of hospices where the poor, the sick, and the homeless could be fed and cared for: the poor of the city, in addition to travelers and pilgrims, were important targets of those institutions that were generally called *xenodochia* (Greek for *strangers' houses*), or *hospitia* (Latin for *guesthouses*).[22] The consecutive decline of urban civilization meant that such institutions did not prosper north of the Alps, and most of them actually disappeared, the principle being revived only in the twelfth and thirteenth centuries, when numerous hospitals and almshouses were established in expanding towns through the initiative of clergy, princes, and rich merchants. We cannot know exactly what the poor would have eaten in late Antiquity *xenodochia,* but we do know that the food in thirteenth-century hospitals was of very poor quality, regardless of the fact that many inmates were actually sick people: salted meat was very common, as well as plain bread and wine, and the fare would have been very repetitive.[23] Charity was at the root of such institutions, but it was a socially conscious charity, which reproduced the hierarchy of society at large and its alimentary aspects in these hospitals.

In the meantime, regular clergy became the main providers of food and drink for travelers and pilgrims. According to the sixth-century *Rule of St Benedict,* which became the norm in a great majority of western monasteries from the ninth century onward, the monks' duty was to feed the *pauperes*—the poor and the weak—as well as the *peregrini*—foreigners and travelers. "All guests are to be received as Christ himself," the Rule goes.[24] This the monks did readily in most monasteries, but we must be aware of the fact that social distinction remained at the heart of the medieval practice of hospitality, even in monasteries: egalitarian treatment of guests was not an option in any early medieval practice of hospitality. In his *Life of Wulfstan,* the Bishop of Worcester in western England († 1095), William of Malmesbury, tells us that the saint, when he was still only the prior of Worcester cathedral minster, received his bishop and some papal legates.[25] He had to refresh them with quality food and to organize a feast, even if it was during Lent, and even if, as a very ascetic person should, he found this a rather shocking thing to do. Such a duty was linked to the status of the travelers, to Wulfstan's own office, and to their relative situation of superiority and inferiority: we can be certain that Wulfstan, for all his generosity and holiness, would not have bothered for more simple travelers, and would have provided them with an allowance of food more appropriate both to their status and to the season of the year.

Another significant illustration of this distinction can be observed in continental monasteries of the Carolingian period, where there were generally two separate *hospitia:* a *hospitium diuitum* and a *hospitium pauperum.*[26] The plan of St Gall, a ninth-century document which maps an ideal Carolingian monastery, shows three of them (at least): one for the rich, one for the poor, and a third for monks.[27]

THE MEANING OF FEASTING

Depending on your social status, on the place where you were received, and on the means and plans of your host, you would have been received very differently in a medieval guesthouse, lay or ecclesiastical. However, receiving guests, whoever they were, was never a small and insignificant feat: there was always a notion of liberality, the idea that, even if strict laws and customs could establish what should be the minimum given to a particular guest, a good host should not be bound by such regulations. The feasting table was a place where hosts could show their status' quality, their generosity, and their lack of stinginess. The appearance of sumptuary laws in southern Europe in the eleventh century is an indirect tribute to that mentality: in Italian or Provençal towns, competition among the rich was such that municipal authorities had to set limits to the possibilities of showing off through food, drink, clothes, and ornamentation. By being too magnificent and too much infused with the mentality of splendor and generosity, those rich townspeople—nobles and commoners alike—threatened to impoverish the city, and challenged the social order by behaving like upstarts and *nouveaux riches,* receiving and dining on a scale which was neither proper, nor adjusted to their social rank.

In the whole of western Europe, rulers were primarily thought of as dispensers of gifts and providers of food and drink. In Old English, the lord was called *hlaford,* or the loaf-warden: he was the one who kept and gave bread to his retainers, who were themselves called *hlafætan,* the loaf-eaters, the lord's wife being the *hlæfdige,* the loaf-kneader.[28] By sharing their lord's bread, warriors acknowledged his superiority and, at the same time, strengthened the link that united them together and with him. Bread was symbolically important there, but also, and maybe even more so, were intoxicating drinks such as wine, ale, and mead: in several vernacular texts such as the Old English epic of *Beowulf,* but also in Latin poems such as the Carolingian story of *Waltharius,* the sharing of the cup appears as a major ritual that unites the prince and his warriors.[29]

In the early Middle Ages, the powerful were expected, through their behavior at the table, to stress the fact that they belonged to a ruling class. In early Merovingian times, with the influence of late Antiquity patterns still strong on consumption patterns, there was in the elite, Roman and barbarian alike, an ideal of moderation and refinement: by inviting each other for dinner, but also by exchanging presents of precious food and drink,[30] members of the lay and clerical elite expressed their common interest for refined food, often incorporating exotic foodstuffs. Bishop Gregory of Tours († 594) tells of a kind of omelet with dates and olives—ingredients that are not indigenous to the Loire region where he was able to taste that dish.[31] However, from the late sixth century onward, this ideal was modified[32]: the elite must now show their status by eating in large quantities—especially large quantities of meat, which became more and more of a status symbol and an important aspect of their alimentary culture.[33] The importance of meat, as a symbol of strength and violence, became part of the elite's mentality, whether it was acquired through hunting (another communal practice of the powerful), or through farming (in which case it could also express economic superiority).[34]

For many young warriors, who did not necessarily come from the richest background (and this was true both of early warbands and of knights in eleventh-century French castles), eating and drinking at their lord's table was a means to behave like members of the lay elite, and to have access to consumption patterns typical of the elite, such as the eating of meat: it was actually a means to join that elite by acquiring its codes and practices. Refinement never disappeared altogether, but it seems to have receded behind quantity as a primary means of showing elite status. Only in the central Middle Ages did refinement in food and foodways again become a major way of affirming one's social status: new ways of receiving guests began to appear in tenth-century German texts such as the epic *Ruodlieb*,[35] but they are particularly well depicted in twelfth- and thirteenth-century Arthurian romances. In Chrétien de Troyes's *Conte du Graal* (c. 1180), the table of the Fisher King is described as a paragon of refinement, where Perceval is splendidly received: the setting is beautiful, with tables of ivory, trestles of ebony, and white tablecloths; the knight is welcomed with warm water to wash his hands; he his offered "dates, figs, nutmeg, cloves, grenades, gingerbread from Alexandria,... sweet wine, blackberry wine and clear syrup."[36] This does not mean that such decoration and such food were actually found at high medieval tables, but the description shows what was ideally thought of as proper for members of the knightly class in late twelfth-century Northern France.

Inviting and being invited were then means of expressing social superiority; but by eating and drinking together in a context that was different from the domestic one, medieval diners also expressed their affiliation to a community. Eating and drinking together strengthened friendship, and this was true of many kinds of communities: monastic, fighting, urban, and so on. All of them had alimentary rites of bonding, which made their members fellow-drinkers, and hence friends ready to uphold, protect, and sometimes avenge each other.[37] The *Rule of St Benedict* insists on the fact that monks should eat together at the same table if they wanted to be a proper community.[38] By mimicking late Antiquity food habits in their feasts, early sixth-century Franks were expressing their "crave for *Romanitas*"[39]: to entertain his guests in a proper Roman way, King Theuderic I (511–534) hired a Greek physician and food expert, Anthimus, whose treaty *On the Observance of Foods* has been preserved.[40] By sharing drink from the same cup or drinking horn, warriors expressed their solidarity and became ready to die together and for their lord: the early Welsh poem of the *Gododdin*, probably composed in the late sixth century, but expanded and modified in the following centuries until it was set on manuscript in the thirteenth century, shows this ideal.[41] In the poem, the warriors of King Mynyddog of Din Eidyn (Edinburgh), having drunk their lord's mead for a whole year, fight together against the Angles at Catraeth (Catterick, north of York) and "pay for their mead" by falling together in battle.[42]

Indeed, this practice of communal eating and drinking was not limited to the ruling classes: the early and late medieval west was full of drinking associations and feasting societies, and in all classes of society, feasting remained a way of building, maintaining and reinforcing communities, just as it had done in Roman and Merovingian times.[43] Guilds, which were a major urban (but also rural) institution of the central and late Middle Ages, had their origins in late Antiquity and in early medieval groups united by oaths and the sharing of meals. From the eleventh century, we begin to see how guilds functioned, with the building of guildhalls where all guild activities would take place, the main one being the (at least) yearly communal meal. All members of the guild were expected to bring an equal contribution, and were fined if they failed to sit at the guild-meal.[44] Missing such a communal occasion was considered unacceptable, because eating together was a gesture of peace—indeed, it was often part of rituals of reconciliation—but refusing to sit with one's fellows meant defiance and enmity. After his humiliation at Canossa, Emperor Henry IV of Germany (1056–1106) is said to have sat for a meal with his former enemy Pope Gregory VII; but he did not eat anything. Whether the story is true or not, the papal chronicler who told it wanted to show that Henry's repentance was not sincere, that his submission was incomplete, and that he did not intend to keep the peace he had just attained with the pope: accepting the sharing of food was "an engagement for the future, a promise to behave in a certain way towards one's table-companions."[45] In guilds also, as in all kinds of confraternities and associations, eating together was a way of establishing peace, friendship, and mutual aid, and rejoicing together was compulsory.

The fact that the feast was a moment and a space of peace does not mean that violence was always absent from it. We have many examples of meals that turned sour, in which guests were injured or killed. The Old

English epic of *Beowulf* explains how such brawls could begin. A guest, sitting next to a warrior of the host's retinue, would see on his fellow-drinker's lap a sword which had belonged to his father, an heirloom lost in old combats: mead and ale helping, he would accuse the other man and provoke him, creating the conditions for a general fight between the host's warband and the guest's friends, ending in strife and despair.[46] However, even if the sources mention it frequently, violence was always seen as abnormal in the context of a feast: a guest had to be fed and honored—not humiliated or killed.

INNS AND TAVERNS: EATING OUT IN TOWNS

When we think today of eating out, we think first and foremost of having a meal in a restaurant—that is, in a place where food is prepared and served in exchange for money. This was not the case in the early Middle Ages: when they ate out, early medieval people stayed in a friend's house, in a ruler's hall, in their guild's meeting place, or in a monastery's *hospitium,* and their meal was generally not paid for with money, but with services and attitudes that linked them together and/or to their host. Inns and taverns were not a typical feature of the early Middle Ages: within an economy which knew minted metal, but did not have an extensive use of it except for paying taxes and buying prestige goods in marketplaces, commercial hospitality was not frequent. Moreover, the decline of urban civilization means that before 1100—that is for most of our period—examples of such hospitality are very rare, even if they are not wholly absent. We find, for instance, regular mentions of taverns in the acts of councils: bishops would forbid to their priests the frequentation of such places—but they actually repeated late Antiquity prescriptions which had existed at least since the 363 council of Laodicea,[47] and it is difficult to assess the actual pertinence of their warnings.

Things become clearer and more documented after 1100, with the rise of towns in all of western Europe. The renewal of urban life meant that new spaces for consumption developed: even if they kept gardens, pigsties, chicken runs, and even orchards (especially within the walls of religious houses) medieval townspeople had to buy most of their food. Bread, which is after all a readily cooked food, was much more important in towns than in the countryside, where cereals were often consumed in the form of porridge and gruel: buying bread from a baker's became standard behavior in medieval towns. This does not mean that all food and drink was bought from professional caterers: many townspeople had several activities, among which was the production of ale, bread, pastries, or wafers, and they sold or bartered those products to each other. If we take the example of the production of ale—an activity that, understandably, was closely linked to the development of taverns—it is only in the thirteenth century that urban brewing in Germany and the Low Countries became more important than rural production, either monastic or domestic.[48] Even in thirteenth-century English towns, most breweries were still held by housewives, who brewed ale for themselves and their families, and occasionally sold the surplus to other patrons. Professional breweries—and the taverns that go with them—were very much a later phenomenon, which really began only in the fourteenth century.[49]

Many townspeople did not have a kitchen within their lodgings, and resorted mainly to takeaway food, bought from small shops or, even more frequently, from roving sellers who *cried* food in the streets. Cries of food became a familiar noise in medieval towns, as in Paris, where such cries are well known from several thirteenth-century texts such as Guillaume de la Villeneuve's *Les crieries de Paris,* one of the poems that evokes the cries of the city.[50] Some of those criers, especially those who dealt in wine and other liquors, were themselves innkeepers, or employed by them to attract patrons. The *Jeu de saint Nicolas,* a mystery composed by the early thirteenth-century playwright Jean Bodel from Arras in Northern France, presents Raoulet, crier of the town, who extols the qualities of the wine he sells in his tavern: a wine from Auxerre in Burgundy, "lively, easy-going, full, strong, climbing like a squirrel in the wood, with no hint of mould or acidity, on dregs, frank, dry and light, clear as a sinner's tear, lingering on the gourmet's tongue."[51] In the Northern town of Arras, in a tavern that was visited by both common people and well-off burghers, Raoulet was selling a good white wine from Burgundy, far superior to anything produced in the neighborhood. Townspeople, as opposed to peasants, had access to quality products and did not limit their consumption to local productions. As Raoulet had it, drinking his wine could be considered a marker of town identity, of belonging to the town of Arras: "no-one else may taste it."[52] Eating and drinking together in taverns thus became a characteristic of town-life, a kind of urban sociability which—except in Italy, where it can be observed quite early—became much more documented after 1300. However, even then, with a practice which looked very much more like our own modern way of eating out, having a meal or a drink in a tavern remained primarily a means of reinforcing personal links, a way to build a community, and a statement of one's social identity, just as it had been for centuries—and still was by the end of the thirteenth century—in a lord's hall, a guild house, or a monastic hostel.

CHAPTER SIX

Professional Cooking, Kitchens, and Service Work

MELITTA WEISS ADAMSON

COOKS AND KITCHEN STAFF

In the late Middle Ages—the period under investigation here, when sources became more abundant—cooks were organized in guilds, and their training followed the apprenticeship system that was the norm for many professions at the time. According to the statutes of the Cooks' Guild of thirteenth-century Paris, the prospective cook was expected to work as an apprentice for two years, and afterwards as a journeyman for a master cook.[1] Once he had completed his training and attained the title of master, the cook had the option to continue working for another master, open his own cookshop, or secure one of the coveted positions in the kitchen of a wealthy aristocratic, bourgeois, or clerical household. Whether self-employed or practicing their craft in an affluent household, cooks generally suffered from an image problem. To us, living in an age of gourmet restaurants and celebrity chefs whose creations command exorbitant prices, it may be surprising that the well-to-do in the Middle Ages went out of their way not to eat out or to buy ready-made food. Even when they were living away from home or traveling, they might perhaps take some expensive spices with them, but would otherwise buy their provisions on the road to have them prepared by their own kitchen staff.[2]

Why this aversion to food prepared outside the home? The general reputation of medieval cooks of being dishonest and unclean likely had a lot to do with wealthy consumers' preference for homemade dishes. The previously mentioned statutes of the Cooks' Guild in Paris already hint at problems with quality control, stating, for instance, that "[n]o one may boil or roast geese, veal, lamb, kid or piglets...or beef, mutton or pork unless the meat is good and proper for selling and eating, and unless its marrow is good" or "[c]ooked meat may be kept only three days for buying or selling, unless it is adequately salted."[3] Ordinances from Britain paint a troubling picture of pies and pasties filled with foodstuffs not, or no longer, fit for human consumption, reheated food, or inferior meat sold as venison at premium prices.[4] A more elaborate scheme from the City of London was that of cooks selling kitchen waste to bakers who used it as fillings for pies that they then sold to hungry consumers.[5] From the sources that have come down to us it would appear that the well-to-do only turned to cookshops as a last resort when unexpected guests arrived, or they had food catered when the quantities needed exceeded what their own kitchen staff and facilities could produce. But even then, the food that was bought ready-made was generally kept to a minimum. Hiring extra cooks for a special occasion, such as a wedding banquet, was a better way to control the quality of the food to be served.

Who, then, were the main customers of the cookshops in medieval Europe? Found primarily in densely populated cities, cookshops catered in particular to the poor whose living quarters had no, or insufficient cooking facilities. In other words, to have a hot meal they had to buy take-out food, much of it of questionable quality. In medieval towns a correlation appears to have existed between high population density, a high number of single-adult households (of poor widows, for instance), and a high number of cookshops, with the latter at times even exceeding the number of bakers.[6] Judging from the street cries heard in Paris in the thirteenth century, the hot foods sold included mashed peas, beans, pasties, cakes, wafers, pancakes, flans, tarts, and simnels (bagels)—all relatively modest fare, which seems to support these findings.[7] If self-employment for medieval cooks meant running a cookshop that mostly sold to the lower strata of society, this clearly was not the place for the ambitious cook intent on rising to the top of his profession. Such a cook did his very best to find employment in a noble household where money was no object. The most famous cook of the Middle Ages, author of the fourteenth-century cookbook *Le Viandier,* Guillaume Tirel (ca. 1310–1395), was known by the name of Taillevent, literally *slice wind.*[8] He served as royal cook for three French kings, Philip VI, Charles V, and Charles VI, managing a kitchen staff of close to fifty persons, plus a dozen or more *maîtres d'hostel.*[9] Little is known of Taillevent's background. He may or may not have come from "a wealthy merchant or *haute bourgeois* family."[10] What we do know is that his beginnings in the royal kitchen were humble. Taillevent started as a kitchen boy in the early fourteenth century, as a scullion performing menial jobs such as cleaning fish, scouring pots, or turning the spits. For scullions it was also not unusual to sleep in the kitchen.[11] At the end of his life, Taillevent, chief cook and *sergent d'armes,* had attained the rank of squire, with his own coat of arms depicting three cooking pots.[12] Enjoying the trust and admiration of his royal masters, he was handsomely rewarded for his services, which extended from the kitchen to the dining room.[13] According to the courtier and chronicler Olivier de la Marche (1425–1502), the master cook under the Valois had the following duties and privileges:

> The master cook had the privilege of carrying a dish to the duke's table, to have a seat next to the fireplace of the kitchen, and to sit there when he wanted. The keeping of the spices was entrusted to him. He commanded everyone in the kitchen; and, in accordance with his title, he carried, when he was working, a great wooden spoon, which he used as much to taste the soups as to correct his subordinates when they were negligent.[14]

Helping the elite sustain their bodies at a time when the spirit was re-garded as higher than the flesh, cooks were often looked down on, and were portrayed in the literature as lacking education, reeking of kitchen odors, being hot-tempered, and having a rough sense of humor.[15] In con-trast, cooks themselves appear to have had a different image of their pro-fession. The chief cook to the Duke of Savoy perceived himself as an artist and a scientist.[16] Occupying a position of trust, aristocratic cooks more than most other members of the court, were responsible for the health and well-being of their employers and frequent guests. While their level of literacy may have varied, some not only knew how to read and write, but also knew some Latin. Working side by side with the court physicians they must have had some knowledge of dietetics, the medical theory of keeping the four humors in the body in balance, or restoring their balance, through food and other lifestyle adjustments.[17] In addition to mastering a variety of cooking methods and keeping up with new developments and techniques, many of them also had considerable artistic talent that manifested itself in their use of colors, shapes, and in fantastic illusion food, designed to both entertain and nourish. Their amazing dishes have come down to us in numerous illuminations, recipes, and chronicles of memorable banquets.

At the same time that Taillevent was dazzling the French court with his creations or nursing those whose bodily humors had temporarily fallen out of balance with his sick-dishes, scribes were busily at work further to the south, recording the operation and food supply of the kitchen at the papal court, located in Avignon, from 1305 to 1378.[18] As in other wealthy households, the trend in the papal kitchen at Avignon was toward self-sufficiency and homemade food. The cooks employed by the popes were all lay people and lived outside the palace. Their pay in foodstuffs, and later money, was higher than the pay for clerics holding food-related offices at court.[19] The early records differentiate between *coqui* or cooks and *brodarii,* likely pottagers or perhaps sous-chefs in today's parlance.[20] Later a *magister coquine* or master cook was added. He and/or an *emptor coquine* or buyer for the kitchen managed the day-to-day operations of the kitchen.[21] The number of cooks hired for luxurious feasts could be as high as thirty-eight plus helpers for the coronation of Pope Urban, or even sixty-five (twenty-four *coqui* and forty-one *brodarii*), as was the case at a two-week-long feast by Pope Clement VI, that also employed fourteen butchers. Fifty thousand tarts were consumed during that feast. Interestingly, the preparation of the three standard sauces for meat dishes (cameline or cinnamon, green, and garlic sauce) was outsourced, as these were bought ready-made in barrels.[22] Although the papal court differed from a secular court in that it was a woman-less court, the types of court offices that dealt with food were similar to those of aristocratic courts.[23] Butlers managed the buttery and were in charge of wine and other alcoholic beverages, and for a while, also fruit. Pantlers were responsible for the pantry and the supply of bread, salt, flour, cakes, pastry, and raisins. The wax office looked after the purchase of wax as well as butter, and the apothecary looked after the purchase of spices and confections. There was also a *speciarius* who produced confections on the premises. A water and a wood office guaranteed the adequate provision of water, firewood, and coal at the court of Avignon. The alms office was in charge of the food that was to be handed out to the poor. The hall master, comparable to the steward in aristocratic households, was the keeper of the silverware. A *pisconarius* looked after the papal fish ponds, and hunters were hired as needed.

The kitchen at the fashionable court of the Duke of Burgundy in the late Middle Ages was staffed in the following way, as Olivier de la Marche tells us: two kitchen clerks were responsible for all expenses related to the provisioning of foodstuffs and kitchen supplies.[24] A master cook and two other cooks were in charge of the preparation of food for the ducal household and they oversaw the work of twenty-five specialists plus a roaster and his helper, a pottager and his helper, and a larderer responsible for the larder where the preserved food was stored. Non-professional workers in the kitchen included fire-tenders and fuellers, potters, and an army of scullions. Two saucers produced the standard sauces and were responsible for adequate supplies of verjuice (*verjus,* the sour juice of unripe fruit), vinegar, and salt. They delivered the sauces and salt directly to the pantler in the great hall. The fruitery employed two fruiters who were in charge of fresh and dried fruits, nuts, as well as wax candles and tapers. Among the professions that operated either from within or outside a wealthy household were bakers, pastry cooks, waferers, confectioners, butchers, and poulterers.[25] In the case of the Burgundian court, bread and meat were delivered by outside bakers and butchers who had term contracts with the duke's household. The papal kitchen, too, bought its bread from local Avignon bakers.[26]

KITCHEN

Hearths in early medieval castles, as in more modest abodes, were centrally located with cooking and dining combined in one room. A change from wood to stone as the primary building material for castles, made the integration of the hearth in the wall possible. This, together with the danger of fire and the smell and noise pollution connected with the preparation of food, were the main reasons why those who could afford it separated kitchen from dining hall, sometimes even going so far as to make the kitchen a separate building altogether that was connected to the living quarters by a covered walkway. The kitchen at the Burgundian court in Dijon, like others serving a household of similar size, was big enough for approximately fifty kitchen staff. It boasted six stone-hooded hearths, two each being built into three of the four kitchen walls. The fourth wall had sinks and above them a big window.[27] There are indications that supplies were transported to the kitchen not just through doors but also through windows in the Middle Ages. Under Pope Clement, for instance, Avignon had a big window and a pulley block installed.[28] For most of the period, the windows across Europe had just wooden shutters. Glass windows were only introduced in Avignon in the latter half of the fourteenth century.[29] The open fires in medieval kitchens that needed a steady supply of oxygen made ventilation one of the top priorities. Chimneys, often capped with lantern-like structures known as louvers, allowed the smoke to escape. Louvers came in different materials and in many shapes and sizes. Slatted ones with a string attached could be opened or closed, pottery ones, especially when made in the shape of a head, produced special effects as the smoke emanated through the mouth, eyes, and ears.[30] The Avignon popes had two kitchens, a *coquina magna* (big kitchen) for big banquets and a *coquina parva* (small kitchen) for everyday meals.[31] Cardinals and clerics at the papal court had their own separate kitchens and kitchen staff. In addition to food, the papal kitchen also bought firewood, kitchenware, and dishes.

An ample supply of water was essential for the cooking and cleaning activities in the kitchen, and in other areas where food was handled, and cooking and dining equipment was cleaned, such as the brewhouse, the bakehouse, the scalding house to prepare poultry, the boiling or seething house, and the scullery.[32] Water was either transported through a conduit system, or drawn from a well or cistern in buckets that water bearers then carried to their final destination in the household. When it came to cooking, the best hearth or oven was worthless without an adequate supply of firewood. Medieval cooks were keenly aware of that. Firewood, and toward the end of the Middle Ages also coal, the latter valued for its long-lasting and even heat, were delivered to the kitchens of Europe's grand households by the cartload. To meet the fuel needs of the papal kitchen in Avignon, firewood was procured from as far away as Burgundy and western Switzerland.[33] The purchase of coal spiked in Avignon in the plague years of 1349 to 1351, which may be attributed at least in part to the advice Pope Clement VI received from his physicians to remain between two basins of burning coal at all times and thereby avoid being infected.[34]

Fire irons and kindling were used to start a fire and bellows or air from the mouths of kitchen staff were used to draw up the flames. Since this was cumbersome, embers were frequently left dormant under a pottery cover with holes for ventilation. This cover was known as a *couvre-feu*, which is the root for the modern English word curfew.[35] Given the value placed on firewood, cooks in kitchens big and small were careful to exploit the heat produced by it as fully as possible. Different foodstuffs and cooking processes frequently required different heat intensity, and medieval cooks were masters in moving even the heaviest cooking pots to and from the fire as they saw fit. Adjustable hooks allowed for the raising and lowering the pot, and with the help of a swinging chimney crane the pot could also be moved horizontally, closer to or farther away from the heat source. Andirons contained the burning logs that could be removed altogether to reduce the heat under a pot. Some andirons were equipped with little metal baskets at the top that served as an extra heat source when filled with burning coals, for smaller, more delicate dishes, or for keeping food warm.[36] Tripods or trivets over the fire would also serve as the base on which big cauldrons were placed. The simplest version of utilizing the heat source was to put a pot directly in the coals, a method cooks used when making fritters, for instance.

Meat was generally roasted and served with the appropriate sauce. Cooks in bigger households would have a wide range of spits and grills in different sizes at their disposal, made of iron or wood. Expected to roast or grill to perfection anything from a delicate fish or bird to a boar or ox, expert cooks knew exactly how to place the animal above, or next to the fire for optimum results. Scullions, sometimes located behind a shield to protect them from the intense heat, would be the ones the cooks called on to turn the spits, often for hours on end. Intent on letting neither any of the heat, nor any of the food being roasted to go to waste, medieval cooks would also put pans under the spits to catch the juices dripping from the roasted animal.[37] In addition to boiling, stewing, roasting, and grilling, the hearth was used for frying. Medieval frying pans, immortalized in the paintings of Hieronymus Bosch (1450–1516), look surprisingly modern. Equipped with one long handle, they were produced in varying sizes and depths. The long handle allowed the cook to fry food fast by holding the pan directly over the fire. Another less tiring option was to place the frying pan on a tripod.

For baking bread and pies, an oven was needed. A small portable oven made of metal or pottery and known as *trapa* appears to have been popular in southern France in the Middle Ages. Mentioned in the only cookbook from Languedoc that has been handed down to us, and in the household records of the papal court in Avignon, that the *trapa* was likely placed in the coals.[38] To build and operate an oven that used up a lot of valuable firewood required permission by the authorities, which is why the majority of the medieval population bought their baked goods from the baker, or had bread or pies baked by him for a fee. As mentioned earlier, even the Burgundian court had its bread delivered by local bakers. Non-commercial, full-sized bakers' ovens built into the masonry of the fireplace, or constructed in a separate bakehouse were only found in wealthy households. To heat the inside of the oven, a fire was lit inside first, and once the desired temperature was reached, the ashes were removed and a hardwood peel was used to lift the bread, pies, and other pastries into the oven.[39] A household rich enough to be equipped with a baker's oven would also usually employ a baker. For pies the cook and baker would have separate tasks, the former to produce the pie fillings and the latter to produce the dough, encase the fillings in it, and bake the pies. Food was also processed in the dairy, where a lack of pasteurization and proper refrigeration made it necessary to turn most of the milk quickly into cheese or butter. Milk was given to children to drink, but its consumption by adults was frowned upon. The standard equipment found in the dairy were the cheese press and a tall butter churn, as well as milk pails and shallow pans in which the milk was first poured when it arrived.[40] Some households would also have their own breweries, complete with big vats and roasting kilns, where ale, more affordable than wine and safer than water, was produced.[41]

Cooks and their various helpers in the kitchen usually wore long aprons. Their primary workspace was a massive wooden table. Chopping blocks were used for the preparation of meat. Dressers, ranging from elaborate pieces of furniture with storage space for food, dishes, or utensils, to simple boards were also found in medieval kitchens, butteries, and serving areas. The final preparation and arrangement of dishes prior to serving was made on those dressers.[42] In addition to the kitchen equipment already mentioned such as the hearth, oven, cauldrons, pots, frying pans, roasting spits, tripods, trivets, chains, chimney cranes, and hooks, a well-equipped kitchen would have assortments of spoons, long-handled basting spoons, and big stirring spoons, ladles, flesh hooks, tongs, as well as containers of varying sizes. Saltboxes and saltshakers were essential, and so were platters, trenchers, basins, and flasks, and a range of different baskets, sometimes with leather covers, barrels, vats, hampers, ewers, rabbit and fish nets.[43] The instruments used included sieves and sieve cloths, mortars and pestles, knives and whetstones to sharpen them, graters, rasps, cleavers, and whisks. Some foodstuffs, such as bone-dry cod known as stockfish, were softened with a mallet.[44] In the papal kitchen in Avignon, copper was the preferred metal for cauldrons and other kitchen and dining equipment such as wine coolers, water basins, and even a foot-warmer for Pope Benedict XII's cold feet.[45] Also mentioned in the sources are waffle-irons, salt and mustard mills, hand querns for grinding grain, a stone basin to store oil in, various molds, and a container for the preparation of Lombardy cake, presumably the famous Parmesan pie found in many upper-class cookbooks of the time. Dijon, the seat of the fashionable Dukes of Burgundy, was the favorite commercial center where the papal court shopped for kitchen and dining equipment.

Kitchens that processed a lot of food also produced a lot of dirty utensils and kitchen waste. Kitchenware was either cleaned in the sink or sinks located in the kitchen proper, or in a separate scullery. Cloth, scouring sand, and ashes were used for scrubbing kitchen and dinnerware clean. The waste water and solid kitchen waste were dumped into the moat below that was occasionally cleaned out when the stench got too offensive, or dumped into the river—if there was one—outside the castle walls. Farther away, and hence more inconvenient, were the municipal dumps that were usually located outside the city. Garbage disposal in our modern sense of the word was still in its infancy in the Middle Ages.

COOKING TECHNIQUES

Two of the biggest challenges for medieval cooks were to get the temperature and cooking time for a given dish just right. Thermometers did not exist yet and clocks, if available at all, were still few and far between. Medieval cookbooks have very little to say on the issue of temperature beyond some vague instructions as to the size or intensity of the fire. We can assume that cooks learnt the proper use of their heat source or sources during their time as apprentices. They may also have used their intuition at times. That accidents did happen, resulting in food burning to the pot or boiling over, becomes evident from the comments found in a number of written sources.[46] Cooking times, if recorded at all in the recipes, were given in activities whose approximate duration was familiar to the common man. They included saying a Paternoster or a Miserere, or walking a certain distance, such as a mile or the length of a field.[47] Experience and intuition were also necessary when it came to the quantities for ingredients in the medieval kitchen. Apart from such relative measurements as half as much or twice the amount, there is occasional reference to a nutshell of this, an eggshell of that, or the length of an arm, or width of a finger in the cookbooks. Medieval recipes were a far cry from our modern recipes that list the precise temperatures, cooking times, weights, and measurements.

Despite its apparent lack of exact cooking instructions, medieval cuisine, at least that of the upper classes was a very sophisticated cuisine that valued a high degree of food processing, judging from the sources. Ingredients were chopped, diced, mashed, ground up, sieved, colored, and shaped to a degree previously unknown in Europe. In addition to knives of various sizes, the medieval cook's favorite tools were the mortar and the sieve cloth, the manual forerunners, one could say, of today's food processors. Both were essential in producing sauces and pastes of supreme smoothness that typically accompanied the roast meats. Or they helped turn meat into forcemeat used for pies, stuffings, meatballs, and the like. Part of the reason why ingredients were so often pureed and pulverized beyond recognition was surely the influence exerted by medieval medicine. Based on humoral theory, it assigned two of the four prime qualities hot, cold, moist, and dry (cold-dry, cold-moist, warm-dry, warm-moist) not just to drugs, but also to foodstuffs. To keep the four liquids or humors in the body in balance, the food consumed also had to be balanced. This could be achieved in two ways: either the ingredients within a dish were in balance, or a hot and dry dish, such as roast meat, was balanced by a cold and moist dish, such as a sauce that possessed those prime qualities. Combining foodstuffs in their finest possible consistency ensured their complete humoral mixture and influence on one another.[48] Another reason for using foodstuffs in a highly processed state was that it allowed for an even coloring and perfect shaping of the substance—two aspects that were of enormous importance for the medieval dining experience. While heavy food processing is still—or is again—with us, the medieval habit of multiple cooking has since waned in popularity. That roast meat was frequently pre-cooked before it was larded and put on the roasting spit should come less as a surprise than the more elaborate triple-cooking of a suckling pig in a German recipe collection which calls for cooking the meat and returning it to the intact raw skin of the animal. This step is followed by boiling and grilling the suckling pig.[49] Making sure the meat was thoroughly cooked was certainly one, but likely not the only motivation behind it, given that fish was also sometimes subjected to multiple cooking.

The extant cookbook manuscripts of the period give us a sense of the preferred taste in food that medieval cooks and their helpers catered to. Acidic liquids from wine, vinegar, and verjuice, to the more exotic and costly citrus fruits were added to many dishes, especially sauces. The thickeners used to produce these sauces were substantially different from the dairy product, flour, or fat and flour (roux) varieties popular in Europe today. Medieval cooks boiled down their mixture of tart liquids and powdered spices and stirred in eggs, breadcrumbs, ground almonds, or rice flour to achieve the desired creamy consistency.[50] Sour or tart flavors in dishes were often combined with sweet ones found in honey, unfermented grape juice, or the more exclusive sugar. It would appear as if sweet-and-sour was the flavor of choice, at least in the later Middle Ages when most of the cookbooks and dietetic treatises were written.

The fats used in the medieval kitchen were animal fats, above all pork fat, on meat days, and olive oil, or a variety of nut and seed oils on lean days. The most versatile nut supplied to upper-class kitchens in large quantities was the almond. It appeared whole or slivered as a garnish on dishes, in ground form as a thickener, or as the base for almond milk, the preferred alternative to cow's milk during Lent. Almonds were also processed into almond oil or almond butter, or combined with sugar and rose water and turned into marzipan. Often ordered together with sugar and almonds for the medieval kitchen were the luxury spices, some of which were more expensive than gold, and all of them locked away in a box to which only the master cook had access. The spices procured for the papal kitchen in Avignon included cloves, ginger, pepper, saffron, and cinnamon. Also part of the papal shopping list were cane sugar, honey, myrrh, cubebs, lavender, caraway, fennel, thyme, and pine nuts.[51] Medieval cooks had the choice of buying ready-made spice mixes in powder form of the strong (*fort*) or mild (*douce*) variety. In doing so they ran the risk of using a foodstuff whose potency was greatly diminished through pulverization or adulteration. For these reasons, aristocratic households frequently opted for grinding spices with mortar and pestle on the premises.

Spices, some of which were originally introduced as drugs and only gradually moved from the apothecary to the kitchen, were valued for their presumed health benefits, their distinctive taste, and, as in the case of saffron, the vibrant colors they imparted on a dish. If there are two features that define the look of medieval European cuisine, they are color and shape. Cooks were expected to conjure up in their kitchen every color of the rainbow and turn dishes into symphonies of color echoing the stained-glass windows of the cathedrals that went up all across Europe.[52] Influenced by the attention to color, in particular gold, red, white, and silver, found in medieval Arab cuisine, and in Arab alchemy, medieval Europe expanded its color palette significantly.[53] Saffron and egg yolk produced the desired golden yellow, and a variety of leafy greens produced darker shades of green that could be brightened when yellow was mixed in. Reds were achieved by adding such ingredients as sandalwood, the dye dragon's blood, actual blood, rose petals, or red grape juice to the food. Aside from blackberries, and columbine blossoms, orchil lichen allowed the cook to color a dish blue. When combined with an acidic substance, this lichen could also be used as a red dye. Cinnamon, blood, and variously toasted bread and gingerbread were used for different shades of brown, and prunes for the color black. For white, cooks combined white ingredients such as the white meat of fish and fowl, almonds, sugar, rice, and ginger. Most of these ingredients feature prominently in the famous white dish *blancmangé* that is a standard dish in cookbooks from across late-medieval Europe. Gold and silver leaf, thought to have medicinal qualities besides their dazzling appearance, also belonged to the repertoire of the medieval cook who applied it, for instance, to a boar's head or to another perennial favorite, Parmesan pies. Like the white dish, some standard sauces were simply referred to by their color: green sauce, white sauce, cinnamon or camel-colored sauce (*sauce cameline*). Clear jellies that were all the rage in Europe in the later Middle Ages, also lent themselves well to coloring and multi-colored patterns.

Highly processed food was not only ideal for coloring but also for shaping. Molds, made of wood or metal, and popular in Europe since Roman times, were standard equipment in the medieval kitchen.[54] Wax molds are mentioned in connection with sugar figurines at the end of the period. Molds in the shape of boxes and filled with confections, notably marzipan, or jellies were popular and are probably the forerunner of our modern chocolate boxes. Stamps were used to press a relief into confections. By far the most widely used mold and one that was also included in the equipment of the papal kitchen in Avignon, was the waffle iron. Consisting of two flat planes with interlocking handles, waffle-irons came in two varieties: for oven or for stove-top use. Either flat or rolled up in sticks, waffles were eaten at the end of a medieval banquet, and were such a standard feature of dining in style that they were also commercially produced, by the waffle-maker, known in France as the *oubloyer*.

The medieval love for colors and shapes found its most artistic expression in the dishes served between courses at a grand banquet, which, in turn, soon became a course in themselves.[55] Known as *sotelties* in England, and *entremets* in France, they were designed to trick primarily the eye of the diner by pretending to be something other than the foodstuffs they were made of. The motivations for cooks to produce these ingenious creations and for diners to marvel at them and indulge in them were manifold. The desire to serve and eat food out of season or food forbidden by the Church during Lent surely played a role, as did the desire by cooks to show their technical skills and artistic talents. The meat of warm-blooded animals, dairy products, and eggs all came in fast-day versions, many of them using fish or almonds as a substitute. To complete the illusion, fake roasts were covered with roasted gingerbread and presented in a pepper sauce, the standard sauce for venison. Dough was used by cooks to prepare gigantic pies, sometimes even containing live birds, or even humans, or to build entire castles and other structures. Special know-how was required to masterfully skin a bird so the meat could be processed, cooked, and stuffed back into the intact plumage, and the animal then mounted in a life-like pose. Cooking a fish in three different ways, one part boiled, one roasted, and one fried, each served with the appropriate sauce, while keeping the whole animal in one piece was another achievement with which a skilled master cook could do his lord proud. More intriguing still were the fowl portrayed as pilgrims or as knights riding into battle on a suckling pig. Even the fabled cockatrice was given shape by inventive cooks by combining half a cock and half a piglet. Tricks that made prepared animals breathe fire or make noises, were a sure way to please the audience. Cooks achieved those special effects by inserting a piece of cotton containing camphor or alcohol in the animal's mouth and lighting it, or filling the neck of the animal with quicksilver and sulfur, tying it, and reheating the creature so it emitted sound. Live animals, too, were sometimes served, much to the dismay of the more squeamish diners. Either simply hidden in covered bowels, or made to look like cooked animals by being plucked and even slightly roasted, these pitiful creatures were medieval party jokes more than culinary delights. As the Middle Ages drew to a close, inedible *entremets* made of wood or metal gradually replaced the edible variety, and the craftsman joined the cook as artist in chief.

As the above description of cooking techniques shows, the late medieval kitchen was a place of experimentation and innovation. European cooks and the diners they catered to were eager consumers of all the new foodstuffs introduced by the Arabs, from exotic spices to citrus fruits, and a variety of new vegetables. They readily adopted the Arab habit of coloring food and developed it further; they perfected clear jellies and experimented with distilling food into essences.[56] While the essence of chicken never really caught on, the invention of an edible short crust certainly did. It revolutionized pie making at the end of the period, by transforming the pie crust from a simple container to be discarded into an integral part of the pie that was consumed together with the filling. Innovation also extended to the place of consumption, the great hall, where those who could afford it dazzled guests with a wine fountain that dispensed different wines.

SERVICE WORK

Servitors transported the prepared dishes arranged on platters or chargers from the kitchen to the great hall where the big banquets took place, or up the stairs to the heated chamber of the lord and lady for more intimate dinners.[57] If the kitchen was in a separate building, covered walkways would make sure the food was protected from the wind and rain.[58] Facilities outside the great hall would allow for reheating, temporarily keeping, and final arrangement of the food before it was served. A big medieval feast would involve many members of the household.[59] Overseeing all aspects of the operation was the steward, with the marshal responsible for the flawless execution of the dinner itself. The usher was in charge of the entrance door to the hall. The serving staff consisted of the head waiter, the *sewer* or taster, the butler in charge of the drinks, the *pantler* in charge of bread and salt, the *ewerer* in charge of the lord's *ewery* or vessel for hand washing, the lord's cupbearer, the carver, and all the respective grooms that served under them. The serving staff would normally wear a livery in the colors of the noble house.[60] Chief cooks, too, were sometimes given a livery and asked to serve their creations in person at the lord's table. On truly memorable occasions such as royal banquets, some of the serving was done by noblemen, who received generous rewards from the king for their efforts. As the records from Avignon indicate, kings and emperors were, in turn, called upon to serve the Pope at banquets, especially during the first course.[61]

Tables, usually temporary trestle tables that were dismantled again after the meal, were arranged in a U shape in the great hall. The serving was done from the inside of the U, with the diners seated on benches on the outside. If there was a permanent table at all, it was placed at the center of the U, on a raised platform or dais, and was occupied by the lord and highest-ranking guests. Individual chairs were rare in the Middle Ages. Located in the middle of the head table, they, too, were reserved for the highest-ranking diner or diners, with the ecclesiastical dignitary occupying the loftiest seat.[62] Facing the guests on the dais was often a musicians' gallery. Under it were the doors used by the wait staff to enter and serve the food. An important piece of furniture in the hall was the buffet, known as the *cupboard* in England. Set against the wall in the proximity of the head table, it was used mainly by the butler and his grooms to keep the pitchers with the drinks that were being served. Special treats and valuable vessels in silver or gold would also be displayed on the buffet. Ensuring that the medieval banquet unfolded according to plan and that all actors in this tightly choreographed spectacle played their part to perfection, etiquette books addressed to diners, wait staff, carvers, and children abounded.[63]

The task of setting the table went to the *ewerer* and the *pantler*. The former spread the tablecloths generously, starting with the best and newest at the head table and working his way down on both sides, leaving the most used and torn tablecloths for the lowest ranking guests at the two ends of the U. He was also in charge of the *ewery* cup and towel. Using a lot of cloth to cover the buffet, table, tableware, and even the cut bread for the lord was a sign of distinction.[64] The *pantler* distributed the bread rolls, trenchers, saltcellars, knives, and spoons, again starting on the dais with the highest-quality items. Lesser folk usually brought their own knives, and forks were not yet a part of the table setting for rich or poor. The meal, announced by blowing a horn, started once the lord had taken his seat and grace was said by the almoner. With poison a concern for the highest dignitaries that attended the banquet, the first step was to have the *pantler* assay or test the bread at the head table for poison. The cupbearer tasted the water in the *ewery*, and once the dishes for the first course arrived in the great hall, the *sewer* or taster had them assayed one-by-one by the chief cook and the steward. Following this ritual, all the diners sat down, the drinks were assayed by the marshal, butler, and cupbearer, and the carver began his work at the head table. At the other tables, diners in groups of two, four, or six shared the food that was brought to them in a serving known as a *messe*, and helped themselves or each other to the food from a common platter, or bowl. Drinking vessels, too, were shared by all but the highest guests. Their materials ranged from cheap earthenware to wood, leather, precious metals, and in rare cases, also glass.[65]

The job of the professional carver was twofold: to cut the trenchers for the lord's table in neat squares and present them at the start of the meal, followed by the more demanding task of carving a wide variety of dishes, from suckling pig and swan, to rabbit, pike, and crab into the appropriate morsels without the food getting cold. Cleanliness, sharp knives, the mastery of a specialized vocabulary, and utter speed and dexterity in handling the food with the left, and cutting with the right, were essential qualities for a successful carver. With banquets ranging from the standard two main courses plus dessert course, to as many as six courses of seven or more savory and sweet dishes each, the carver also had to possess a lot of stamina. For the guests of lesser status, the food either came to the table already precut into bite-sized pieces, or they carved it themselves with carving knives provided by the host. Food left over from carving or discarded by the diners, such as used trenchers, was collected in special containers or *voyders*.

Generosity by the host was valued highly, and so was charity, which expressed itself at the medieval banquet table in the form of alms collected by the almoner in the alms dish, either once or several times in the course of a meal. The food that was later distributed among the poor consisted of offerings ranging from the lowly loaf of bread to the most elaborate dish served to the lord. Alms were a way of soothing the conscience of the rich, and giving the needy a taste of upper-class living. Far from being a modest container, the alms dish was often as luxurious in material and design as the other showpieces displayed on the buffet.[66]

When the last course was consumed, the tables were cleared by the hall staff in reverse order from the way they were set. Utensils and leftover food were collected starting at the end and gradually moving up towards the dais. Then the dessert course, typically consisting of fruit and cheese, wafers, and aromatic spices, and accompanied by spiced wine known as *hippocras* was served. Finally, drinking vessels, trenchers, napkins, and saltcellars were removed from the table, the hand-washing ritual was repeated, grace was said, and the lord got up from the table, thereby officially ending the banquet. It was not unusual for dinnerware, especially when made of precious metal, to be stolen by diners. For this reason, the papal court in Avignon and other courts of Europe took to locking their doors during the meal, and only allowed diners to leave after all the tableware was accounted for.[67]

Overall, the Middle Ages was a time of increased professionalization in the kitchen, as more and more cooks were trained in the apprenticeship system and organized in guilds. A distinct preference for eating in, over eating out, meant that the most successful cooks were those employed by a rich household, while self-employed cooks operating their own cookshops more often than not sold fast food to those of modest means. Making up in specialized manpower what they lacked in modern transport and kitchen equipment, medieval cooks were masters in logistics, inventors, nutritionists, and artists all in one. Along with the diners they sought to please, they were open to a wide range of new foodstuffs, cooking practices, and forms of presentation. Sweet–sour was the preferred taste, and a high degree of processing that allowed for the coloring and shaping of the food, along with special effects were particularly valued. The wait staff in charge of executing a medieval banquet, far from being looked down on as lowly servants, consisted of well-trained personnel who were familiar with the rules of etiquette and were often of noble birth. Together, those working in the kitchen and related food offices, and those serving their creations in the great hall produced some of the most memorable dining experiences in human history.

CHAPTER SEVEN

Family and Domesticity

GABRIELLA PICCINNI

Charles Hindley

THE HOUSE WITHIN A HOUSE

To cook together is to be a family. In the medieval village of Montaillou, in the Pyrenees, the kitchen was called a house (*chas*); that is, it was a "house within a house,"[1] and even today, this is a saying in the Tuscan country-side and in other European regions. In past centuries all this evokes the image of fire burning in the fireplace, an everyday scene pervaded by smells and steam from a saucepan, or from a grill, or spit above their embers, a vigil after the evening meal devoted to shelling legumes and seeds, mending, spinning, gossiping, or telling stories. Around the fire revolves the existence of a group of people, living under the same roof, cooking, and taking meals together.

From very ancient times, the fireplace was used as a metaphor of do-mestic unity. Already in 20 BC the Roman poet Horace (*Epistles* I, 14, 2) spoke of the five *fires* composing a small property of his. Eight centuries later and a few thousand miles away, between 811 and 826, the Abbot of Saint-Germain-des-Prés also used the same term, *fires,* for some properties in the countryside near Paris. Especially widespread from the twelfth cen-tury and up until the beginning of the twentieth, in Normandy, Armagnac, Catalonia, or Italy, and in many other areas of Europe, taxes of various kinds go under the name of *focaticum,* or *focagium.* In Italy, in times much closer to our own, when to say hearth and home already simply meant a metaphor to indicate the unifying power of television, in front of which the family gathered for their evening meal, the term *focatico* was revived for a family tax of a new kind paid by the *focus;* that is, the household. And this in 1992, when only old songs or grandparents' stories evoked that patriarchal idea of domestic unity![2] The fires, in other words the kitchens, *are* the families.

It is not always easy to reconstruct how people lived, cooked, and ate around the firesides of the past. Up until the last few centuries of the Middle Ages, there is much less written evidence for what took place inside the house than for what occurred outside of it; for what happened in the countryside rather than in the towns, and in the houses of the poor than in those of the rich. For more ancient times, for the less well-off classes, and in general the places of the less privileged, the laconic tone of the written sources and the literature is not compensated for even by evidence drawn from iconography, which has left us very few images to draw upon concerning kitchens or pantries, this literature preferring instead to focus on the abundance or decorum of upper-class meals, or on those of religious environments. In the same way the history of women who prepared the food is much less well-known than that of the men who sat round the table, even though it was to them that the traditional division of labor between the sexes attributed most of the domestic economy. Finally, the cookery books which were written from the thirteenth century onward, and the first records of accounts of home expenditure, primarily record the diets of the upper classes, the high bourgeoisie of the towns, and the well-off classes in general, and do not allow us to enter the kitchens where, for generations, the meals for so many ordinary families were prepared.

Consequently, in order to begin to unravel the everyday diets of the ordinary families of the time, we need to begin by examining the objects that were used in the preparation of their meals. Those objects that are listed in wills give us insight into the relevant kitchen utensils, what was used for the fireplace, the table, or the larder, enabling us to imagine the dynamics unfolding around them: how people tried to store their food, to prepare it, and eat it. Those actually found in the great investigations of rural archaeology of the 1960s in France and England, and afterwards in other European countries and in urban areas, have brought to light the way of life of the poorest, in the humblest houses, and in the huts that for centuries represented the everyday environments of most of the population.

THE SONG OF THE FIRE

When seeking for a common denominator within the variety of diets in the European Middle Ages, we can start from the fireplace, this time not as a tax unit or term for census calculation, but as a materially central feature in most houses, though gradually enriched with cultural and symbolic significance.

In the early Middle Ages throughout Europe, most people lived in buildings of a modest size, with just a single room, built using poorer quality materials such as wood, reeds, dried clay, or branches, and sometimes having cellars, or basements. Cooking environments were therefore extremely rudimentary. Sometimes, as has been shown in central-northern Italy, small, individual buildings—for example, one in which to live, prepare meals, and make wine; one for use as a storehouse, granary, larder, and cellar; and another in which to keep animals and tools—made up a unit the people of the time saw as one place. This was an enclosed space bordered by hedges, fences, or ditches, within which one could also find a vegetable garden, and sometimes a well. The dwelling place, strictly speaking, was a room lit up at the entrance where you went in. People moved from one part to another to work, to sleep, and to prepare and eat meals.[3]

In the Mediterranean area, archaeologists have found fireplaces out in the open. The first indoor fireplaces were very simple affairs, at ground level on earthen floors, dug out of the earth or slightly raised, with the smoke finding its way out of a hole in the roof or the door.[4] People had already invented some means of delimiting the area where the fire was lit, and anxiety over reducing its dangers had led them to pave or surround their fires with small stones or bricks arranged in a regular pattern. In Tuscany, up to the twelfth century, the few fireplaces found in peasant houses were in the center of the room or against the side walls, dug out of the earthen floors, surrounded by stones, and sometimes with a work surface for cooking.[5] In a mosaic dating from between 1163 and 1165 in the Abbey of St. Nicola in Otranto, in Puglia, the cold month of February is represented by a low fireplace over which a large pot hangs, and a pig is being roasted whole on a spit. It is clear that in these cases people cooked by crouching down in front of the fire, or by sitting on very low stools.

From the twelfth to thirteenth centuries, from houses made only with materials available locally, we gradually find slightly more complex buildings, utilizing some stone and brick. In the English village of Wharram Percy, in Yorkshire, however, many of the houses were still just modest rectangles from 39 to 88 feet long and 13 to 19 feet wide, with a door at the center of the longer side, and a fireplace with the smoke coming out of a hole in the roof. On average, a family had around 377 square feet in which to live, so their crowded centerpiece was the fire, where they cooked and warmed themselves. This may be compared to the Burgundy village of Dracy, brought to light by some thirteen digging campaigns by French and Polish archaeologists: there, in the peasants' houses, the fireplaces were very small, less than 24 inches, often near to the entrance and set against the wall, whereas only in the houses of the much better off would a square fireplace, in the center of the room, reach 6 × 6 feet.

In the early Middle Ages, throughout most of Europe, the houses in towns, by then clearly impoverished, resembled those of so many country villages, if we exclude the buildings of the local authorities, the eminent, and other dignatories. For example, in Italy, in Brescia (Lombardy), people lived in basement complexes, similar to those in much of Europe; and in Luni (Liguria), in the area where there were monuments surviving from the time it had been a Roman city, people lived in buildings that comprised of just one room, with earthen floors.[6] In these extremely simple dwellings, from the twelfth and thirteenth centuries, first of all north of the Alps, and then in the towns that bordered the countryside, the building of chimneys appeared and slowly spread, with flues for channeling the smoke built into the walls above the fireplaces. There is already some trace of these in tenth-century documents where the term *caminata* is used to describe a room with a fireplace and a chimney, in prestigious buildings and built along quite complex lines.

With the spread of fireplaces and chimneys, cooking in the home resembles that of the current day a little more. Images of intimacy and warmth emerge from the decorated calendars of the thirteenth and fourteenth centuries, where in January, the bourgeoisie or peasants warm themselves by the fire, maybe with a glass of wine in their hands, while over the fire hangs a pan with something cooking inside. Sometimes there is a peasant couple warming themselves by the fire; the husband may have his clothes pulled up to warm his private parts, flaunting his genitals.[7] Again in the fourteenth century, Geoffrey Chaucer describes the house of a poor widow who eats and sleeps in the same room covered in soot.[8]

With time, the house is transformed into a place to live in, containing two or three rooms, until we find, quite late on, a separate kitchen. Within this general evolution, the houses in the country and of the poorer classes tend toward the horizontal, whereas those of the town and the better off tend more often to be vertical, with living space organized on more than one floor, marking the separation between the fireplace on the ground floor and the upper area where meals were eaten.

SIMILARITIES AND DIFFERENCES

Before passing on to describing how families usually cooked and ate, we first have to briefly visit the two basic diets that the Middle Ages inherited from the ancient world[9]: the first was adopted by the people of southern and Mediterranean Europe, rich in products of vegetable origin, bread, wine, oil and vegetables, completed by cheeses and a little meat; the second diet, of the Celts and Roman-Germans, whose economy was based on hunting and wild livestock, centered on food of animal origin. In the early Middle Ages, the differences between both types of diet diminished: the consumption of meat shifted towards the south, encouraged by the renewed availability of uncultivated lands and woods, while the three basic features of the Roman diet—bread, wine, and oil—spread towards the north via the image promotion brought about by the Christian sacraments,[10] up until the emergence of a mixed diet, when cereals and legumes began to find themselves on the same plates as meat and fish.

Other differences emerged, however. From the eleventh century and with increasing intensity, the growth of population and of areas under cultivation, the diminished area available for hunting, and the concentration in the hands of the upper classes of landed property meant that the consumption of meat became a privilege of a small, rich part of the population, while the more numerous lower classes fed primarily on cereals, legumes, vegetables, and cheeses. Thus, it happened that, once again, a meat culture differentiated itself from a cereal culture, this time to mark the differences between social classes and between the inhabitants of the towns (more beef and mutton, white wheaten bread) and those of the countryside (less meat, mainly pork and chicken, black bread because of the inferior cereal mixed in, cheeses, chestnuts). Pork, in particular, not eaten by Jewish families or in Muslim areas, became a real distinguishing mark of Christian Europe.[11]

Beside these social inequalities, a series of other differences (in space or time, or between various social and productive contexts; the place of trade in making available basic cooking materials; forbidden food in Muslim areas and within Jewish communities) determined taste and very different methods of preserving food, of combining the various components in the kitchen, and of sitting down at the table. Here we can only mention a few isolated examples.

If French and Italian cookery books at the end of the Middle Ages offered a great variety of dishes—boiled and roast meats (*allesso* and *arrosto*), pies (*torte*), fried food (*frittelle*), jellies, soups, broths of meat and fish, pasta of many kinds[12]—bread, milk (boiled, as prescribed by Aldobrandino da Siena, who was a doctor in France in the thirteenth century), eggs, and cheeses were the normal food among the peasants in the north of France, according to the *Fabliau du meunier et les deux clercs*. The great role of dairy products in the French diet is exalted even in a short poem, in a version put together from the thirteenth century, where Lent fights against Carnival, guiding an army at whose head is butter, followed by sour cream, hot pastries and pies, custard, fresh cheeses, processed cheeses, and hard cheeses.[13] According to the chronicler Ranulf Higden (1280–1363), the Welsh ate great, round oat and barley pies, and panfuls of porridge, while the thirteenth-century Italian Riccobaldo da Ferrara lingers over a description of the frugal dinner of a married couple in the town who eat from one plate, yet who, despite this hapless scene, eat fresh meat three times a week (roast beef, goose seasoned with garlic, and rabbit stuffed with carrots) with vegetables and beans.

Baking bread is not the only way to make use of cereals, and in fact the kitchens produced polentas (recommended for women who had recently given birth) and porridges of barley and millet, gruels of oats and foxtail millet, soups of cereal broken up and mixed with fresh or dried legumes, and savory pies in which pasta was stuffed with cheeses, meats, and greens.[14] Soups were also very important on the tables of the Jews, although what went into them varied a good deal depending on the area. In Toledo they were made from chickpeas, broad beans, meat, coriander, cumin, and onions; in Murcia from chickpeas, with just a little meat and oil; and in Catalonia they were made with spinach, chickpeas, mutton, salted meat, and eggs.[15]

What one does not eat every day, finally, is also what one would like to eat eagerly: poor Calandrino, the protagonist of *novella* VIII-3 of Giovanni Boccaccio's *Decameron*, dreamed of the sausages which went with the vineyards, the geese, the ducks, the mountain of grated Parmesan cheese, the *maccheroni* and *ravioli* cooked in capon broth, and the *vernaccia* wine that flows in the rivers.

WOMEN AND THE BASIC HANDLING
OF EVERYDAY FOOD

Up until fairly recent times, to cook meant to assemble and utilize the seasonal produce, in more or less tasty ways, and according to regional, cultural, and climatic conditions, together with the provisions that you had the technical ability and financial means to preserve. To have a meal every day the women had to turn to their larders and bread bins, their cellars or granaries, and then fetch the water by dropping their buckets into wells, or going down to the nearest stream, and carrying their various mixes and uncooked food toward the ovens.

If, before the law, to possess a fire meant being a *male* head of a family, in front of that fireplace, in the cellars, in the vegetable gardens, in the kitchens, and around the table, there were legions of *women* bustling around. Of course, this is hardly surprising. A very ancient tradition attributed a complementary character to the relation between men and women, reserving to the men the task of working outside the house to maintain the family, while the women worked at home, busying themselves with preserving food and preparing meals: and they were first of all mothers and then wet-nurses.

It was in the houses, where women of several generations worked, that the young women learnt the manual and technical skills that the family needed, some of them essential to human life, such as cooking in general, but also rearing the children, preparing the medicines for the sick members of the family, or the food suitable for women who had just given birth. In the peasant family, women's work at home included grinding or pounding the grain by hand, looking after the vegetable plot and the chicken run, making the ale, doing the cooking, serving up the meals, bringing the water, washing up, and going to the market.

Of course, they looked after the fire. In many *fabliaux,* the fine stories written in verse between 1180 and 1330 in the provinces of northern France, and revolving around the family of the small land-holding peasant, the fire in the home is presented as a reassuring and welcoming presence. A woman lights it in the morning, looks after it, and keeps it going, or, if a gentle lady is involved, she makes sure her servants carry out these tasks. Men rarely do any of this, and when they do, it is clumsily done and with bad grace.

In the last centuries of the Middle Ages, bread regained its pride of place on the table, leading to the bringing together of other foods under the name of *companatico* (literally: accompaniment of bread). The lower the social position, the higher, percentage-wise, was its consumption compared to that of other foods. Throughout medieval Europe, to make bread was always primarily a domestic event—in the country, bread was the final phase of the transformation of cereal occurring around the house or even inside it. This was the case even when the upper classes promoted the spread of mills and bakeries (to get paid by those who had to use them), and even if in the towns, the baker's trade was among the first to have its own organization. In many cases, and for several centuries in the Middle Ages, the grain was transformed into flour in the mortar or ground in small amounts with a small quern or grinder, following a very ancient technique to be found around the Mediterranean in biblical times. Pounding the wheat (and also other cereals and chestnuts) in household mortars continued, indeed, to be a part of everyday activities, even when the hand-driven mills, or those using animals or water power, started spreading (from the seventh century, but with a sharp increase in the tenth to twelfth centuries) and windmills began to be used for the purpose (from the twelfth century).[16] Still in the fifteenth century a *Tacuinum sanitatis,* which describes the characteristics of plants and gives advice on diet, illustrates spelt—a cereal similar to wheat—with a woman pounding the spelt seeds in a mortar that a man had brought her in a little basket.[17]

Whether escaping or not from the expense of the lord's mill or the swindling of the miller, the flour was ready to be transformed into bread. Having a well near the house meant one was fortunate: without water, very few foods can be produced, and carrying water home from streams was an exhausting business. Some town houses, at the end of the Middle Ages, had their own well, with its bucket and rope to draw up the water, but even without this privilege, the wells or public water tanks, maintained at the expense of neighbors or the community, were a common enough feature by the thirteenth century; for example, they were common in Bologna, Piacenza, Florence, Venice, Siena, and other Italian towns.[18]

Before the end of the Middle Ages, domestic ovens made from clay were still quite widespread: simple *calottas* or canopies in the shape of truncated cones that were not very big; or *testi* (baking dishes), that were used to cover the dough placed directly on the floor of the fireplace/hearth, with embers around them, with some holes for ventilation to eliminate the damp inside the chamber where the cooking occurred. Isidore of Seville (c. 560–636) described various kinds of bread: fermented, not fermented, or slightly fermented (*fermentatus, azymus, acrozymus*), placed like a *focaccia* under the ashes (*subcineratus* or *focatius*), or under a *testo* (*sub testo coctus*), made to adhere to the walls of a bell (*clibanitius*), or, finally, placed in the oven (*de furno*).[19]

To bake bread in the oven, in a manner similar to today, only very few things and very little action was required: sifting, to reduce the amount of bran or other impurities left from the crude grinding or pounding of the cereal; mixing it with water and a little fermented pasta kept from the previous batch; waiting an hour or two; and then heating the oven carefully so as to guarantee a uniform baking. The verses of the *Oustillement au vilain* (a thirteenth-century poem that began a successful tradition, and which lists the utensils in a well-kept home) describe a peasant's house where the necessary equipment was kept to prepare the bread and bake it, with various sieves for the flour with some string to hang them up, and how it did not really matter if now and again the bread burnt a little while baking. In the inventories of objects, too, we normally find the tools or containers necessary for the baking of bread in the home: cloth bags to preserve or carry the flour, sieves, and then bread bins or boards to mix and preserve the dough, and spatulas or scrapers to scrape the dry flour from the bin,[20] with one part widened, and one end thicker to grip it. All these tools, in particular the bin and the board to mix the dough, were in the kitchens, whether of the rich or the poor, and only in certain cases of the really well off was there space devoted specifically to flour and bread. In Valencia, for example, only the families important enough to have an oven to bake their own bread in also had a room where the flour was sifted and made into dough. In many cases, especially in urban areas, the bread's dough was prepared in the home, by the lady of the house or servants, according to social status, but the baking occurred in an oven elsewhere, public or private, and had to be paid for.[21]

THE PRESERVATION AND USE OF RESERVE SUPPLIES

Preservation techniques were very important—to salt, to smoke, to put into sacks, or bags, or skins, to ferment or leaven, to dry or desiccate[22]—allowing for the storage of the food in people's houses or the immediate vicinity for the months to come, defending them from animals, parasites, damp, mold or mildew, heat, and lessening the risks involved in sudden food shortages.

In the *Oustillement au vilain,* the ideal peasant house is the one consisting of more than one building, following the model we have already seen: the peasant would put his grains in one room, his hay in another, and in a third would live together with his family. However, even if we exclude the granaries and the pits for the preservation of grains in significant quantities from our picture, there is not just one type of place where products were stored. The inventories of goods in town houses give the impression that only some of the food was to be found in the kitchens, small amounts, whereas most of the reserves were to be found in cellars or granaries.

In the town, however, space was almost always lacking, so builders learned to make use of the ground underneath the houses to preserve food. So it might well have been necessary for people to go down into subterranean cellars, occasionally impressive complexes, even built at several levels, with stone steps and subterranean connections between individual rooms, used for plentiful reserves of cereal and other products. Such was the case, for example, in Lille, Provins, Besançon, Laon, Arras,

and Strasbourg (France), in Valencia (Spain), and in Siena (Italy).[23] In
the houses of Jews, the subterranean cellar led to the courtyard and was
ventilated via small windows in the lower part of the frontage.[24] In the
countryside, once again, things were simpler: from a small storeroom next
to the kitchen one would take dry legumes, wine, flour, and fats preserved
in terracotta vases or other containers.[25] Clearly, cooking on the ground
floor meant simplifying the carrying of the heavier things needed for the
process: the food from the cellars, the water from the well, and the wood
to keep the fire going.

Every culture, every kind of cuisine, and every latitude had its own kind
of cellar and storeroom, with variable amounts of dried legumes (broad
beans, chickpeas, beans), flour or cereal, dried fleshy fruits (grapes, figs,
and so on), eggs and olives under salt, salted meat and fish, dried meat,
wine or beer prepared in the home, salt, cheeses, vinegar, and spices, which
in the last centuries of the Middle Ages were added to dishes in massive
doses despite their often high price.[26] The latter, used alongside local sea-
sonings, were available according to the social and geographical context.
Pepper, cinnamon, cloves, nutmeg, ginger, cumin, and saffron are all well
to the fore in cookery books, in medical works, and in documents to do
with trade, showing the wealth and economic links of the centers where
they circulated: for example, in the thirteenth century an anonymous
Genovese poet pointed out the extensive use of pepper, ginger, and nutmeg
in the kitchens of his city, a city well connected to the Levant, a producer
of spices.[27]

At some point in time prior to the thirteenth century and probably
introduced by the Arabs, dried pasta appeared in many Sicilian kitchens,
which could be preserved. The Arab geographer, al-Idrisi (of the twelfth
century), described Palermo as a center exporting this product to Calabria
and to other Mediterranean regions. We meet dried pasta again in the thirteenth century in Genoa, Pisa, and Cagliari, going under various names
such as *maccheroni, lasagna,* and *vermicelli,* and then, gradually, and
above all during the fifteenth century, in other Italian and Mediterranean
cities such as Barcelona, Mallorca, and Valencia.[28] The first women appear
in calendars at this point, spreading out pasta to dry on apposite wooden
supports.

LOOKING AFTER THE VEGETABLE GARDEN
AND THE CHICKEN RUN

One of the women's tasks was to look after the dovecote and the chicken runs, which, even more importantly than their meat, supplied eggs, a very cheap food[29] given that the hens were fed from leftovers and by pecking worms from the ground.

In the family's vegetable plots, normally next to the peasant's house and also in town houses,[30] women grew a wide range of greens. It was a great material help to the family. The *Capitulare de villis* (the eighth century text by Charlemagne, giving instructions on the management of royal estates) already recommended that on the king's property all greens should be grown, and it listed a score or so of them (water melon, honey melon, marrow, lettuce, fennel, endive, beet, various kinds of cabbage and onions, leeks and shallots, radishes, and garlic),[31] as well as a series of medicinal herbs. The vegetable garden, for the family's use, was a space shared and co-managed within the area of small properties or as part of the life of the community, as, for example, it was in German areas; according to the *Oustillement au vilain* the community vegetable garden supplied broad beans, cabbages, turnips, chives, garlic, and also fruit (pears), which until the thirteenth century was rather rarely eaten by the lower classes.[32] Vegetables were also economically important where dependent country laborers worked, as, in general, vegetables were not subject to a levy by the lord or the landowner.[33] Vegetables also played a leading role in the life of monasteries and convents as food compatible with a sober diet, and labor in the vegetable gardens was believed to harmonize well with the practice of humility.

Soups were prepared with vegetables, and pies were stuffed with cabbage, beet, garlic, onions, leeks, marrows, and were sometimes mixed with meat: cookery books abound with detailed descriptions of savory pies. To give a highly colored example, a record of this was left in the description of the stall of "eggs with cheese, to make the herb pies, or ravioli or other things" in the verses of the Florentine poet Antonio Pucci (*Le proprietà di mercato vecchio*). The wife of a vegetable gardener of Barcelona, worried by the thought that after her death no one would look after her vegetable plot, enjoined her husband and heir to re-marry or, at least, to employ a servant.[34]

THE KITCHEN AND ITS OBJECTS

The objects used in kitchens of the time reveal not only how food could be preserved, but also how it was cooked, and by examining them we can imagine the life of the people who used them. Utensils, and what was used to hold food in the kitchen—emerging from archaeological digs, listed in the inventories, reproduced in miniatures, in paintings, and frescoes—can help us move on from food products to the domestic kitchen, where women's hands transformed basic items into dishes, from the plain to the elaborate.

What, then, do the objects making up the stock-in-trade of domestic kitchens tell us? There were iron chains with oval or circular rings supporting holding hooks that ended in a barbed fashion in order to suspend a cauldron or cooking pot in copper or copper alloy; iron rings to support containers without handles; trivets in wrought iron to place convex-bottomed pots on; and unusual shovels to help control the fire: all of this Spartan paraphernalia completed the medieval fireplace, especially in houses in the countryside. Andirons and bellows were used when there was a fireplace, with spits for roasting and, more rarely, grills or gridirons for the better off. Archaeological traces of these objects have emerged from terrain where destroyed or abandoned houses have been found, and they are listed in many inventories of objects to be found in wills. Shifting cooking activities to beneath the cowl of the fireplace certainly had an influence on the preparation of meals, encouraging roasting to develop in close proximity to the boiling and stewing foods.

The peasant women described in the *fabliaux* were good cooks, using kitchenware of pottery, metal, or wood, and little casserole pots where they also cooked garlic sauces or *peverate* (sauces made with pepper) to accompany the food on the table. In the *Oustillement au vilain* we find the pot for boiling the soup, items that were required for grilling food, a hook to extract the cooked meat from the pot without burning oneself, tongs and bellows to stoke up or kindle the fire, a mortar, a small and large pestle, and a small grindstone, evidently for the household grinding of cereal.[35] There was no lack of kitchenware in the house and various instruments are listed rather at random: chalices and bowls, plates, bowls of various sizes, which when they broke were carefully repaired, knives, scissors, and items for fishing with a basket for carrying the fish. There was a strong interest in the products of the vegetable garden, and no wine to drink (it makes one drunk), only water.

In the same period and area, a miniature shows the typical possessions of a rich town house neatly arranged on shelves: next to bags of money, furs, precious cloth and stones, wooden boxes, sheep and horses, we see glass chalices, pans, terracotta containers, a mortar, barrels of wine, and reserves of grain. A little later (in the fourteenth century), another image illustrates the moral disorder of the woman through that of her home, where kitchen objects, such as a box for the salt and two pots, are mixed up with old chairs, spindles, and broken chests.[36]

The pottery that has emerged from excavations in many European medieval villages enables us to reconstruct certain activities in more concrete ways. The round earthenware pots and pans of various sizes, whose fragments are preserved underground so well that they provide the large majority of archaeologists' finds, were used by families of all classes, and tell us of cooking soups and legumes on a slow fire, or of the boiling and stewing of meats.[37] In a fourteenth-century Sicilian village the bones of animals (including game) were cut into three- to four-inch pieces to make them correspond to the size of the pots, leading us to imagine that most of the meat cuts, perhaps not so very tender as the animals were no longer young, were boiled.[38]

The "monopoly of boiled food" seems to have been one of the distinctive characteristics of ancient and medieval cooking,[39] although boiling was not the only way people cooked. In one of the *fabliaux* already mentioned, there is an amusing portrait of a peasant excited by the fact that his wife, with great care, is roasting two partridges that he managed to pick up by chance; but the wife is also attracted to the unusual food, and bite after bite, she ends up eating both the partridges while they are being cooked, throwing her husband into the deepest despair, which then turns into aggressive behavior. The literary sources, thus, show that game was a very unusual part of the peasant's diet. Nonetheless, gridirons and roasting spits, with copper or terracotta dripping pans to collect the juices, not only in the homes of the upper classes and in the towns, reveal a diet also consisting of quality meat and fish. Handmade metal artifacts, many of which had been repeatedly repaired, worn out, or broken from overuse or poor quality[40]—such as iron pans, saucepans, cauldrons, large cooking pots in copper or bronze, and skimmers—were found in the villages of Burgundy, Tuscany, or Catalonia.[41] Illustrated in miniatures[42] and listed in inventories, these objects enabled people to prepare fried foods, stews, and fricassees,[43] while small pans may have been reserved for the *farinate* (gruels) for the latest newborn baby, for the sick, or for mothers who had just given birth. Little stockpots endowed with small feet spread through France from the thirteenth century onward and served to isolate the pot from the embers to avoid the meat sticking to the bottom and acquiring a burnt flavor. Simple ovens could be used for cooking beneath the ashes. A large, round, long-handled pan was even used as a religious metaphor in the miniature decoration of a French manuscript of the eleventh century.[44]

Archaeological digs also provide evidence that the meat of cattle and sheep was eaten more than was believed until a short time ago.[45] Pork was a very popular with peasants. Pigs were easily reared at home following the rhythm of the seasons, because they are omnivorous and very prolific. In domestic environments, pork could be boiled, made into sausage meat, salted, and smoked—work done at the beginning of winter following a calendar preordained by nature—and finally preserved in cellars. In the thirteenth and fourteenth centuries, many inhabitants of the Tuscan cities had peasants rear pigs for them in the nearby countryside,[46] a custom that indicated both the familiarity of city dwellers with the process and the close relation between urban and rural areas. In the illustrations of the *Tacuinum sanitatis* of the *Biblioteca Casanatense* in Rome (fourteenth century), we see a man, seated beneath a truncated, cone-shaped fireplace from which chains and hooks hang, blanching little pigs' trotters in a cauldron or a large cooking pot, with a few objects—a glass and a jug for drinks—visible on the shelves. Another man turns a spit on which spleens are cooking and a woman cleans tripes hung from a hook, while another bends down to keep an eye on the cooking and yet another stirs a soup in a large container. There is a warm atmosphere, and the shared domestic work is done almost in a party mood, somehow anticipating what would be written at the end of the fourteenth century by the Florentine short-story writer Franco Sacchetti: "when the pig dies everyone in the house joins in the party."[47]

Methods according to area, centered on their use for frying or browning, or preparing sauces with pig's lard, or with butter (which, present in a thirteenth-century cookery book, makes its appearance quite late), or else with oil. While pigs also provided fat, several other kinds of fat were used in the kitchen. In the Middle Ages different fats were associated with various cooking methods, partly depending on the geographical area. Pork's lard, butter (which, present in a thirteenth-century cookery book, makes its appearance quite late), or oil could be used for frying, browning, or preparing sauces. However, none of these cooking customs is necessarily exclusive (also because of the Church obliging people to alternate, in the various liturgical periods, fat foods with lean ones of animal and vegetable origin, respectively), showing substantial variations even in areas that were quite near to each other[48]: for example, in the eleventh-century kitchens of Tuscany, home of the olive, you could find knives specifically for cutting lard, pans to melt it, or pans with holes to strain it.[49]

Of course in the well-equipped kitchens of well-off families, as in those of abbeys, convents, or hospitals, kitchen utensils were more specialized than among the peasantry. In one of the finest English medieval kitchens that has been preserved from the fourteenth century, with fireplaces in the corners, meals were prepared for the Abbot of Glastonbury's guests.[50] Kitchens of a high technical quality are in evidence in Venice at the end of the thirteenth century, and in the fourteenth century they can be found in all the houses of a certain importance.[51] One or more mortars of stone of various sizes could be found (indispensable for reducing cereals to flour when there was no grindstone, or to pound herbs and spices for the sauces that accompanied the meats),[52] together with graters for cheese or bread, ladles and big spoons, gridirons to toast bread, irons for *cialde*, strainers to filter sauces and broths, pottery vases to keep grain, dried legumes, or fats, and vases with spouts to carry liquids, and knives of various types and sizes.[53] There would be wooden objects, lids, bowls, large wooden spoons, or ladles.

AT LAST, "TO THE TABLE"

Given that eating is in itself a social phenomenon as well as a biological necessity, the literature conveys images of cooking and the dining table as a time for people to get together, when human beings satisfy their desire to communicate with others as well as their need for nourishment. Sharing the dining table becomes then a symbol of fraternity, of integration in a group, and of the harmonious relationship of a couple. Sharing your bread is a symbol of friendship and loyalty, and if sometimes it was necessary to eat alone or in silence, as in many religious refectories, this was considered a form of privation and asceticism. So in the end, one went *to the table*, although the table was not always there, even in the houses of the well-off: the poet Jean Bodel (1167–1210) writes of a merchant of Douai who, after an absence of three months, was welcomed by his wife before a fire which burns without smoking, and, sitting on a cushion, is brought meat, fish, and fine quality wine to soothe his weariness, as an advance and promise of more secret pleasures to come.[54]

There is a good deal of documentary evidence from the twelfth century onwards about the great northern French families of the rural aristocracy, in which a public area on the first floor—where the lord in great pomp and ceremony is shown in the act of serving his friends, lit up and warmed by a gala or banqueting fire—was separated from a private quarter, where the kitchen, with a fire for cooking, and the dining room for the family meals were located, united together in privacy.[55] Only in the refined houses of the rich or in towns did separate rooms exist, provided with a rectangular table, placed near to the fireplace and supported by trestles (if big enough), or having four table legs (if smaller). Covered by a tablecloth, this table was laid with bowls in pottery, wooden boards on which food was placed, shared between two diners, various knives, some spoons, sometimes goblets of glass (in the Mediterranean world), or cups made of metal or wood (more to the north). Diners ate with their hands, a practice deplored by the thirteenth-century Bonvesin da la Riva of Milan, and in the fourteenth century, also by the Florentine Antonio Pucci.

The poorest houses and those in the countryside did not have a room specially set aside for eating, and meals took place in the kitchen where tables were also fairly unusual, and were placed beside the fire or near to the door of the house, depending on the season, sometimes simply consisting of a bench or a chest.[56] In the *fabliaux*, too, owning a table to eat on is a mark of being well off. It would seem that most people ate two meals a day, the daytime one consisting of bread, cheese, and wine or beer (both nutritious drinks), depending on the area. The evening dinner, the main meal for adults, included the same food with the addition of a hot dish (soup, broth, or stew). Weaned children would receive their baby's bottle of milk, like the one shown in a thirteenth-century French miniature.[57]

We can imagine that also on more solemn occasions the meals of the lower classes, who did not have much choice in the matter, took place in the same, everyday places, unless the summer season allowed them to get together outside, on the occasion of weddings or funerals, when family and friends met together at the house of the dead person. We know that there were people who went to the trouble of indicating to their heirs what kind of food should be served at their funeral, above all wine, bread, and meat: in 1143 a small Catalan landowner reserved a considerable quantity of cereal and salted meat, sheep, pigs, and an ass for his funeral meal; in 1193 a poorer peasant limited himself to two pigs, two rams, corn, barley, and a barrel of wine.[58]

Cooking for guests meant bringing out the very best the larder could provide, although this might just mean milk, cheese, and compote—ordinary food, but served in plentiful amounts, as can be read about in more than one *fabliau*. The Tuscan writer, Francesco da Barberino *(Documenti d'amore)*, recommends that male guests avoid looking at the faces and hands of the women as they eat. However, when the guest is especially loved, things may take on a different complexion: in the text entitled *Le prestre comporté*, with the complicity of the servant, the lady of the house prepares an especially refined meal for her lover, including a salted pie brushed with egg yolk and browned with eggs.[59] A couple of centuries later, the protagonist of a short story by the Lucca writer Giovanni Sercambi is also expecting particularly tasty pleasures from her lover, and hence serves up capon and pasticcio of meat, whereas her husband just gets millet, broad beans, garlic, and leeks.[60] Personal social relations expressed themselves through customs and rituals: in the warmth of the fireside, affections, sexuality, and food are inseparable.

CHAPTER EIGHT

Body and Soul

ALLEN J. GRIECO

The relationship between body and soul is central to philosophical thought in the Western tradition, even prior to Aristotle's treatise on the soul. Any attempt to approach this topic in such a way as to communicate the endless diversity of ideas that have been expressed on this topic in a short chapter, even restricting it to the period covered by this volume, is doomed to failure. What can be done, with a better chance of success, is to try and give a succinct idea of how food in the Middle Ages was perceived to be a physical necessity that represented a moral and spiritual danger of considerable importance to the soul. For a variety of reasons, food was considered to be a potential source of perdition. Its presumed influence on the body was such that certain dietary habits were thought to determine, quite literally, sinful behavior, for which the soul would ultimately be condemned. Given the association between food and sin, it is hardly surprising that medieval tales often cast the devil in the role of cook. Depictions of hell, up until the fifteenth century, more often than not portray it as a kind of horrific kitchen in which devils of various kinds roast on a spit, boil, or butcher human beings as if they were animals to be dismembered.[1] The association between cooks and the devil lingered on for a long time in Western culture, to the extent that, as late as 1628, John Earle could write about cooks in his *Micro-cosmographie,* creating a highly suggestive conflation where the subject and the object were confused in a very telling manner: "The kitchen is his hell, and he the devil in it, where his meat and he fry together."[2]

Because of this attitude to food, much attention was paid to understanding it, classifying it, and disciplining what people ate, when they ate, and, above all, how they ate. Although the main culprits for sinful behavior were thought to reside in the consumption of foodstuffs that were considered to be rich and luxurious, this was not the only danger. The selling by Esau (the son of Isaac) of his birthright for a plate of lentils was often mentioned by medieval theologians to remind everybody that even as simple a dish as lentils could have far-reaching effects.

The importance that food was invested with in the realm of the medieval moral economy is hard to overstate and is particularly conspicuous in terms of the link that was perceived to exist between an excessive or incorrect behavior in eating, gluttony, and another physical sin, lust. Linked in theological, philosophical, literary, and iconographic representations of the torments undergone in hell, gluttony and lust, two of the original eight capital sins,[3] were closely associated from the second half of the fourth century, when they were dealt with in the works of an influential Christian monk and ascetic: Evagrius Ponticus (c. 345–c. 399). As has been pointed out repeatedly, the conceptualization and the ordering of the so-called vices have to be attributed to this late Antiquity, Christian authority, who absorbed, and went on to transmit Palestinian and Egyptian late, fourth-century monastic spiritualism. It is thanks to, "his numerous works on evil thoughts and on the methodology the monk is to employ to confront and dispel them that one can first speak of the existence of the genre in Christian literature."[4] This first ordering of the vices persisted into the Middle Ages and the Renaissance with hardly any modifications, even though parallel and slightly different traditions of classifying the vices grew up alongside this first ordering of them. Although there is a complex history surrounding the formulation of the various vices and the capital sins, here it will suffice to point out that the link between gluttony and lust is common to all of them, even though the weight they are accorded might be slightly different.

According to Evagrius Ponticus, there were eight main categories of sinfulness: gluttony, lust, avarice, sadness, wrath, sloth, vainglory, and pride.

The order usually followed in listing them was not a casual one, and was often referred to with an acronym GLATIAVS, which used the first letter of each one of the different vices in Latin as a kind of shorthand: Gula, Luxuria, Avaritia, Tristitia, Ira, Acedia, Vana gloria, and Superbia. The order was a highly significant one and was meant to reflect the spiritual progress required of monks. The first two, gluttony and lust, confronted all monks at the beginning of their career when they were meant to control the coarse desires of their bodies, while the others were more closely linked to the realm of "spiritualized temptations," culminating in vainglory and pride.[5] As Evagrius pointed out, the connection between gluttony and lust was particularly intimate, since it was considered quite impossible for someone to fall into the sin of lust without having first been defeated by gluttony. In fact, a progressive and linear connection existed not only between these two vices, but more generally between all of the others too, since there was "a concatenation of evil thoughts by which each one of them was linked causally to those before and after."[6] These concepts, which were initially intended exclusively for the monastic context, ended up permeating civil society as of the later Middle Ages.[7]

The link between gluttony and lust seemed to be implied even in the biblical account of the Fall of Man, which was much commented upon by medieval theologians (even though St Augustine excluded such a reading). The verses of the Ancient Testament describing this event (Gen. 3.6 and 7) were interpreted as drawing, quite simply, a link between cause and effect, between the transgressive act of consuming forbidden food and the subsequent mutual recognition of their sexuality: "And when the woman saw that the tree was good for food, and that it was pleasant to the eyes, and a tree to be desired to make one wise, she took of the fruit thereof, and did eat, and gave also unto her husband with her; and he did eat. And the eyes of them both were opened, and they knew that they were naked; and they sewed fig leaves together, and made themselves aprons."[8]

With respect to the theological debate unleashed around this issue, Casagrande and Vecchio have pointed out that: "From Cassian to Alanus de Insulis and from Peraldus to Gerson the idea that gluttony was the first sin of man, and that due to gluttony all of the ills and all of the faults entered the world, became the inescapable point of departure to construct a proper relationship with food."[9] In that the first man and woman were thought to have been responsible for succumbing to gluttony and, as a consequence, also fell into the graver sin of lust, it was this theoretically spurious interpretation that inspired the many artists who portrayed the Original Sin. The apple (the fruit that was usually chosen to carry the responsibility for man's fall) was often a thinly disguised visual metaphor for Eve's breast. In fact, artists employed a number of ways to transmit the significance of tasting this forbidden fruit and the sensual appetites it unleashed.

However, it is worth mentioning exactly how the link between these two original sinful acts was explained, other than circumstantially. Pope Gregory the Great (c. 540–604), who was responsible for changing the order of the capital sins as well as for reducing them to the canonical number of seven, drew attention to the dangerous proximity existing between the stomach and the genitals of a person, asserting that "when the first fills up excessively, inevitably, the others also are excited to sin."[10] Theologically, as well as physiologically, food was therefore the object of special concern, since it was potentially nothing less than the door to all vices. Certain foods, especially rich dishes, were seen to be particularly dangerous for the moral well-being of those who consumed such dangerous foodstuffs. Church authorities had written on the link between gluttony and lust for a long time, developing a complex moral discourse whose primary, but not sole object, was to closely regulate any incorrect or excessive food consumption. More generally, food was believed to have the "side-effects"[11] that, according to Aristotle, "every natural agent suffers in acting." According to this idea, the human body is the agent of digestion, converting food into itself. In other words, the body was thought to turn food, which was potential flesh, into actual flesh, but in the process it became tainted and gradually corrupted by the very food it assimilated. Interestingly for us, not all foods were held to have the same effect on the human body. As has been pointed out by Reynolds, quoting the Franciscan theologian Peter of John Olivi (1248–1298), the various components of one's diet "retain much of the virtue of their prior forms…[so that] nutriment from wheat has one virtue, from barley another, from fruit another, from meat another, from fish another, and likewise from other things; hence also the physicians in their diets consider carefully the prior nature of foods."[12]

From such a point of view, it seemed quite logical that different foods would have different effects on the human body, even though this was ultimately a subject that was dealt with more by doctors than by theologians and scholastics. Doctors who composed dietary treatises and who classified food, above all, in terms of its impact on human bodies, were writing treatises as early as the sixth century, as was the case of Anthimus, a Byzantine doctor employed at the Ostrogoth court of Theuderic the Great.[13] This early example, linking Antiquity to the early Middle Ages, was followed by, at first, a slowly developing concern with dietary considerations, and then an increasingly rapid development as of the late thirteenth century. The interest doctors, dieticians, and their readers demonstrated for what became nothing less than a highly successful medical/literary genre bloomed after the plague of 1348, and greatly benefitted from the invention of the printing press, and is clear proof that eating right was a major concern throughout the period under examination.[14]

Food remained potentially dangerous because "school-men entertain[ed] the disquieting thought that what looks attractive and appeals to one's appetite through the senses of smell and taste might contaminate one's body through harmful residues or influences" and that "no food has been entirely safe since God expelled Adam and Eve from the garden of Eden...but some foods are more unhealthy than others."[15]

Food could be dangerous and unhealthy in at least two different ways: it could represent both a moral and a physical danger, even though the two sometimes overlapped. The moral danger represented by gluttony came to be defined above all as the consumption of excessively luxurious foods and, in particular, as it turned out, the consumption of fowl, while the physical danger was linked to a way of eating that disregarded the many and sundry rules that the dietary dictates of the time continuously repeated. The dietary concepts broadcast by this literature have to be seen as nothing short of a fully integrated system, where everything had its place, and where parameters such as age, sex, location, seasons, social class, and so on were all part of the rules that dictated a proper way of eating. Every different type of foodstuff had well-defined characteristics that were derived, above all, from the way they fit into the classification system that was used at the time.

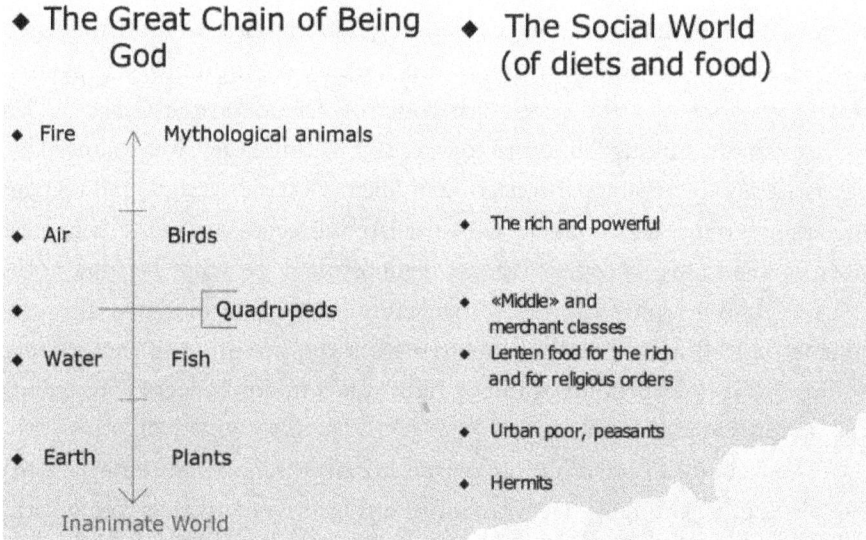

FIGURE 8.1: The Great Chain of Being and the Social World. (Figure summarizes information provided in Grieco 1991 and 1999).

In order to understand how both moral and physical dangers were derived from this system, it will be necessary to briefly examine how food was classified in the Middle Ages.[16] This system, derived in part from classical Antiquity but re-read and modified in the course of the Middle Ages, not only classified all foodstuffs but also introduced, as a corollary, the rules that regulated what was to be considered appropriate consumption and what was not. According to the prevailing worldview, a series of analogies existed linking the natural world created by God and the world of human beings. It seemed self-evident that God had created the universe and had inspired the laws that governed human affairs in such a way that both were structured by a vertical and hierarchical principle. Human society was ordered in a hierarchical manner, but nature too had a similar hierarchical ordering, usually referred to as the Great Chain of Being. This system, inherited in part from classical Antiquity but modified in the period between the high and the low Middle Ages, connected the world of the inanimate objects to God. Between these two extremes were all of the animals and plants of creation, whether edible or not. The chain could also be subdivided into four distinct segments that represented the four elements (fire, air, water, and earth), to which all plants and animals were linked. While fire contained mythological animals, the element air was populated by birds, water by fish, and earth by plants of all kinds. Each kind of plant and animal had a precise position on this ladder whereby it was thought to be nobler than what was below it and less noble than what was above it.

The hierarchical structure of both society and nature suggested that these two worlds mirrored or even paralleled each other in such a way that society had a *natural* order while nature had a *social* order. The outcome of this parallelism was that it was commonly thought by doctors, moralists, authors of agricultural treatises, and others, that the upper strata of society were destined to eat the foods belonging to the upper reaches of the realm of nature. By the same token, the lower classes were thought to be destined to eat from the lower reaches of the realm of nature, which explained why they were best off consuming vegetables and plants more generally, as opposed to birds. The eminently classist system, bolstered by medical and moral discourses of some complexity, assigned different parts of the Chain of Being to different parts of the social body. According to these, not practicing the diet that was considered best for the social group to which you belonged was not only a moral transgression, but also a source of sickness, as most of the writers of dietary treatises underlined in their well-circulated work. Thus, physical and spiritual problems were closely connected via the food that people ate.

CHAPTER NINE

Food Representations

BRUNO ANDREOLLI

Charles Hindley

READABLE, BUT SLIGHTLY OUT-OF-FOCUS
PICTURES AND IMAGES

One would expect that the images of food we get from the Middle Ages come to us mainly via iconographical sources. Yet, this is not the case, as evidence of this kind is almost overwhelmed by the omnipresent representation of the sacred, to the extent that this may even cloud our perspective. It is no surprise that, for the most part, these pictures offer stereotypes, overloaded with symbolic values.[1]

The Cycles of the Months, so numerous and morphologically various in the Romanesque era, are a good example. In miniatures, statues, mosaics, frescoes, and glass, all offering a wealth of detail from which to glimpse everyday life in the Middle Ages, much is made of work outdoors, in the fields, with pruning, haymaking, harvesting, threshing, and then the grape harvest, wine making, the beating down of acorns with a pole, the fattening, killing, and butchering of a pig, and wood cutting. All of these outdoor jobs led to the preparation of food that, nevertheless, is never, ever shown. If anything, it is the animals who are seen to be eating, as in the month of May in the mosaics of St. Savino at Piacenza,[2] where the horse is intent on cropping the fresh grass; or in November, where the pigs are rooting about under the oaks laden with acorns for their last and decisive fattening period.[3]

In the well-known Cycle of the Months framing the portal of the *Pescheria* in Modena cathedral, September is shown in the act of treading the grapes and bringing a bunch of them to its mouth, or more probably a glass of must, which has the air of a technical wine-tasting operation, concerned with the quality of the product, and not a gesture of contented appreciation.[4]

In the pictures of banquets, too, mostly on religious subjects, such as the Last Supper and the Wedding at Cana, the dishes, cutlery, bread, meat, and fish are waiting on the table, but Christ and the Apostles seem to be thinking of anything except eating. In some of the pictures from the later Middle Ages, those truly interested in the food are the dogs and cats around the table legs, which the human actors seem to think of as an altar, on which the ritual of Holy Communion is being performed.

Medieval iconography embodies a detached attitude to food, almost as if it was ashamed of it. A good example is the twelfth-century Last Supper of the Evangeliary at Nonantola near Modena, showing an apostle on his feet, receiving the bread from Christ under the vigilant eyes of the other eleven apostles, with the illustrator interested in the Eucharist as an institution. A similar petrified, suspended rituality can be seen in the later Last Supper at Avignon, at the *Musée du Petit Palais,* where, very unusually, a few apostles are actually shown with a glass in their hands (one with a glass at his mouth), or in the act of reaching for a knife.[5] Similarly, in the mid-fourteenth century so-called moralized Bible in Naples, episodes such as the distribution of the bread and the fish, and Mary Magdalene wiping the feet of Christ with her long, blond hair, the food and the banquet are represented as simply background to events whose significance lies elsewhere. Among the Weddings at Cana there is one of a rare, expressive efficacy narrated by an illuminated missal at Salzburg in 1104, where the expectation of the miracle leaves to one side any concern over the absence of wine.[6] For breast-feeding Madonnas we have to wait until the last two centuries of the Middle Ages, while the very tender Madonna of the *canapé* we owe to Lippo del Dalmasio, a fourteenth-century Bologna painter.

Taking into account the fact that today it is no longer possible to make use of iconographical sources in such an ideological way as in the past—as Emilio Sereni managed to do,[7] though art historians would urge him to be more cautious over an excessively uninhibited use of his sources[8]—it is nonetheless worth underlining that some of the ideas created by that intense dialogue between history and iconography are not to be thrown away, well aware as we are of the very close relation between autonomy and heteronomy in art.[9]

A wooded reaction (the strong emergence of wood that covers the landscape that before was cultivated), landscape disintegration, and regrouping, as well as fortifications and defensive works, are by now certainly exaggerated ideas that have to be streamlined and either used with more care or less often. However, the boar in a field of sorghum, drawn from a fourteenth-century miniature of the *Tacuinum Sanitatis* at the *Biblioteca Casanatense* in Rome,[10] is an excellent viewpoint from which to interpret the early medieval regime of open fields, the close interrelation between *cultum* and *incultum*, between wild and domesticated, with its strategic importance for the economy of the time, in a mixed-cereal agriculture that knew how to integrate winter and spring sowing, moreover procuring harvests especially suitable to blends of flour and blends of bread.[11]

If anything, the limits of iconographical sources lie in the fact that they sometimes tend to establish standardized or repetitive models; as a result, the model may be of some use, but the *passe-partout* it claims to be works only to a limited degree. So inevitably the scholar finds himself needing many more images, even the contradictory ones provided by written sources, especially narrative and literary in nature, for which we will be trying here to offer a persuasive, if not comprehensive summary.

The image of food in these texts permits us to make other and more complex interpretations, on the basis of the principle that food is mankind, but is also the thing: mankind, as in role, hierarchy, profession, social condition; thing, meaning circumstance, liturgy, ceremonial, and message. There is the frugal meal of the ascetic or the hermit, the crowded and ostentatious banquet of the lord's court: both are strongly characterized by rituals and menus in which the gastronomic gesture is presented as distinctive, identity revealing clothing. The poor people relieved in the monasteries mostly eat a dish of stew consisting basically of meat, bread, and legumes, but we know that this meal is an explicit reference to the Last Supper. Indeed, the number of those receiving charity was often fixed at twelve, the number of the apostles present, and not unusually the washing of the feet was also on the menu.[12]

The monks ate fish, legumes, eggs, cheese, sometimes white meat (chicken), but in this case too, the ritual nature of the meal often prevents us from seeing the difference between North and South (in Ireland, for example, beer was drunk instead of the much wished for wine); nor are cases of monks living frugally and beyond the requirements of the rule lacking, or greedy monks, going against their rule. It would seem, for example, that the monks of St Gall, in present-day Switzerland, were gluttons for bear meat, their forests being full of bears, so that Hildegarde of Bingen (1089–1179) reminds them that the meat of this animal fosters sexual desires, and it would be better to avoid it.[13]

Adelchis, son of the last Lombard king, Desiderius (in the second half of the eighth century), having sneaked into the enemy camp, is recognized because of his ability to crush the bones of the meat at a banquet, and Charlemagne is unable to deprive himself of the robust roast meats of game, as his biographer Einhard[14] scrupulously informs us. Conversely, the frugal Guy of Spoleto, aspiring to the throne of the Franks, sees himself denied the imperial crown by the bishop of Metz, who requires better nourished shoulders and heads more vigorously wetted.[15] In recalling this second episode, Liutprand of Cremona perhaps had to be thinking of the emperor of the East, whose dietary behavior he had also stigmatized, when alleging that "the king of the Greeks is long-haired, with his tunic, broad sleeved, and his mantle or cloak; he is a liar, fraudulent, ruthless, astute, proud, falsely humble, mean, greedy garlic, onion and leek eater, drinker of mineral water; the king of the Franks, on the contrary, wears his hair nicely cut, wears clothes different from those of a woman, wears a pileus cap, is truthful, loyal, very merciful when necessary, severe likewise, always and truly humble, never mean, doesn't eat garlic, onions and leeks to thus be able to save his animals, and not having eaten them, to sell them to amass money."[16]

Liutprand, as usual, exaggerates and is prejudiced, but on food we can lend him some credibility, because while his reflections refer to the black and white image of two opposing dietary models, whose moral and ideological reasoning or justification may be rejected, underlying information is relevant.

Similar interpretative precautions can be extended to wine descriptions, which in a mirror-like fashion present the ancient Greek and Roman tradition and the medieval one, of which the disgusted ambassador makes himself the spokesman: "to our misfortune, it happened again that the wine of the Greeks turned out to be undrinkable, given the mixing in of pitch, resin and chalk."[17]

THE PRIMACY OF WINE AND MEAT

Benedict, on the insistence of his monks, having once put behind him the radical asceticism typical of eastern monasticism, permitted the daily consumption in his Rule of around half a liter of wine, though in particular circumstances a father superior could increase the prescribed amount, as long as this did not result in drunkenness.[18] In some monasteries the permitted increase must have been quite considerable, since it has been calculated that Austrian monks in the fourteenth century drank from two to four liters of wine a day.[19] Yet apart from these very evident exaggerations, maybe to be linked to the fear of water as a carrier of plagues and endemic diseases, it does seem to be the case that between the Middle Ages and the Modern Age there was an actual, sometimes considerable increase in the consumption of meat and wine at monastery tables.[20]

For his part, Alcuin, among the most prominent of intellectuals of the Palatine School established by Charlemagne, while condemning excesses, loved an abundance of good food and preferred wine to beer. In a couplet about a bell, it is hoped that it always diffuses a noble harmony, but the tolling of the cooks also resounds benevolently or pleasantly, while in a verse letter he complains that Friesland produces neither oil nor wine.[21]

The great Rhenish abbess, Hildegarde of Bingen, a prophetess and mystic admired for her visions, had no doubts: "Wine cures and gladdens mankind with its goodly warmth and its great merit...Whereas beer fattens up people's flesh and gives a high colour to the face, thanks to the strength and goodly juice of the cereal. Water on the contrary weakens people and generates the livid mucous around the lungs of the sick, because water is weaker and does not possess strong virtues."[22] She also points out, however, as something of an expert, or with maybe a promotional intention, that "strong and fine wines unhealthily agitates [sic] people's veins and blood, attracting all humours to itself as well as every humidity/moistness/damp...This does not happen with Rhenish wines, which lacks [sic] the properties to agitate excessively people's humours. The strengths of fine wines diminish if they are accompanied with bread or if they are mixed with water...It is never necessary to lessen the strength of Rhenish wine, however, because it lacks very strong properties."[23]

In the first half of the ninth century, when Sicily was conquered by the Arabs, the Muslims imposed a ban on drinking alcohol. The vineyards were replaced by gardens, and flourishing vegetable plots and orchards, with new cultivation of crops such as sugar cane and pistachio nuts. But wine was attractive, and before long the vine made a big comeback, accompanied by Bacchic poetry with the excesses we may imagine, just as the poet Muhammad Ibn Al-Qattâ assures us:

> The liquor helps you and brings you joy,
> So stop mounting
> the strong young camels,
> No longer shed tears
> On where you bivouac
> Already by now destroyed,
> Even the ruins vanished,
> And come in the early morning
> To wine
> On which years upon years
> have already passed.[24]

It should be clearly recalled that, as Lilia Zaouali has emphasized, "it is above all the abuse of alcoholic drinks that the Koran condemns, and not a moderate consumption of it."[25]

In medieval societies, wine and meat represent almost an hendiadys, as the Salerno School assures us, which on mentioning the pig says that its meat, taken together with wine, actually transforms itself into a medicine: "Pork meat without wine is worse than mutton, but if you add wine, then it's good food and medicine."[26]

It is by now generally accepted that the men of the Middle Ages were mostly carnivorous. Even for peasants' diets, scholars have now discarded the old cliché that they only ate cereal and vegetables. In the upper classes, indeed, the abundance and ubiquity of animal resources, domestic and wild, in no few cases provoked the onset of diseases linked to meat monophagism, such as gout.

On this central reality, Hugh of St Victor (1096–1141) expatiates in his *Didascalicon,* when he sets out the seven mechanical arts one by one, giving hunting (*venatio*) a very prominent place, understood as the culinary art par excellence: "To the art of hunting belongs the proper preparation of all food, of sauces and drinks: the general term 'hunting' now indicates all the activities of this art, because in ancient times people usually nourished themselves mainly by what they hunted, as still happens in some areas, where the use of bread is still very unusual, and the principal food is still meat."[27] He concludes: "So hunting includes all the bakers', butchers', cooks' and tavern keepers' activities."[28]

All meat was appreciated, but for most of the Middle Ages red meat from game and, among domesticated animals, pigs, bred in a wild or semi-wild state in the extensive oak forests throughout Europe, enjoyed great prestige. From this derives the high status the master swineherd enjoyed among the Lombards, while the trenchant image law number 351 of the Edict of Rothari (the earliest Lombard legislative text, from the year 643) compares the strongest boar of the herd to a kind of warrior, calling him *sonorpair* "the one who fights all the other boars and wins."[29]

Einhard, the biographer and collaborator of Charlemagne, wrote, "he was sober in his consumption of food and drink, especially drink, because drunkenness disgusted him...He was unable to be frugal or parsimonious with his food, often complaining about the negative effects of fasting on his body...His dinner usually consisted of four dishes, not including the roast meat hunters were in the habit of skewering on a spit and which he preferred to any other kind of food."[30]

Again on Charlemagne, in chapter 24 of his book *On the Palace and the Court*, Hincmar of Reims wrote that four hunters and a falconer, by mutual agreement, made available the number of men required to provide the game for the emperor's table.[31] Notker Balbulus, the St Gall monk, dwells on Charlemagne's eating habits to emphasize his moderation, but the flattering nature of his work is only too clear.[32]

If royalty and the aristocracy enjoyed flaunting a wealth of game at their banquets, the peasantry especially appreciated pork, also because some parts of this valuable animal (an animal for food par excellence) could be preserved throughout the year in the form of sausages or salted meat, which also reached the tables of the landowners as payment for rent or as gifts.[33] And these preserved items would arrive in great quantities at Christmas, Easter, or on the patron saint's day.

In the Romanesque images of the Cycles of the Months, the pig is certainly the animal most commonly seen, and between November and

January his glorious end is consummated via the fattening up, the killing, and the butchering. In the mosaic cycle of Otranto cathedral, there is a remarkable, rare month of February represented by a figure placing a cauldron over the fire at the same time as he turns the handle of the spit on which a young pig is skewered.[34]

Monks were forbidden or advised not to eat pork (and meat in general), but the Church did not consider it impure nourishment, as the Scriptures would nevertheless suggest. Indeed, they promote its hagiographical value, evident from the fact that the pig, the faithful companion of St Anthony the Abbot, from being the personification of the devil quite early on in the west, is transformed into a protected animal, also because of the potentially healing qualities of its fat, used against shingles.[35]

Fish were always well regarded, especially fresh-water fish, promoted by monastic culture as an image of Christ, since the first letters of "Jesus Christ, Son of God, Savior" translate into *fish* in Greek; in addition, not to be underestimated were the miraculously multiplying fish by the Sea of Galilee, as well as the fact that the first apostles were fishermen on the lake before they became fishermen of men's souls.[36]

Near Ravenna, among the precious mosaics of the sixth-century *S. Apollinare Nuovo,* Jesus' calling of Peter and Andrew sees them busily hauling a net full of fish onto their boat, while dominant in the image of the Last Supper is a great dish on which two big fish are lying. In the refectory of the Pomposa abbey, again near Ravenna, where there is a very frugal Last Supper, there is also a fresco featuring the well-known episode of the abbot Guido transforming water into wine, but on the table there are two fish dishes, which given the rich fish ponds and marshes of the district will come as no surprise.[37]

THE PUMPKIN OF WALAFRID STRABO

In her commentary on the Benedictine Rule, Hildegarde of Bingen stresses that monks would do well to eat with moderation, and the food she refers to are soups and broths (those foods that while they are being cooked have to be continuously stirred with a ladle so that they don't burn), as well as greens and legumes, fruit, fish, cheese, and eggs. With the exception of birds, meat was forbidden.[38]

So, in Benedictine monasteries it is taken for granted that the vegetable garden had priority over everything else, which the monks looked after, even using the garden as a research laboratory for their experiments. It comes as no surprise that in the so-called plan of the monastery of St Gall, there is an actual theoretical project for the building of an abbey worthy of the name, with the vegetable garden neatly set out in eighteen plots, in two lines of nine, on each of which is written the name of the greens growing there, both for food and for medicinal purposes.[39]

The importance of this intellectual territory is confirmed by the fact that even monks admired and well known for their studies in the fields of morality, theology, and exegesis, devoted careful attention to the growing of vegetables. This is true of Walafrid Strabo (808–849), one of the most important students of Abbot Rabanus Maurus in the Carolingian court, and author of a famous and much-appreciated annotation of the Bible, but also the author of some short poems, including one in hexameters about his own little vegetable plot just behind his cell. All the descriptions take the form of miniature pictures, where he reveals himself to be a passionate and expert vegetable gardener, with precision and warmth in his descriptions of each plant, its cycle of growth, its uses, and in certain cases, its symbolic significance. For the experts of middle Latin literature, there is a wonderful piece on the pumpkin, whose delightful fruits the poet evokes, his mouth watering after a long and analytical description: "when they are still tender, before the juice hidden in its depths begins to diminish in the late autumn, while all around the outer skin has remained dry, they are often brought to the table of plenty among other good things, absorbing the rich fat in the hot pan, and often, cut into juicy slices, offering their sweet flavour to the second course."[40] He ends by pointing out how pumpkins are used as containers for grain or wine; but it is also well known that they were used as floats or lifesavers.[41]

Fasting and abstinence sharpened ingenuity, especially in sophisticated monks such as the Cluniacs, who knew a great variety of ways of cooking eggs, and who in due season allowed themselves five bunches of grapes each; even mussels would reach their table from time to time.[42] Of course, wine and meat generate a generous licentiousness, but even in the delicate leaves of vegetables the vegetarian devil could conceal himself; Gregory the Great refers to this in his *Dialogues,* recalling the novice who greedily tucked into the lettuce of the monastic vegetable garden, forgetting to bless it with the sign of the cross. As a result she was attacked by the devil, driven out soon afterwards by the Abbot Equitius.[43]

TOWARD GOOD MANNERS

The poems of chivalry are representative of what we may call an intermediate phase, in which meat still occupies an important place, yet within a context presenting other behavioral models with other choices of food. The problem does not seem to be chronological but, rather, depends on the cultural context. In fact, there is no lack of later poems where the life of the knight is still mainly shown as rooted in wild and unmannerly behavior.

This is the case with the poem about *Sir Gawain and the Green Knight*, which has come down to us in just one manuscript, probably from around the end of the fourteenth century, containing a wealth of events taking place in forests or marshes, filled with dragons, wolves, bears, red and fallow deer, and wild boar, ogres, and giants. There are detailed scenes dealing with the ability of the main characters and their servants in butchering and dismembering or quartering their prey and cutting the meat up into pieces. And yet even in this text, though imitating the archaic, we have a sophisticated banquet of exquisite soups and a great variety of fish courses, with fish cooked in bread, roasted, boiled, in stew with spices, and all garnished with ingenious sauces.[44]

Ruodlieb, a knight that a poetic fragment talks about (from the second half of the eleventh century), exhibits codes of behavior in which the fish is prominent (fresh-water fish, of course), as well as bread (preferably white). In the *Tristan* of Béroul, from around the end of the twelfth century, the forest provides a large number of red deer, fawns, and roe deer to the knight and Queen Isotta as they flee, but the two unfortunates suffer because "in the wood there was no bread; the fugitives eat only meat, and nothing else."[45] In a thirteenth-century novel about the search for the Holy Grail, Lancelot, about to embark on his adventures, accepts the orders of a hermit not to eat meat, not to drink wine, and if his whereabouts allowed him, to go to church every day and listen to the divine office.[46] So what we follow in the poems of chivalry, from Siegfried to Parsifal, leads us from the boisterous and joyful banquets out in the open, with bear, red deer, and boar killed and butchered on the spot, to more sophisticated and composed meals.

In the *Novel of the Fox,* a minor and ruthless fox called Renart (metaphorically representing noblemen), whose greed for power manifests itself in violence, robbery, and gluttony, when offered a peasant's buttock by the wolf Primasso, replies: "Never on your life! Peasant meat, white or black, raw or cooked, is always bad in any season. I prefer duckling: the meat is fatter, more tender, more tasty."[47] And at another point, the gluttonous villain exclaims: "Come on, quick, to the hunt! Don Gomberto, the rich churl, is rearing the plumpest of geese, which he wants to celebrate Christmas with. But if I have anything to do with it, he will never see it cooked. It will be in my own belly by the end of the day, and I will be licking my chops over it. It is absolutely shameful that a mere peasant should nourish himself with the meat of a goose! He should feed himself on thistles only, and only to knights like ourselves should such juicy morsels be permitted, for we eat them without harming anyone else."[48]

In the *Perceval* of Chrétien de Troyes there is a detailed description of a banquet, with a first course of a well-peppered thigh of venison cooked in its own fat, the meat cut up and served on a great piece of flat bread. Other meat dishes follow, always accompanied by clear wine and must. At the end of the meal, dates, figs, and nutmegs are offered and pomegranate, cloves, and electuary; then Alexandrian ginger paste and spiced jelly, with various drinks, aromatic wine without honey or pepper, good blackberry wine and clear syrup.[49]

In the same poem, Sir Gawain is served according to the desires of a brave fellow; plovers, pheasants, partridges and other game; wines strong and clear, white and red, new and old.[50]

The knight Bohor, in his search for the Holy Grail, finds himself confronted with a sumptuous encyclopedia of a banquet, in which, with the aim of giving adequate merit to the virtues of privation, nothing may be lacking: "all the most refined meats, geese, roast capon, chicken, swan, peacock, partridge, pheasant, heron, and bittern; every kind of game, venison of red and fallow deer, wild boar, roe deer, hare; fish in abundance, sturgeon, salmon, plaice, conger eel, mullet, cod, turbot, grey mullet, bass, sole, bream, fat mackerel, chubby hake, and fresh herring; all the sauces spiced in the best way, with pepper, cameline, verjuice, and in many other guises; pike and lamprey in galantine; eels and turtle-doves in pies; a thousand varieties of pastry, cream tarts, wafers/waffles, cornets filled with cream, cheese cakes, pies, cakes made with honey, almonds, candied peel and spices, little pancakes, puffs, éclairs; the most precious wines, pepper wine, ginger wine, wine from flowers, rosé, *morello*, hyssop wine, claret, wine from Gascony, Montpellier, la Rochelle, Beaune, Saint Pourçain, Auxerre, Orleans, of the Gâtinais, of the Léonais." Faced with such evidence of God's grace, the chaste knight "contented himself with cutting three slices of bread, which he ate after dipping them in a silver goblet filled with water."[51]

His recipe was well known and widely shared: "Do not eat meat and do not drink wine: it is with bread and water that the celestial knights must refresh their bodies, and not with those other strong foods that lead mankind to licentious behaviour and mortal sin."[52]

In this process tending towards the dematerialization of food, conferring a rather smug detachment to the act of eating, we have the appearance of the fork. But its reception must have been slow and difficult, as often happens with such a new departure, so vulnerable to being stigmatized as so evidently vain and exotic. The austere monk, Pier Damiani, was disapproving of the Byzantine princess who had come and married the Doge Domenico Silvio (1071–1084), because from Byzantium to Venice she had brought with her the use of the fork (with two and three prongs).[53] Yet it is precisely from a monastery that we have the first iconographic evidence of the fork in use, since in an illuminated manuscript of Montecassino, apparently from the first half of the eleventh century, there are two people seated at a table both with a big, two-pronged fork, not just for keeping the food steady, but also to bring it to their mouths.[54]

However, it took the fork a long time to break through the meat-eating etiquette that regarded it as superfluous, preferring the use of one's hands. And this, despite the inevitable burning of the fingers the story-telling tradition had so much fun with, so that even in one of Franco Sacchetti's short stories, on the end of the fork the *maccheroni* continued to "smoke a lot."[55] However, it was precisely the coming of pasta and its gradual spread that promoted the use of the fork, even in the more traditional places in Italy such as convents and castles.

In the castle of Appiano in the province of Bolzano, we find a woman intent on cooking a saucepan full of *gnocchi* (which given the area might well have been *canederli*), and that tastes one of them, bringing it to her mouth on the end of a utensil that might be a big fork.[56] At Sulmona, in the convent of the order of the Clares, in a cycle of frescoes from the end of the thirteenth century, Christ is shown as guest of his friend Lazarus at Capernaum; Mary Magdalene, prostrate, is drying Christ's feet with her long, blond hair, while on the table, beside the guest's plate, a twin-pronged fork awaits.[57] Both seductive, the fork and Mary Magdalene form a pair at Jesus' service, discreetly suggesting the everyday and most intimate aspects of a society that was slowly changing.[58]

CHAPTER TEN

World Developments

FABIO PARASECOLI

The chapters in this volume have illustrated different aspects of food culture during the Middle Ages in Europe and in the Mediterranean world. This last section is an overview of the techniques, products, food-related behaviors, social structures, and concepts in cultural environments that have traditionally been marginal in relation to the studies on Western history. Without any pretense at being exhaustive, the chapter will focus on various cases and examples—on different scales and registers, from the continental to the local—to achieve a better understanding of the cultural and culinary trends in some major areas of cultural innovation during the period.[1]

THE ISLAMIC AND JUDAIC WORLDS

While the consequences of the movements of Germanic populations were still being felt in western Europe, the Eastern Mediterranean saw a growing conflict between Byzantium, which considered itself as the heir of the Roman Empire, and the blossoming Muslim power. In terms of food and gastronomy, this contrast exemplified the tension between different traditions, one looking—at least ideologically—toward the west and the Roman world, and the other ready to absorb and transform elements not only from the western Mediterranean, but also from various Asian and African cultures. The Muslim Empire, whose beginning was marked by the *hijra,* Muhammad's flight from Mecca to Medina in 622, grew in less than two centuries from its original territory in the Arabic Peninsula, to become an extensive area stretching from Spain and Sicily to North Africa, and the Middle East, all the way to Central Asia. However, the political unity of the Islamic community was short lived. In 661 the Umayyad dynasty took control of the empire, moving its capital to Damascus, a city at the center of an important agricultural region, whose production allowed for the development of a courtly life that was inspired by the luxury and the splendor of the traditional Eastern kings, from Byzantium to Iran.[2] In 749 a new dynasty, the Abbasid, moved the center of the empire to Baghdad, opening itself to Central Asian, Turkic, and Iranian cultural influences, also in terms of food, cooking techniques, and dining style for the elites. The political unity of Islam was lost forever at the beginning of the ninth century, when parts of its territory became autonomous under local dynasties, while areas of modern Turkey fell under Turkic tribes from Central Asia, who had converted to Islam, embracing its most orthodox version.

Despite the ethnic fragmentation, the Islamic world maintained a strong cultural identity, which helped in making it an integrated economic space where commerce flourished, reaching out to India, South East Asia, and Eastern Africa, and exploiting preexisting routes over the Indian Ocean.[3] Spices coming from India (pepper), Sri Lanka (cinnamon), and as far as the Moluccas Islands (clove and nutmeg), were sold all over the Islamic world, reaching the Mediterranean and the Christian kingdoms of western Europe, where they were considered as luxury items.

Thanks to its territorial expansion and its religious influence, the Islamic cultural and political impact reached Sub-Saharan Africa, the Russian steppes, and South East Asia. From the technological point of view, the Muslim civilization extended practices based on intensive cultivation, irrigation, canalization, and drainage that often increased agricultural outputs, while facilitating the adoption of plants of various origins. Despite recent debates about the actual role Islam played in reviving western European agriculture through the introduction of new crops and technologies, some of which were already known in the area, there is no doubt that a territory that stretched from Central Asia to the Atlantic facilitated the movement and adoption of diverse agricultural techniques, ingredients, dishes, and cooking styles.[4] For instance, eggplants, spinach, citrus, pomegranate, rice, saffron, and indigo were introduced into western Europe.[5] The cultivation of sugar cane, which the Muslims had absorbed from India, spread west to Syria, Lebanon, Cyprus, Sicily, and even Spain. In today's southern Iraq, sugar-cane production was organized for the first time in its history in efficient plantations manned by slaves, mostly from East Africa. These slaves, known as *Zendj,* embraced a non-orthodox sect of Islam and revolted against their masters in 869. It took fifteen years for the rebellion to be quashed.[6] Also, the oases found in many desert areas in Muslim territory became important for agricultural production, with cultivation organized so that the tall palm trees (especially date-producing ones) offered shade and protection to shorter plants, such as fruit trees, around which, in turn, ground-level vegetables could grow.

Sedentary agriculture was just the extreme of a continuum of food production that had, at the other end, nomadic pastoralism; in the Islamic world, all possible solutions in between could be found. From the political point of view, it was important for caliphs and other functionaries to protect and expand agriculture, which guaranteed products to feed cities and provided taxable revenues; however, tribal feuds, natural disasters, and political turmoil could easily push sedentary peasants to switch to herding, if the natural environment was suitable for it. Grain constituted the main staple, especially wheat when available; governments went to great lengths to guarantee its distribution to the main cities, in order to avoid riots among the populace because of scarcity, or increases in food prices. Olive oil, borrowed from the Mediterranean tradition, was also considered very important for cooking; however, it could be replaced by other vegetable oils (such as sesame), clarified butter, or sheep fat.

Within areas under Muslim control, numerous cities expanded or were founded anew. New cooking styles developed in these refined urban environments, which highly impressed the often uncouth Christian knights during the Crusades in the eleventh and twelfth centuries. Meals were served on large trays placed on small trestles and were usually consumed with the hands; spoons and knives were available only among the upper classes, among which, culinary texts seem to indicate a great care for food presentation, especially decorations and colors, with gold, white, and green being particularly relevant.[7] Probably out of a concern for purity and cleanliness, recognizable in other features of Islamic culture, great care was given to scents and perfumes, both in the dishes and among those who shared meals, who were always expected to be perfectly clean and fresh (an aspect which baffled Westerners). As for the recipes, Islamic cuisines were the result of the encounter of various culinary cultures, among which were the Byzantine, committed to Mediterranean products, and the Persian, with its use of fried meats, the presence of fruit and nuts (including almonds) in meat dishes, and the relevance of rice consumption.[8] Due to the availability of sugar, candy making and pastry reached very high levels: sorbets, non-fermented and sweetened fruit juices were often added to ice, marking the origin of sorbet. Sugar was mixed to ground almonds to make marzipan. Techniques to candy fruit and to model sugar for decoration slowly spread through the Mediterranean, and through Italy they would eventually reach all of Europe.

Whatever the differences due to status or local traditions, some food-related principles were—and still are—common to the whole Muslim world, dictated by the Holy Book, the Qur'an: one of the five pillars of Islam was in fact the fast, *sawm*, to be kept during the month of Ramadan to commemorate the revelation of the book to Muhammad. All Muslims older than ten years of age were required to abstain from food, drink, and sex from dawn to dusk; pregnant women, sick people, and travelers were excused, but they were expected to fast later for a number of days equal to those during which they had not respected the *sawm*. Festive meals were prepared every evening after sunset, culminating with the celebration of the 'Aid al Fitr, where lavish banquets were organized in every family according to their economic means. On that day, no Muslim was supposed to go hungry, so that the better off would take care of the less fortunate. The custom was a reflection of another pillar or Islam, the *zakat* (alimony), which was considered an expression of the spirit of sharing uniting all Muslims in the *Umma,* the community of the faithful. The Qur'an also warns against the excesses caused by alcoholic drinks, often connected to gambling and disturbance; however, wine will flow in Paradise together with milk and honey. Other prohibitions regarded the consumption of pork and all animals sacrificed to gods other than Allah. Complex rules about butchering, similar to the Jewish *kashrut,* were also imposed, as was the taboo—based on the Bible and shared by both Jews and Christians in the first millennium—about the ingestion of blood and animals found already dead.

The Islamic world played a fundamental role in the transmission of the medical science and the dietary principles codified by Galen and other Antiquity authors. While this corpus of knowledge had disappeared from western Europe, it had been handed down in the Byzantine Empire, later translated by Nestorian refugees into Syrian, and then brought into Persia, where it was made available to the local scholars and became part of Islamic sciences, in whose framework it was developed and enriched by authors such as Averroes. The ancient texts were translated back in Latin only from the twelfth century, in the Salerno School of medicine and in the scholarly circles of Toledo.[9]

Jewish communities, considered as *dhimmi* (protected subjects), thrived in many major urban centers under Muslim control. Their foodways, which are at the root of what became later known as Sephardi cuisine, were very influenced by the Muslim environment in terms of techniques, ingredients, and the sensual appreciation of flavors. While Judaism enjoyed a period of peace and prosperity in the Muslim territories, in Central Europe Jews were increasingly subject to persecution, in particular during the Crusades. They started moving East toward today's Poland, Ukraine, and Russia, bringing with them many food traditions such as their taste for soups and substantial food, dumplings and dark breads, fresh-water fish, pickles, and also spices, dried fruits, and nuts whose use they had learnt through their contacts with their Mediterranean brethren. In Eastern Europe they settled in countryside villages known as *shtetl* where they developed dishes that would become mainstays in Ashkenazi cuisine, such as bagels, bialy, and blinis.[10]

The diffusion of the Islamic Sunni faith reached Central Asia, precipitating the formation of Turkic states, among which was the Seljuq dynasty (from the eleventh to the twelfth centuries), whose territory stretched from Anatolia to Persia. In this culture, food was at the core of political relationships, reflecting the strength of the connection between subjects and their ruler, who was supposed to ensure their sustenance (often referred to as *bread and salt*). The famous Seljuq minister, Nizam al-Mulk, underlined in its book *Siyasat-nama* how the sultan was to use large meals as a representation of his generosity and his power, a concept that was probably a derivation of both Persian court etiquette and Central Asian tradition (in the steppes, providing food for his followers had been a not-so-symbolic duty of the tribal leader).[11] These customs may be at the origin of the Ottoman traditions of the soup kitchen (see volume 3, chapter 10 for further detail).

AFRICA

The introduction of dromedaries in the Sahara, probably from the Arabic Peninsula via Somalia and Egypt between the second and fifth centuries AD, and the integration of the area to the Muslim commercial and cultural networks marked the development of long-distance, trans-Saharan trade routes that connected Mediterranean Africa with the Sahel, the Niger basin, and the West African coasts. While this commerce focused on high-value goods such as iron, gold, and slaves, it also included diverse food items from the various ecozones of the areas, including salt, dates from the oases, groundnuts from the savannah, and even tropical crops such as palm oil, yam, malagueta pepper, and kola nuts.[12] Most exchanges in Africa were over a short distance, and goods traveled through a system of relay stations and market places that often constituted the core for the development of kingdoms and, occasionally, larger empires like Ghana and its successors Takrur on the Senegal river, and Mali along the Niger river. However, also before the contact with Islam, urban cultures, such as Jenné and Gao, developed thanks to the surplus from the cultivation of areas naturally flooded by water and from pastoralist production, with transportable grains traded all the way to Timbuktu at the edge of the desert.[13] Further south, the rotational, bush-fallow agriculture close to the rain forest and the domestication of trypanosomiasis-resistant dwarf cattle allowed the establishment of power centers such as Ife and Benin.[14]

The emergence of state formations is also connected with the intense exploitation of local products in the upper valley of the Nile; the cultivation of barley and sorghum, together with intensive animal husbandry, provided the foundation for the Christian kingdoms of Nubia from the sixth through to the fourteenth centuries.[15] Further South, the locally domesticated *teff* (a kind of grain typical of Ethiopia), cultivated in irrigated terraces with the help of oxen for pulling ploughs (unique in tropical Africa), and the abundance of livestock, together with the access to the Red Sea trade routes, favored the growth of a complex urban culture under the Christian kingdom of Aksum, which flourished between the first and the tenth centuries; after that period, probably due to the lack of constant supplies of food and firewood, the local rulers adopted a semi-nomadic life, establishing camps that have been defined as "moving capitals."[16] On the East African coast, the exchange of different products between the communities on the shore and in the interior—among which were hunter–gatherers, agriculturalists (sorghum), pastoralists (sheep and cattle), and fishing people—stimulated the development of coastal urban centers, which were then integrated in the commercial maritime routes of the Indian Ocean, often dominated by Muslim and Indian merchants.[17]

INDIA

In the Indian subcontinent, before the contact with the Muslim customs, cultures and governments inspired by Hinduism, Buddhism, and Jainism reached high levels of refinement. In the third century, the north had been unified by the Gupta dynasty (320–550), under which agriculture developed widely, producing fruits and vegetables such as mangoes, coconuts, bananas, sugarcane, fruits of Chinese origin such as plums and apricots, but also grapes, melons, and pomegranates originally from Persia. Spices were at the center of a flourishing trade both with the east and the west, and salt was under the direct control of the state. While in many coastal areas of the south and in Bengal fish acquired growing cultural relevance, consumption of meat was still limited, with vegetarianism embraced by Brahmins as a mark of power.[18] Following the crisis caused by the invasion of Central Asian populations, the Gupta Empire fragmented into smaller kingdoms. It is probably in this period that traditional religious offerings (*puja*) involving all kinds of foods, above all fruits and sweets, developed into their classic forms. This period also saw the spread of tantric ceremonies, new forms of devotion that often included orgiastic elements, and the ritual consumption of meat and alcoholic drinks.[19]

The Indian subcontinent entered into close contact with Islam since its inception, mostly through the trade connections in the Indian Ocean, where not only precious goods such as spices played a huge role, but also bulk commodities such as flour. Eventually, the area was conquered by Muslim Turkic dynasties, the Ghaznavids and the Ghurids, who kept the Mongols out of India, centralizing the production and distribution of food, and applying price controls on grains when necessary.

CHINA

After centuries of division, China was unified again in 580 by the Sui dynasty (581–618). One of the first acts of the first emperor, Yan Qian, was the introduction of a land system called *chun tian* (equal field), establishing the state as the owner of all the territory, which was redistributed equally among the population, with larger allotments for government officers, nobles, and Buddhist temples. Taxes were paid in grain, cloth, and labor, which allowed for public granaries to be reinstated.

Meanwhile, the introduction of barley in Tibet from the fifth century determined a boom in population and trade exchanges, which, in turn, allowed the expansion of the new Tibetan state into Central Asia, where it clashed with the Arabs, Turks, and Chinese.[20] To this day, barley is the main Tibetan staple: toasted, fermented to make beer, or ground into flour, or made into dough called *tsampa,* it is the basis for many traditional dishes. Tea was an essential part of the Tibetan nomads' diet; drank in large amounts, it helped cure illnesses resulting from the lack of fruits and vegetables.[21]

In 618 a new dynasty, the Tang dynasty (618–907), took power. With the exception of the huge landholdings belonging to Buddhist monasteries, the new government tried to maintain the *chun tian* system for more than a century, but from the middle of the eighth century the system collapsed, due to its intrinsic complexity, and to a series of famines and revolts, caused in part by cold and dry weather. The result was the rise of giant estates, which continued to flourish also during the following Song dynasty (960–1279). While millet remained the main staple in the north, the use of wheat, till then considered as a luxury, kept on spreading, also due to the introduction of new methods of milling that made flour available for dishes like noodles, dumplings, and *shaoping,* a Chinese version of the Central Asian bread covered with sesame seeds and baked on the sides of the oven.[22] Frying was also a common preparation method for flour dough products.[23] The Tang nobles often had Central Asian ancestors, and they frequently maintained forms of connection with those cultures. The influence of Central Asian Buddhism, for instance, is evident in the increase of dairy products, the decrease in the use of beef, the diffusion of vegetarianism (which was already the actual diet of large sections of the population due to the scarcity of meat), and the growing popularity of tea, which had probably first appeared in China after the Eastern Han dynasty (25–220).[24] It is during the Tang dynasty that the scholar Lu Yu wrote the famous *Chajing,* the Book of Tea. In this period, leaves were pressed into a brick and then baked; the brick was then broken in pieces, ground, and boiled with water.[25]

From the west, several new crops were introduced into China, such as spinach, lettuce, almonds, figs, and the yellow peaches from Samarqand, among other luxury products that highlight the Tang dynasty's love for the exotic.[26] The dynasty also extended its control over the southern provinces, where the cultivation of rice expanded enormously and the Chinese settlers also adopted taro and yams, which, however, were considered as coarse and unrefined, and raw-fish consumption.[27] From the south came fruits such as oranges (the bitter variety would be later introduced in the Mediterranean by the Arabs in the tenth century, the sweet one in the thirteenth century, during the Crusades), tangerines, kumquats, pomelos, litchis, longans, and bananas.[28]

After the fall of the Tang dynasty in 907, China was left in disarray until the Song dynasty took power in 960. Favored also by a change in climate, which marked the end of a cold and dry period, agriculture expanded. The south became the core of the empire after 1127 when the north fell under the control of Altaic and Tungus populations. The Song were forced to move their capital from Kaifeng, in the Yellow River Valley, to Hangzhou. Despite attempts at enforcing monopolies on alcohol, salt, and tea, the Song dynasty followed decentralized policies in agriculture, leading to the expansion of large estates especially in the south, which became the cultural heart of the country. This shift was accompanied by the growing importance of fish (fresh, salted, and fermented), soybean sauce, tofu, vinegar, and even tea, which was no longer considered as a luxury.

Following the expansion of a merchant class and of local elites of officials depending on the state, the later Song dynasty saw the development of a bourgeois cuisine, in which regional differences and styles emerged from the outset. Specialized restaurants offering different regional delicacies opened in the largest cities. Local differentiation grew, together with a strong nationalism that tended to exclude anything that felt non-Chinese and, especially, nomadic. Because of these sentiments and the presence of various populations pressing at the northern and western borders, the Song dynasty expanded their maritime trade with Japan, the China Sea, South East Asia, and even India. Seafaring commerce, much less expensive than caravans crossing the desert, was not controlled by the state, but by independent merchants. China's internal commerce for commodities such as rice, salt, and tea, grew so much that by 1024 the government printed money for large, long-distance trades, although not for everyday transactions.[29]

From the technical point of view, book printing, invented during the Tang dynasty but expanded under the Song, made the diffusion of the new agricultural techniques more effective. Among these, we can mention the adoption of rice varieties from South East Asia that allowed for double-cropping, also made possible by the improvement of hydraulic techniques, better preparation of the soil, and erosion control.[30] The latter had become an urgent problem due to the expansion of agriculture and deforestation, brought about by the need for wood for the iron, printing, and ceramics' industries, and by the timber demand for the construction of buildings and ships. New crops were introduced, among which were sorghum and watermelons in the area occupied by the northern tribes, cotton, which changed forever the way in which the Chinese dressed, as well as sugar-cane, which originated efficient agribusiness and widespread commercialization.[31] Fujian acquired a preeminent position in the sugar business, not only assuring production, but also exporting the commodity and the best techniques to grow it all over South East Asia thanks to a massive diaspora of both farmers and merchants, who also made sure that the emigrants overseas could buy rice and other Chinese products.[32]

Tea, previously confined to the higher classes, under the Song Emperor Huizong (1101–1125) also spread to the new bourgeoisie connected with trade. In Sichuan and other provinces, fallow lands were converted into tea plantations.[33] A new use of tea became prevalent: tea was dried, ground, and then mixed with boiling water to obtain a frothy drink, similar to the tea style used to this day in the Japanese tea ceremony. Tea was also employed as an important instrument of diplomacy, since Central Asian populations grew to enjoy it to the point that they exchanged precious war horses for it.[34] In the south, the diffusion of tea gave origin to teahouses, which at first served free, salted pine nuts, walnuts, or melon seeds, and in time saw their culinary offering grow to include snacks, and light meals, the ancestors of dim sum.[35]

At the beginning of the thirteenth century, the pressure coming from the newly formed Mongol Empire finally prevailed over the Song dynasty: the north fell in 1234, while the south resisted till 1279. The Mongols had inherited the nomadic traditions developed by the Central Asian populations over centuries, which included the consumption of the blood of their horses, if necessary; the use of dried or boiled meat (which was cut up in pieces with knives at the table, a custom considered unacceptable by the Chinese); the relevance of dairy products, including *kumiss* (fermented mare's milk); animal fats such as butter or the rendered fat of sheep tail; the popularity of tea; and lavish banquets to entertain guests and display power.[36]

China became a mere province within an immense empire, which established connections with the outside world: foreigners trading with the Mongols settled in China, and many merchants, such as Marco Polo, visited from all over the world. Commerce, both maritime and inland toward Central Asia, flourished. This dynamism had a positive influence over commercial products such as wine, vinegar, and sugar (all subject to taxation). If agriculture as a whole had a hard time recovering from the invasion, especially in the north, the Mongols created an Office for the Stimulation of Agriculture, which pioneered new crops that proved most appropriate for the different areas, while selecting new varieties of traditional Chinese products such as rice, millet, and even tea.[37] However, in China proper, the great estates dominated by the rural gentry from the Song era were left undisturbed under the Mongols, who were only interested in levying taxes from them. The Mongols kept themselves apart from their subjects, sticking to their steppes' tradition. As a consequence, their customs had little impact over the foodways of the Chinese population, especially in the south. The nomadic influence was more visible in the north, where dairy products and mutton became more culturally acceptable.

KOREA

The Chinese influence over Korea, which was unified under the Koryo state between 918 and 1392, grew through both diplomatic channels and the increasing relevance of Buddhism. Korean monks who studied in China came back, bringing with them the consumption of tea to improve meditation. The drink was also considered a medicine, and over time was employed to mark important events, both social and religious.[38] Koryo was very involved in international trade, thus opening the country to foreign influence until the Mongol occupation, which left behind it some culinary elements that are now considered to be traditional, such as grilled meat dishes, noodle making, the use of black pepper, and *mandu*, or stuffed dumplings.[39]

JAPAN

The period starting with the sixth century, which marks the introduction of the imperial political and social system, has been considered as the so-called formative period of Japanese culinary culture, when Japan adopted and often imitated many foods and foodways from China, and more often from Korea, which often functioned as the cultural intermediary and where Japan had held a small colony until 663. By that time, the Japanese court, first in Nara and later in Heian (present-day Kyoto), had established direct contact with the Tang dynasty in China. Several cultural elements were imported from the west that had an important impact on diet and food-related customs: among the most relevant were Buddhism, which facilitated the diffusion of vegetarianism (the first imperial edict against meat consumption was issued in 675), tea, and techniques for high-temperature production of earthenware, metal, and glass objects. It is only from the tenth century, when diplomatic contacts with the Chinese imperial courts were interrupted but commercial ties had become regular, that ingredients, dishes, and eating habits coming from abroad were integrated, and adapted to the native culinary traditions.[40] As aristocratic families affirmed their political power over the emperor, they appropriated large estates in the provinces that, together with the vast monastic properties, came to be known as *shoen*. Rice, mostly used to pay taxes, became harder to find on the market and was adopted as the staple for the higher classes, while the rest of the population relied on crops such as buckwheat and millet. Rice (and sake, distilled from it, which was considered a sacred liquid able to protect one from evil spirits) assumed important functions in *shinto* ceremonies. Tea leaves had been imported by monks starting from the eighth century, but seeds were only brought to Japan later. The monk Eisai, usually known for having introduced Zen Buddhism from southern China at the end of the twelfth century, and later his disciple Dogen, turned tea drinking into an important aspect of monastery life and into a spiritual experience, thus setting the path for the development of the tea ceremony.[41] From the monasteries, the popularity of tea also spread among the samurai warriors, who from the twelfth century created their own culture, the *bushido*, and established a political system in some way similar to European feudalism, with great military families fighting each other to gain control of the country.

Starting from the thirteenth century, the feudal lords introduced new techniques to increase agricultural yields and, therefore, their revenues. As a consequence, rice became more available for larger strata of the population. Salt with which to season food also circulated in greater quantities, but the extractive techniques were often not very advanced, so that the lowest quality salt was often mixed together with other ingredients in what was called *hishio,* a fermented food based on animal protein (fish or meat), cereals, pulses, other vegetables, and also seaweeds, considered as the ancestor of many Japanese specialties such as *miso,* soy sauce (*shoyu*), and *tsukemono* (fermented, pickled vegetables).

CENTRAL AMERICA

The main cultures in Mexico at the beginning of the Christian era were Teotihuàcan in the west and in the central plateau, the Zapotec, whose most important city was Monte Alban, located in the Valley of Oaxaca, and the Mayan city-states, whose influence in the east spread all the way to Yucatan and Guatemala, and which established a system of canals and drainage to create elevated fields from the surrounding wetlands. However, by the end of the ninth century, the Mayan cities were practically abandoned and the whole society collapsed. The prevalent theory is that the Mayans caused one of the first ecological catastrophes in the history of humanity. Deforestation and the excessive exploitation of agricultural lands led to erosion and floods that, in turn, curtailed food provisions available for the urban population, which had boomed thanks to the success of maize cultivation. A decrease in the level of precipitation that started around 800 gave the final blow to agricultural production, forcing the urban dwellers to abandon the southern cities. On the other hand, cities in the north of Yucatan such as Chichén Itza and Uxmal, apparently adapted to the new conditions, producing cotton, cacao, and salt that were exchanged with crops from other areas (including the staple maize) through a wide trading network.

Around the ninth century, waves of hunters and gatherers moved from the semi-arid plateaus of northern Mexico, giving birth to cultures such as the Mixtec, the Toltec, and the Aztecs, who adopted crops from the previous civilizations, especially maize and beans, but also chili peppers and pumpkins. The Aztecs also developed very efficient commercial routes; their capital city, Tenochtitlàn, was full of lively markets where products from all over the empire were sold, such as honey from Yucatan and cacao from today's Honduras, despite the fact that only humans could transport goods, in the absence of large beasts of burden. The relevance of trade is clearly indicated by the privileges enjoyed by the merchants' corporation, the *pochteca,* who operated as government officials.[42] Special cultural significance was attributed to maize, almost identified with the body of the Aztec people and already used to make tortillas, an everyday staple, and tamales, more of a festive dish.[43] Corn-based dishes and cacao, together with blood offerings, were employed in religious ceremonies. Cacao was ground and mixed with water and spices such as chili peppers and vanilla, which was exacted as a tax from the area around Veracruz (today home of the Papantla vanilla). Food was a cultural marker for class, gender, and ethnicity, with women in charge of food preparation and the upper classes having access to better and more abundant provisions.[44]

SOUTH AMERICA

Between the eighth and the eleventh centuries, a series of city-states developed in the high valleys of the Andes, which are actually composed of two rows of mountains going from northwest to southeast, with plateaus in between. The area between the two ranges was exploited in different ways according to the height where the plots were located. The agricultural system developed in all its complexity after the adoption of Mesoamerican plants including beans, maize, and pumpkins in the first centuries of the Christian era. In the plateaus and the lowest slopes of the Andes up to 11,800 feet above sea level, irrigated cultivations of maize, beans, and quinoa were prevalent. In the areas up to 13,800 feet above sea level, known as *suni,* and covered by prairies and steppes, potatoes were the main crop, while the highest areas, the *puna,* were only suitable for raising animals.[45]

Only in the thirteenth century did the Incas start developing into a powerful and well-organized state. They inherited and perfected an agricultural system that was structured around kinship-based farmer communities called *ayllus:* to minimize risk, each *ayllus* cultivated small plots in very different environmental conditions, planting multiple crops in each of them. Despite the absence of large domestic animals providing manure, a fertilizer rich in nitrates and phosphates was found in the guano produced by thousands of marine birds along the coast of Peru. Guano was gathered and brought inland on llamas, and used also in very high areas.

In the Amazon basin, where slash-and-burn had proved to be the most efficient and environmentally sound form of agriculture, a complex culture developed between 800 and 1400 on the island of Marajò, at the mouth of the river. While some scholars believe that this culture slowly deteriorated because of an inability to limit its own growth, which led to the overexploitation of the environment,[46] others argue that Marajò developed fully, with public works and intensive subsistence.[47]

NORTH AMERICA

In North America, from around 950, a sedentary civilization flourished around the city of Cahokia, located near the confluence of the Illinois, Missouri, and Mississippi rivers. This center was built on a huge earthen mound, a model that had already been employed from the third millennium BCE in many areas of North America, from southern Canada to Louisiana. It seems that the increase in population that led to the new cultural formation was based on the widespread adoption of maize varieties of Mexican origin that were adapted to the local climate and daylight length. The population never acquired an urban character, mostly living on agriculture, with few artisans and merchants; however, the position of the city also allowed some fishing and exchanges with the hunters from the prairies, who at times brought large prey such as elk, bison, and bear. It seems that many hunter tribes had developed advanced systems to control the environment with wildfires in order to avoid the excessive growth of thick forests, not favorable to the large mammals constituting an important source of their food.[48] It seems that from the end of the first millennium, many tribes all over the east coast started using deforested plains to plant orchards for fruits and trees such as hickory, and native chestnut (now almost extinguished), while closer to mound cities they cultivated vast areas of maize. As a consequence, bison and deer almost disappeared,[49] and in some areas flooding became a constant problem. It appears that Cahokia was severely hit by floods, and eventually an earthquake razed it to the ground in the thirteenth century.

NOTES

Introduction

1. Montanari 2004, 9–10.
2. Montanari 1993, 13–14.
3. Montanari 1993, 17–19.
4. Montanari 1993, 12 ff. (drawing from the idea of Duby 1973, chapter 1).
5. Montanari 1993, 98–100.
6. Montanari 1979, 63–65; Montanari 1993, 36–40.
7. This was one of the main topics of the famous Pirenne thesis, which, though criticized, remains a stimulating one. See Montanari 1995, for a re-reading of Pirenne in the context of food history.
8. Montanari 2005.
9. The role of the Arabs in helping to create the European (food) culture of the Middle Ages has been much discussed: Rodinson 1949 described it as decisive; Rosenberger 1997 and Laurioux 2005c prefer to play it down. I personally do not agree with either of these excessively reductionist views.
10. On the history of pasta: Sabban and Serventi 2000. In particular on Italy: Capatti-Montanari 1999, 59–67.
11. On the increasing number of spices used in cuisine, from Roman to medieval times, see Laurioux 2005b. On the role of spices in the medieval economy, see Freedman 2008.
12. Montanari 1984, 8.
13. Montanari 1998b.
14. Montanari 1993, 104 ff.
15. Montanari 1979, 174–77; Montanari 1984, 55–85.
16. Montanari 1993, 51 ff.
17. Montanari 1984, 32 ff., 156 ff.
18. Montanari 1993, 53.

19. Montanari 1993, 57–62.
20. Montanari 1984, 159 ff.
21. Hilton 1973.
22. Montanari 1993, 107–9; Montanari 2008a.
23. Montanari 1993, 67–69.
24. Montanari 1984, 191 ff.; Pinto 1978.
25. Biraben 1975, 147.
26. Montanari 1993, 93.
27. Braudel 1982, 168 ff.
28. Abel 1937. On Abel's thesis, see Mandrou 1961.
29. Montanari 1993, 94–96.
30. Stouff 1969; Stouff 1970.
31. Montanari 1993, 94.
32. Montanari 1993, 96–97.
33. Nada Patrone 1981, 381–82.
34. Montanari 1993, 104; Campanini 2006.
35. Montanari 2000.
36. Montanari 1993, 104 ff.
37. Arikha 2007.
38. Montanari 1993, 109–10.

Chapter 1

1. Comba 1978, 78.
2. On the variety of uses of woodland and uncultivated land see Andreolli and Montanari 1988a; *Ambiente vegetale* 1990.
3. *Chasse* 1980; Montanari 1984, 174–90.
4. Montanari 1979.
5. *Olio e vino* 2007.
6. Montanari 1979.
7. For the various contexts: Finberg 1972; Andreolli and Montanari 1983; Pasquali 2002; Verhulst 2002; Devroey 2003; a critical summary with detailed bibliographical material in Pasquali 2006.
8. For Italy see *Inventari* 1979.
9. Pasquali 2002, 19.
10. As well as the contributions on the *curtis* already cited, see also Toubert 1983.
11. The debate on the origin and development of the *curtis* has been frequently summarized and commented on; perhaps just three references are needed here: Toubert 1983; Andreolli and Montanari 1983; Wickham 1998.
12. Comba 1988, 93.
13. Among the very numerous references, see Russel 1972; Ginatempo and Sandri 1990; Pinto 1996.

14. The general outlines of the phenomenon, still valid, are in Duby 1962. For the various contexts: Cherubini 1984; Rösener 1985; Hallam 1988; García de Cortázar 1988. We refer to the works cited for more detailed analysis of the subjects dealt with on the pages below.

15. Montanari 1993.

16. To the texts already cited should be added, for France, Duby 1975.

17. Important interpretative studies are Postan 1972, and Hilton 1983.

18. Fumagalli 1976.

19. Some suggestions for a synthesis in Cortonesi 1995.

20. To the texts already cited should be added, for Portugal, Oliveira Marques 1978.

21. More detailed analysis in Cortonesi 1999.

Chapter 2

1. Devroey 1986; Menant 2007, 25–26.

 2. McCormick 2001, 639–81.

 3. Montanari 1979, 211–18; Desportes 1987, 29; Neveu 1973, 371.

 4. Cortonesi 2004, 544–45, 566.

 5. De La Roncière 1985a; Pinto 1978, 73–79, 317.

 6. Romano 1953, 2:149–61; Wolff 1959, 147–64; Cuvillier 1974, 161–70.

 7. Palermo 1997, 228.

 8. Hübner 1997, 351–64; Balard 1985, 64–80.

 9. Del Treppo 1972, 340–52; Dufourcq 1966, 535–38, 565–69; Riera Melis 2007, 139–40.

10. Wolff 1985, 20.

11. Van Uytven 1985, 76–80; Tits-Dieuaide 1975, 144–66.

12. Duby 1962, 2:232; Tits-Dieuaide 1975, 143.

13. Postan 1952, 120–23; Tits-Dieuaide 1975, 144–66.

14. *Annales Sancti Rudberti Salisburgensis,* 786.

15. Reglero 2011.

16. Menant 2007, 41.

17. Pinto 1978, 107 ff; Palermo 1997, 262.

18. Palermo 1997, 251.

19. Riera Melis 2007, 147, 156–57.

20. Van Uytven 1985, 80–81.

21. Faugeron 2006, 57.

22. Mutgé 1987, 76.

23. Zylbergeld 1982, 263–304; Zylbergeld 1991, 791–814.

24. Stouff 1970, 33, 48.

25. Van Uytven 1985, 90–91.

26. Riera Melis 2007, 140–42.

27. De La Roncière 1982, 72.

28. Langdon 1991, 424–44.
29. Wolff 1959, 27.
30. Cortonesi 2004, 561–62, 566–68.
31. Desportes 1987; Desportes 1996, 435–36; Stouff 1996, 11–18; Stouff 1994, 39–50.
32. Riera Melis, Perez-Samper, Gras 1997, 296.
33. Three to four times higher than today's consumption, according to Pini 1989.
34. d'Andeli 1881, 23–30.
35. Dion 1959; Renouard 1959; Wolff 1959, 22–23.
36. Postan 1952, 173.
37. Devroey 2003, 224.
38. Postan 1952, 172.
39. Laurioux 2002, 88.
40. Cortonesi 2004, 554; Moulin 1984.
41. Grieco 1993.
42. Al-Idrisi 1970–1984, 541.
43. Constable 1994, 181–83; Bolens 1993.
44. Cortonesi 2004, 552.
45. Constable 1994, 358.
46. Braudel 1967, 79, 142.
47. Stouff 1970, 169–94.
48. Montanari 1993, 97.
49. Montanari 1979, 211–18, 425–56.
50. Faugeron 2006, 57.
51. Redon 1984, 2:121.
52. Anes Alvarez de Castrillón 1994, 49–92.
53. Laurioux 2002, 86.
54. Postan 1952, 171.
55. Stouff 1970, 130–32.
56. Faugeron 2006, 60.
57. Cortonesi 2004, 571–72.
58. Stouff 1970, 132–34.
59. Cortonesi 2004, 564–65.
60. Riera Melis 2005, 194.
61. Derolez 1968.
62. Montanari 1993, 102; Laurioux 2002, 81; Riera Melis 2005, 193.
63. Postan 1952, 171.
64. Mollat 1968, 11–19; Montanari 1988a, 183–91.
65. Wolff 1959, 18; Laurioux 2002, 83–84.
66. McCormick 2001, 698.
67. Hocquet 1987.
68. Wolff 1959, 19.
69. Hocquet 1978.

70. Riera Melis 2000, 1078–79.
71. Wolff 1959, 16–17; Freedman 2008.
72. Wolff 1959, 16–17.
73. Riera Melis 2002, 1028–29.
74. Montanari 1993, 36–49; Montanari 1997b.

Chapter 3

1. Dupâquier 1997, 247.
2. Carpentier 1962.
3. Procopius of Caesarea 1974, 124 (II, 3).
4. Procopius of Caesarea 1974, 167 (II, 20).
5. Procopius of Caesarea 1974, 167 (II, 20).
6. Montanari 1993, 13–15.
7. Montanari 1993, 36–40.
8. Schofield 2007, 242; Pinto and Sonnino 2007, 490; Bulst 1997, 178.
9. Cherubini 1981; Bruneton-Governatori 1984.
10. Gregory of Tours 1981, 227 (VII, 45). See a commentary in Devroey 2003, 87.
11. Glaber 1982, 140 (IV, 12).
12. Pinto 1982, 355.
13. Stouff 1970, 33–34; Pinto 1978, 146; Nada Patrone 1981, 110–11.
14. Curschmann 1900; Corradi 1894.
15. Menant 2007, 31.
16. Benito Monclús 2005, 97–99.
17. Salrach 2009: 119.
18. For these kinds of descriptions see Le Goff 1969, 291.
19. Villani 1995, 416 (III, 76, vol. I).
20. Salvatico 2004; Palermo 1997.
21. As happened, for example, in 1303 in a part of Tuscany. Pinto 1978, 84, note 53.
22. Le Goff 1969, 291.
23. Le Roy Ladurie 1967; Fagan 2000.
24. Le Goff 1997.
25. Procopius of Caesarea 1974, 167 (II, 20).
26. Gregory of Tours 1981, 125 (VI, 45).
27. Le Goff 1969, 288; Gregory of Tours 1981, 119 (VI, 44).
28. A Florentine case (year 1329–1330) in Pinto 1978, 402.
29. Biraben 1975.
30. Le Goff 1969, 283–85, 401.
31. Cracco Ruggini 1995, 157–71, 468–84.
32. Salrach 2009, 72, 76–77.
33. Gregory of Tours 1981, 227 (VII, 45); Bede the Venerable 2008–10, 222–23 (IV, XIII, vol. II).

34. Biraben 1975, 27–48.
35. Quoted in Montanari 1993, 11.
36. Rouche 1997, 147–49.
37. Salrach 2009, 81; Devroey 2003, 76–77.
38. Salrach 2009, 106–10; Benito Monclús 2005: 108–10 (for the period 1000–1199).
39. Pinto 1978.
40. Lucas 1930; Van Werveke 1959; Jordan 1996; Schofield 2007; and a broad synthesis in Salrach 2009, 164–69.
41. Blockmans and Dubois 1997, 192.
42. Pinto 1982, 333–34; Stouff 1970, 71; Titow 1960, 399–400, 403.
43. Villani 1991, 467 (XIII, 73, vol. III).
44. Salrach 2009, 175.
45. Menant 2007, 32–33; for Italy in particular see Peyer 1950.
46. Faugeron 2009.
47. Salrach 2009, 121.
48. Abel 1973; Titow 1960; De La Roncière 1982; Dyer 1989; Zulaica Palacios 1994.
49. Gaulin and Menant 1998, 56–57; Schofield 1998, 92; Benito Monclús 2007, 89.
50. Pinto 2008, 342.
51. Pinto 1978, 127–30.
52. Pinto 1982, 353–54.
53. Pinto 1978, 128; Pinto 1982, 352, 355; Schofield 2007, 235.
54. Cohn 2006.
55. Fiumi 1956, 49.
56. Salimbene de Adam, 1966, 904–5 (II). See also Menant 2007, 33.
57. Pinto 1978.
58. Le Goff 1969, 289.

Chapter 4

1. Garnsey 1988.
2. Smith 2005, 240.
3. Bray 1999, 111.
4. Van Werveke 1967.
5. Le Goff 1992.
6. Desportes 1981.
7. Van Uytven 1985.
8. Britnell 1996, 27.
9. Pirenne 1951; Hibbert 1965.
10. Britnell 1996, 26.
11. Zylbergeld 1973, 778.
12. Van Uytven 1985, 79.

13. Van Uytven 1985.
14. Britnell 1989; Faugeron 2006.
15. Pinto 1978, 78.
16. Abulafia 1981, 382.
17. Britnell 1996.
18. Schubert 2006, 13.
19. Cohn 2006.
20. Curschmann 1900, 10; Schubert 2006, 40.
21. Blanshei 1976.
22. Zylbergeld 1973.
23. Britnell 1996, 26.
24. Schmitz 1968, 122.
25. Tits-Dieuaide 1984.
26. Fichtenau 1991, 7.
27. Le Goff 1992, 142–43.
28. Montanari 1979, 459–60.
29. Gautier 2006b, 42.
30. Devroey 2006, 505.
31. Bloch 1939, 247 (vol. 1).
32. Gautier 2006a, 246.
33. Montanari 2004.
34. Fichtenau 1991, 59.
35. Magennis 1999, 35 ff; Gautier 2006a, 183–84.
36. Gauvard 1992.
37. Guerreau-Jalabert 1992.
38. Lorcin 1984, 230–32.
39. Bloch 1940, 17 (vol. 2).
40. Montanari 1979, 460.
41. Fichtenau 1991, 61–62.
42. Campanini 2006.

Chapter 5

1. Peyer 1987, 1.
2. Simms 1978.
3. McKitterick 2008, 178–86.
4. Brühl 1969; For Ottonian Germany, see also Reuter 1991, 110–11.
5. Lobbedey 2003.
6. Leidrad, *Letters*, n. 30; quoted by Brühl 1969, 25.
7. Sierck 1995, 20–28.
8. Notker of St Gallen 1969, 107–8 (I, 15).
9. *Vita Dunstani* 1874, 17–18 (B, 10).
10. Paul the Deacon 2003, 38 (VI).

11. Kerr 2002; Kerr 2006.
12. Goscelin 1965, 2.
13. Gautier 2006b.
14. Baschet 2006, 489 ff.
15. Ganshof 1927, 82–83.
16. Zeumer 1886a, 7.
17. Dion 1959, 189–90.
18. Tacitus 2006, XXI.
19. Hellmuth 1984, 69–82.
20. Peyer 1987, 39.
21. Gautier 2009, 23–44.
22. Mollat 1992, 56–58.
23. Mollat 1992, 184.
24. Penco 2008, 53 (1).
25. William of Malmesbury 2002, 10 (I).
26. Goetz 1995, 478; Willmes 1976, 38–39, 69–70.
27. Horn and Born 1979, 139 (II).
28. Benveniste 1969, 27–28 (II).
29. Enright 1996.
30. Shanzer 2001, 217–36.
31. Gregory of Tours 1951, 785–86 (79).
32. Dierkens and Plouvier 2008, 18.
33. Montanari 1985, 641–42.
34. Gautier 2010.
35. Fichtenau 1991, 63–64; Nicholls 1985, 52.
36. de Troyes 1994: *Le conte du Graal,* 3322–32. See Baldwin 2000, 177–78.
37. Bullough 1991.
38. Vogüé 1964.
39. Hen 2006, 109.
40. Anthimus 1996.
41. Gautier 2006a, 200–204.
42. Jarman 1988.
43. Effros 2002.
44. Oexle 1979.
45. Althoff 1988.
46. Heaney 1999, 65–66 (2029–62).
47. Peyer 1987, 79.
48. Unger 2004, 37–42.
49. Bennett 1996.
50. Franklin 1984 [1874], 153–64.
51. Bodel 2005, 642–49.
52. Ibid., 650.

Chapter 6

1. Scully 1995, 236 ff.
2. Carlin 1998, 27–51.
3. Scully 1995, 237.
4. Carlin 1998, 39 f.
5. Henisch 1976, 78.
6. Carlin 1998, 50 f.
7. Carlin 1998, 29.
8. Taillevent 1988 (critical edition of the *Viandier* by T. Scully).
9. Weber 1998, 156.
10. Weber 1998, 146.
11. Adamson 2004, 59.
12. Weber 1998, 146.
13. For the remuneration of cooks in England see Woolgar 1999, 32–35.
14. Quoted after Wolgar 1999, 151.
15. For the portrayal of cooks in the literary sources see Henisch 1976, 59–67.
16. Scully 1995, 40.
17. Adamson 1995.
18. Weiss 2002.
19. Weiss 2002, 167, 172.
20. Weiss 2002, 85.
21. Weiss 2002, 140, 137.
22. Weiss 2002, 297–99.
23. The court offices at Avignon are described in Weiss 2002, 76–91. Their tasks, personnel, location, and changes during the different pontificates in ibid., 132–68.
24. Scully 1995, 243–45.
25. Adamson 2004, 58.
26. Weiss 2002, 211.
27. Scully 1995, 86 f.
28. Weiss 2002, 144.
29. Weiss 2002, 197 f.
30. Henisch 1976, 96.
31. For this and the following see Weiss 2002, 85–88, 132.
32. On the water supply in England see Woolgar 1999, 144 f.
33. Woolgar 1999, 403.
34. Weiss 2002, 406.
35. Henisch 1976, 89.
36. Scully 1995, 94.
37. Ketcham Wheaton 1983, 24.
38. Lambert 2002, 73; Weiss 2002, 207.
39. Black 1993, 110.

40. Black 1993, 110.
41. Woolgar 1999, 144.
42. Woolgar 1999, 142.
43. Woolgar 1999, 143 f.
44. Henisch 1976, 87.
45. Weiss 2002, 206–8.
46. Ketcham Wheaton 1983, 23 f.; Henisch 1976, 41 f.
47. A German cookbook from c. 1350 contains a mead recipe that lists as a cooking time walking the length of a field and back: see Adamson 2000, 61 (recipe 14). See also Scully 1995, 92.
48. Scully 1995, 99 f.
49. Adamson 2000, 58 f. (recipe 8).
50. Redon, Sabban, and Serventi 1998, 23 f.
51. Weiss 2002, 412–14.
52. Pray Bober 1999, 258.
53. On the Arab influence on food coloring see Wilson 1991, 17 f. Useful information on medieval food coloring is also found in Scully 1995, 113–16.
54. Adamson 2004, 69–71.
55. Lafortune-Martel 1992, 121–29; Scully 1995, 104–10; Adamson 2003, 83–102; Adamson 2004, 71–77.
56. Santich 1995, 61–81. The new techniques discussed in detail are the clarification of jelly, an edible short crust, filled pasta, and the distillation of meat.
57. Private dinners in the chamber were generally frowned upon as the comments by Bishop Grosseteste, and Piers Plowman illustrate. See Woolgar 1999, 145.
58. Henisch 1976, 97; Scully 1995, 167.
59. Much of the following on serving in the great hall is indebted to descriptions found in Black 1993, 115–19; Hammond 1993, 111–16; Scully 1995, 170–74; and Gies 1979, 114–18. For details on estate management in medieval England see ibid., 95–108.
60. Scully 1995, 169.
61. Weiss 2002, 240.
62. Scully 1995, 169; Gies 1979, 115.
63. A collection of such etiquette books is contained in Furnivall 1868.
64. Woolgar 1999, 149–50.
65. Woolgar 1999, 151–54.
66. Woolgar 1999, 154–55; Hammond 1993, 115.
67. Weiss 2002, 164.

Chapter 7

1. Contamine 1985; Le Roy Ladurie 1975.
2. Nascimbeni 1992, 9.

3. Galetti 1997, 20; Beresford and Hurst 1971, 111; Pounds 1989, 175.
4. Galetti 1997, 22; Pesez 1984; Fossati and Mannoni 1981, 414; Chapelot and Fossier 1980.
5. Valenti 1996, 191–217.
6. Gelichi 1997.
7. A choice of images and all quotations for *fabliaux* can be found in Alexandre-Bidon and Lorcin 2003.
8. Quoted by Pounds 1989, 171.
9. See a synthetic view in Montanari 2003.
10. Montanari 1993, 24.
11. Montanari 1997, 247.
12. Flandrin and Redon 1981, 397.
13. Galoppini 2006, 427–28.
14. Nada Patrone 1981, 117–18.
15. Motis Dolader 1997, 295.
16. Comet 1992, 330, 375–76, 390–91, 447.
17. *Enrichiridion*, quoted by Comet 1992, 377.
18. De La Roncière 1985b.
19. Quoted by Comet 1992, 480–81.
20. For example Nada Patrone 1981, 98–99.
21. Desportes 1996; Garcìa Marsilla 1993, 151; Nada Patrone 1981, 100.
22. Montanari 1979, 242–44.
23. Bidon and Lorcin 2003, 71, 216–18; Garcìa Marsilla 1993, 151.
24. Motis Dolader 1997, 290.
25. Piponnier 1997, 412.
26. Montanari 1988a, 187; Galoppini 2006, 420; Piponnier 1997, 412; Garcìa Marsilla 1993, 151.
27. Anonimo genovese 1978, 244.
28. Montanari 1988a, 167; Galoppini 1999, 117.
29. Bidon and Lorcin 2003, 260.
30. Galetti 1997, 45–46.
31. Montanari 1979, 351.
32. Bidon and Lorcin 2003, 137.
33. Montanari 1979, 310.
34. Garcìa Marsilla 1993, 152.
35. Bidon and Lorcin 2003.
36. Bidon and Lorcin 2003, 14 (fig. XI), 153 (fig. 84).
37. Piponnier 1997, 410.
38. Beck Bossard 1981, 311–20.
39. Montanari 1979, 406.
40. Bidon and Lorcin 2003, 145.
41. Garcìa Marsilla 1993, 149.
42. Bidon and Lorcin 2003, 145.

43. Piponnier 1997, 410; Bidon and Lorcin 2003, 142–43.
44. Bidon and Lorcin 2003, 13 (fig. VIII), 142.
45. Ceschi 2003, 103.
46. Galoppini 2003, 36.
47. Sacchetti 1970, 113 (*novella* 41).
48. Montanari 1979, 390–94.
49. Galoppini 2003, 45.
50. Pounds 1989, 275.
51. De la Roncière 1985b.
52. Mortars with a radius between 13 and 27 cm in Comet 1992, 376.
53. Piponnier 1997, 410–11; Citter 2002, 115–68.
54. Bidon and Lorcin 2003.
55. Duby 1985, 51–53.
56. Piponnier 1997, 414.
57. Bidon and Lorcin 2003, 9 (fig. 1).
58. Riera Melis 1997, 323.
59. Bidon and Lorcin 2003, 220.
60. Sercambi 1972, 75–78 (*novella* 14).

Chapter 8

1. Concerning depictions of hell, see Baschet 1993.
2. Earle 1628, chapter 20.
3. Concerning the confusing issue of eight versus seven vices see Rigotti 1999.
4. Newhauser 1993, 99.
5. Concerning this progression and the competing system based on what ultimately became the more canonical version based on seven sins developed by
   Pope Gregory the Great, see Newhauser 1993, 99–104, 181–91.
6. *Capita XXVII de diversis malignis cogitationibus.* Quoted in Newhauser 1993,
   104.
7. On this migration of an idea to civil society see Delumeau 1983, 498–508
   (III, 16).
8. The quotation is from the King James version. The same passage in the Latin
   Bible says that: "vidit igitur mulier quod bonum esset lignum ad vescendum
   et pulchrum oculis aspectuque delectabile et tulit de fructu illius et comedit
   deditque viro suo qui comedit, et aperti sunt oculi amborum cumque cognovis-
   sent esse se nudos consuerunt folia ficus et fecerunt sibi perizomata."
9. Casagrande and Vecchio 2000, 125–26. See also Montanari 1988b, 3–12.
10. Gregory the Great, *Moralia,* 89, 1611 (XXXI, XLV). Quoted in Casagrande
    and Vecchio 2000, 136, 152.
11. The following discussion concerning the effects that food was thought to have
    on the human body is based on Reynolds 1999, 19–20.

12. Ibid.
13. For a recent edition and translation see Anthimus 1996.
14. Much has been published on this literature in the past ten years. The most readily available volume for the English-language reader remains Albala 2002. See also Nicoud 2007.
15. Reynolds 1999, 19–20.
16. A somewhat more complete account of the classification system might be found in two articles I published several decades ago: Grieco 1991; Grieco 1999.

Chapter 9

1. On the specific features of sacred art, see Chenis 1991.
2. This mosaic cycle is reproduced in Andreolli 1999b.
3. Mane 1983. For more limited sampling, Andreolli 1999b and Galetti 2002. A good survey is in Baruzzi and Montanari 1981, and is fleshed out with Andreolli 2008. For the dietary aspects see Pucci Donati 2007.
4. Frugoni 1996.
5. Mane 1994.
6. Pirani 1966, 24 (n. 9).
7. Sereni 1961.
8. Romano 1991, 3–84.
9. We owe this phrase to Anceschi 1976.
10. Sereni 1961, 86 (context and commentary, 85–87).
11. For all these aspects see Montanari 1979 and 1988a.
12. For a well-documented sample, Andreolli 1983, 95–112.
13. On the sexual behavior of the animal, Pastoureau 2007, 97–102.
14. Both episodes are mentioned and commented upon in Montanari 1989, 127, 130.
15. Quite rightly, the behavior of these two is linked by Montanari 1979, 457–64.
16. The translation is drawn from Liutprand of Cremona 1945, 252. Another version is in Liutprand of Cremona 1998, 238.
17. Liutprand of Cremona 1945, 227; Liutprand of Cremona 1988, 219.
18. Among the numerous editions and translations I would recommend Penco 1958.
19. Schmitz 1942–56, 29 (V).
20. For the Middle Ages, see Andreolli 2000. For later centuries, D'Ambrosio and Spedicato 1998.
21. Alcuin 1995, 23, 53. On the widespread ubiquity of the vine and vineyards in this era, see Andreolli 2007.
22. von Bingen 1997a, 224–25.
23. von Bingen 1997a, 181–82.
24. Corrao 2008, 5.

25. Zaouali 2004, 38.
26. Firpo 1972, 88.
27. Hugh of St Victor 1987, 111.
28. Hugh of St Victor 1987, 112.
29. Azzara and Gasparri 1992, 92–93.
30. Einhard 1993, 37.
31. Einhard 1993, 83n.129.
32. *Gesta Karoli Magni* 49.
33. For a well-documented sample, see Andreolli 1999a, 201–9.
34. Recent commentary and publication in Fasano et al. 2009, 127 (profile of Laura Pasquini).
35. Fenelli 2006.
36. Among the more recent essays on this see Andreolli 1997 (with an extensive bibliography).
37. Volpe 1999, 95–149.
38. von Bingen 1997b, 88–91.
39. Strabo 1979; Strabo 2004.
40. Strabo 1979, 120–23.
41. Strabo 1979, 122–23.
42. Moulin 1993, 87–88.
43. Gregory the Great 1924, 31. For the context of this episode, see Montanari 1979, 340.
44. Boitani 1991, 70–71, 75, 85, 90–91, 93–94, 99.
45. Béroul 1983, 45, 50.
46. *Cerca (La) del Santo Graal* 1996, 111–12.
47. Battaglia 1988, 181.
48. Battaglia 1988, 229. On the satire of the villain see Lizier 1895.
49. de Troyes 1983, 46.
50. de Troyes 1983, 101.
51. Agrati and Magini 1981, 36–37 (III).
52. Agrati and Magini 1981, 27 (III).
53. Lisini 1911, 3–4. More precise detail is shown in Pertusi 1983, 5.
54. Petrone 2007, figs. 4a–4b.
55. Commentary in Montanari 1989, 211.
56. For the frescoes see Marassi 1927; for the *canederli* Mastrelli 2003, 19.
57. Petrone 2007, fig. 3.
58. Extremely useful, at the level of comparative anthropology, Levi-Strauss 1990.

Chapter 10

1. For a general introduction to the period, see Montanari and Sabban 2004.
2. Hourani 1991, 49.

3. Abu-Lughod 1989; Hourani 1995.

4. Watson 1983; Decker 2009.

5. Wright 1999.

6. Sourdel 1983, 70.

7. Marìn 2000, 205–14.

8. Zaouali 2007.

9. Albala 2002, 14–47.

10. Roden 1998, 41–50, 211–20.

11. Singer 2002, 145–51.

12. Curtin 1984.

13. Connah 1987, 113–33.

14. Connah 1987, 144–73.

15. Connah 1987, 46–53.

16. Connah 1987, 72–93.

17. Connah 1987, 181–221.

18. Smith 1990.

19. Achaya 1994.

20. Beckwith 1987.

21. Blofeld 1985, 4.

22. Sabban and Serventi 2002, 271–344.

23. Chang 1977, 117.

24. Sterckx 2005, 186–236.

25. Martin 2007, 37.

26. Schafer 1963.

27. Anderson, 67.

28. Chang 1977, 95–97.

29. Pomeranz and Topik 1999, 14–16.

30. Kiple 2007, 44.

31. Mazumdar 1998.

32. Pomeranz and Topik 1999, 9–14.

33. Evans 1992, 52.

34. Martin 2007, 54.

35. Evans 1992, 60–61.

36. Chang 1977, 203–10.

37. Weatherford 2004, 227–29.

38. Martin 2007, 56–58.

39. Pettid 2008, 15.

40. Ishige 2001, 46.

41. Martin 2007, 63–66.

42. Pomeranz and Topik 1999, 21–23.

43. Fussell 1992, 29–58.

44. Pilcher 1998, 7–24.

45. Mazoyer and Roudart 2002.

46. Meggers 1954; Meggers 2001.
47. Roosevelt 1991.
48. Mann 2005, 251.
49. Mann 2005, 262–65.

BIBLIOGRAPHY

CONTEMPORARY SOURCES

Agrati, G., and M. L. Magini, eds. 1981. *Romanzi (I) della Tavola Rotonda*. 3 vols. Milano: Mondadori.

Alcuin. 1995. *Carmi dalla corte e dal convento,* ed. C. Carena. Firenze: Le Lettere.

Al-Idrisi. 1970–1984. "Opus Geographicum," eds. E. Cerulli, F. Gabrieli, G. Delia Vida, L. Petech, and G. Tucci. Naples-Roma: Istituto Universitario Orientale di Napoli, 5:541.

d'Andeli, Henri. 1881. "Oeuvres," ed. Alexandre Héron. Paris.

Annales Sancti Rudberti Salisburgensis. In *Monumenta Germaniae Historica, Scriptores,* 9.

Anonimo genovese. 1978. *De condicione civitate Ianuae.* In *Poeti del Duecento. Poesia didattica del Nord,* ed. Gianfranco Contini. Torino: Einaudi.

Anthimus. 1996. *De observatione ciborum (On the observance of foods),* ed. Mark Grant. Blackawton, Totnes: Prospect Books.

Azzara, Claudio, and Stefano Gasparri, eds. 1992. "Le leggi dei Longobardi." In *Storia, memoria e diritto di un popolo germanico.* Milano: La Storia.

Battaglia, S., ed. 1998. *Romanzo (Il) della volpe (The romance of the fox).* Palermo: Sellerio.

Bede the Venerable. 2008–2010. *Storia degli inglesi (Historia ecclesiastica gentis Anglorum),* vol. 2, ed. M. Lapidge, trans. P. Chiesa. Milano: Fondazione Lorenzo Valla/Arnoldo Mondadori.

Béroul. 1983. *Il romanzo di Tristano,* ed. L. Cocito. Milano: Jaca Book.

Bodel, Jean. 2005. *Le jeu de saint Nicolas,* ed. Dufournet.

Boitani, P., ed. 1991. *Sir Gawain e il Cavaliere Verde (Sir Gawain and the Green Knight).* Milano: Adelphi.

Capita XXVII de diversis malignis cogitationibus. In *Patrologia Graeca* 79: 1201.

Cerca (La) del Santo Graal. 1996. Milano: Rusconi.

Corrao, F. M., ed. 2008. *Poeti arabi di Sicilia nella versione di poeti italiani contemporanei.* (Arab poets of Sicily translated by contemporary poets.) Milano: Arnoldo Mondadori.

de Adam, Salimbene. 1966. *Cronica,* ed. G. Scalia. Bari: Laterza.

de Troyes, Chrétien. 1983. *Perceval,* eds. G. Agrati and M. L. Magini. Milano: Mondadori.

de Troyes, Chrétien. 1994. *Romans,* ed. J. M. Fritz. Paris.

Dunstani, Vita. 1874. *"Auctore 'B'."* In *Memorials of St Dunstan.*

Earle, John. 1628. *Micro-cosmographie. Or, a peece of the world discovered in essayes and characters. Newly composed for the northerne parts of this kingdome.* London: Blount.

Einhard. 1993. *Vita di Carlo Magno (Life of Charlemagne),* ed. G. Carazzali. Milano: Bompiani.

Gesta Karoli Magni Imperatoris. 1960. *MGH Scriptores,* 2.

Glaber, Raoul. 1982. *Storie dell'anno mille,* eds. G. Andenna and D. Tuniz. Milano: Fondazione Lorenzo Valla / Arnoldo Mondadori.

Goscelin. 1965. "Life of Wulfhild," ed. Colker. *Studia Monastica,* 7: 418–34.

Gregory the Great. 1924. *Dialogi,* ed. A. Moricca. Roma: Fonti per la Storia d'Italia.

Gregory the Great. "Moralium libri, sive expositio in librum b. Job." In *Patrologia Latina,* 76.

Gregory of Tours. 1951. "Liber in gloria martyrum," eds. B. Krusch and W. Levison. *Monumenta Germaniae Historica. Scriptores Rerum Merovingicarum,* 1.

Gregory of Tours. 1981. *La storia dei Franchi (History of the Franks),* ed. M. Oldoni. Milano: Fondazione Valla.

Heaney, S., ed. and trans. 1999. *Beowulf.* London.

Hugh of St. Victor. 1987. *Didascalicon,* ed. V. Liccaro. Milano: Rusconi.

Inventari altomedievali di terre, coloni e redditi. 1979. Roma: Istituto Storico Italiano per il Medio Evo.

Liutprand of Cremona. 1945. "Liutprando da Cremona." In *Tutte le opere,* ed. A. Cutolo. Milano: Bompiani.

Liutprand of Cremona. 1988. *Italia e Bisanzio alle soglie dell'anno mille. Liutprando da Cremona,* eds. M. Oldoni and P. Ariatta. Novara: Europìa.

Notker of St Gallen. 1969. "Life of Charlemagne." In *Einhard and Notker the Stammerer. Two Lives of Charlemagne,* ed. and trans. L. Thorpe. London.

Paul the Deacon. 2003. *History of the Langobards,* ed. W. Foulke. Philadelphia.

Penco, G., ed. 1958. *Sancti Benedicti Regula.* Firenze: La Nuova Italia.

Procopius of Cesarea. 1974. *La guerra gotica (The War of Goths),* ed. F. M. Pontani. Roma.

Sacchetti, Franco. 1970. *Il Trecentonovelle,* ed. Emilio Faccioli. Torino: Einaudi.

Sercambi, Giovanni. 1972. *Novelle,* ed. G. Sinicropi. Bari: Laterza.

Strabo, Walahfrid. 1979. *Hortulus,* ed. C. Roccaro. Palermo: Herbita.

Strabo, Walahfrid. 2004. *Hortulus, de Klostertuin van Walafried Strabo,* ed. Vincent Hunink. Warnsveld: Uitgeverij Terra Lannoo.

Tacitus. 2006. *Agricola. Germania,* eds. J. B. Rives and H. Mattingly. London: Penguin Books.

Taillevent. 1988. *The Viandier of Taillevent. An Edition of All Extant Manuscripts,* ed. Terence Scully. Ottawa: University of Ottawa Press.

Villani, Giovanni. 1991. *Nuova cronica,* ed. G. Porta. Parma.

Villani, Matteo. 1995. *Cronica, con la continuazione di Filippo Villani,* ed. G. Porta. Parma.

von Bingen, Hildegarde. 1997a. *Cause e cure delle infermità,* ed. P. Calef. Palermo: Sellerio.

von Bingen, Hildegarde. 1997b. *Il centro della ruota. Spiegazione della Regola di San Benedetto,* ed. A. Carlevaris. Milano: Mimesis.

White, Caroline, ed. 2008. *Sancti Benedicti Regula (The Rule of St Benedict).* London: Penguin.

William of Malmesbury. 2002. *Vita Wulfstani,* ed. Winterbottom and Thomson.

Wolfram von Eschenbach. 1989. *Parzival,* ed. G. Bianchessi. Milano: TEA.

Zeumer, K., ed. 1886a. "Formulae imperiales e curia Ludovici Pii." In *MGH Leges V.* Hannover.

Zeumer, K., ed. 1886b. "Formulae Merowingici et Karolini Aevi." In *MGH Leges V.* Hannover.

SCIENTIFIC LITERATURE

Abel, Wilhelm. 1937. "Wandlungen des Fleischverbrauchs und der Fleischversorgung in Deutschland seit dem ausgehenden Mittelalter." *Berichte über Landwirtschaft. Zeitschrift für Agrarpolitik und Landwirtschaft* 12 (3): 411–52.

Abel, Wilhelm. 1973. *Crises agraires en Europe (XIIIe-XXe siècle).* Paris: Flammarion.

Abulafia, David. 1981. "Southern Italy and the Florentine Economy, 1265–1370." *The Economic History Review* 34: 377–88.

Abu-Lughod, Janet L. 1989. *Before European Hegemony: The World System AD 1250–1350.* New York: Oxford University Press.

Achaya, K. T. 1994. *Indian Food: A Historical Companion.* Delhi: Oxford University Press.

Adamson, Melitta Weiss. 1995. *Medieval Dietetics: Food and Drink in Regimen Sanitatis Literature from 800 to 1400.* Frankfurt: Peter Lang.

Adamson, Melitta Weiss, ed. 1995. *Food in the Middle Ages: A Book of Essays.* New York: Garland Publishing.

Adamson, Melitta Weiss, ed. and trans. 2000. *Daz buoch von guoter spise (The Book of Good Food): A Study, Edition, and English Translation of the Oldest German Cookbook.* Krems: Medium Aevum Quotidianum.

Adamson, Melitta Weiss. 2003. "Imitation Food Then and Now." *Petits Propos Culinaires* 72: 83–102.

Adamson, Melitta Weiss. 2004. *Food in Medieval Times.* Westport, CT: Greenwood Press.

Albala, Ken. 2002. *Eating Right in the Renaissance.* Berkeley: University of California Press.

Alexandre-Bidon, Danièle, and Marie-Thérèse Lorcin. 2003. *Le quotidien au temps des fabliaux. Textes, Images, Objets.* Paris: Picard.

Althoff, Gerd. 1988. "Der frieden-, bündnis- und gemeinschaftstiftende Charakter des Mahles im früheren Mittelalter." In *Essen und Trinken in Mittlelalter und Neuzeit,* eds. Irmgard Bitsch et al., 12–25. Sigmaringen: Jan Thorbecke.

Ambiente vegetale (L') nell'alto Medioevo. 1990. Atti della XXXVII Settimana di studio, 2 volumes. Spoleto: Centro italiano di studi sull'alto Medioevo.

Anceschi, Luciano. 1976. *Autonomia ed eteronomia dell'arte. Saggio di fenomenologia delle poetiche.* Milano: Garzanti (written between 1930 and 1936).

Andreolli, Bruno. 1983. *Uomini nel Medioevo. Studi sulla società lucchese dei secoli VIII–XI.* Bologna: Pàtron.

Andreolli, Bruno. 1997. "Le peschiere di San Colombano di Bobbio e l'attività di pesca sul Garda nei secoli centrali del Medioevo." In *Il Garda, l'ambiente, l'uomo. Il priorato di San Colombano di Bardolino e la presenza monastica nella Gardesana Orientale,* 13–19. Centro studi per il territorio benacense, Caselle di Sommacampagna.

Andreolli, Bruno. 1999a. *Contadini su terre di signori. Studi sulla contrattualistica agraria dell'Italia medievale.* Bologna: Clueb.

Andreolli, Bruno. 1999b. "Agricoltura e mondo rurale nel Codice 65 dell'Archivio Capitolare della Cattedrale di Piacenza." In *Il Libro del Maestro. Codice 65 dell'Archivio Capitolare della Cattedrale di Piacenza (sec. XII),* ed. Pierre Racine, 145–70. Piacenza: Fondazione di Piacenza e Vigevano.

Andreolli, Bruno. 2000. "Un contrastato connubio. Acqua e vino dal Medioevo all'età moderna". In *La vite e il vino. Storia e diritto (secoli XI–XIX),* 2 vols., ed. Mario Da Passano, Antonello Mattone, Franca Mele, and Pinuccia F. Simbula, 2:1031–51. Roma: Carocci.

Andreolli, Bruno. 2007. "Paesaggi della vite e paesaggi dell'olivo nell'Italia dell'alto Medioevo." In *Olio e vino nell'alto Medioevo,* 1:317–57. Spoleto: Fondazione CISAM.

Andreolli, Bruno, ed. 2008. *Il maiale alla corte e nelle terre dei Pico.* Mirandola: Comune di Mirandola.

Andreolli, Bruno, and Massimo Montanari. 1983. *L'azienda curtense in Italia. Proprietà della terra e lavoro contadino nei secoli VIII–XI.* Bologna: Clueb.

Andreolli, Bruno, and Massimo Montanari, eds. 1988. *Il bosco nel Medioevo.* Bologna: Clueb.

Anes Alvarez de Castrillón, Gonzalo, ed. 1994. *Mesta, trashumancia y vida pastoril.* Valladolid: Junta de Castilla y León.

Approvisionnement (L') des villes de l'Europe occidentale au Moyen Âge et aux Temps modernes. 1985. *Cinquièmes Journées internationales d'Histoire, 16–18 septembre 1983.* Auch: Centre Culturel de l'abbaye de Flaran.

Arikha, Noga. 2007. *Passions and Tempers. A History of Humors*. New York: HarperCollins.

Aurell, Martin, Olivier Dumoulin, and Françoise Thelamon, eds. 1992. *La sociabilité à table. Commensalité et convivialité à travers les âges*. Rouen: Publications de l'Université de Rouen.

Balard, Michel. 1985. "Le commerce du blé en mer Noire (XIII^c-XV^c siècle)." In *Aspetti della vita economica medievale. Atti del Convegno di Studi, Firenze-Pisa-Prato1984*, 64–80. Firenze: Le Monnier.

Baldwin, John W. 2000. *Aristocratic Life in Medieval France: The Romances of Jean Renart and Gerbert de Montreuil, 1190–1230*. Baltimore: Johns Hopkins University Press.

Bardet, J.-P., and J. Dupâquier, eds. 1997. *Histoire des populations de l'Europe. I. Des origines aux prémices de la révolution démographique*. Paris: Fayard.

Baruzzi, Marina, and Massimo Montanari. 1981. *Porci e porcari nel Medioevo. Paesaggio, economia, alimentazione*. Bologna: Clueb.

Baschet, Jérôme. 1993. *Les Justices de l'au-delà. Les représentations de l'enfer en France et en Italie (XII^c- XV^c siècle)*. Rome: École française de Rome.

Baschet, Jérôme. 2006. *La civilisation féodale. De l'an mil à la colonisation de l'Amérique*, 2nd ed. Paris: Flammarion.

Beck Bossard, Corinne. 1981. "L'alimentazione in un villaggio siciliano del XIV secolo, sulla scorta delle fonti archeologiche." *Archeologia Medievale* 8: 311–20.

Beckwith, C. I. 1987. *The Tibetan Empire in Central Asia*. Princeton, NJ: Princeton University Press.

Benito i Monclús, Pere. 2007. "Et si sterilitas, ut solet, in terra illa fuerit…Frequencia, longevidad y gravedad de las carestías en Cataluña durante la 'fase de crecimiento' de la economía medieval (siglos XI–XIII)." In *Crisis de subsistencia y crisis agrarias en la Edad Media,* eds. H. R. Oliva Herrer and P. Benito Monclus, 79–110. Sevilla: Universidad de Sevilla.

Bennett, Judith M. 1996. *Ale, Beer and Brewsters in England: Women's Work in a Changing World, 1300–1600*. Oxford: Oxford University Press.

Benveniste, Émile. 1969. *Le vocabulaire des institutions indo-européennes*. Paris: Minuit.

Beresford, M. W., and J. G. Hurst, eds. 1971. *Deserted Medieval Villages*. London: Lutterworth.

Berthe, Maurice, ed. 1998. *Endettement paysan et crédit rural dans l'Europe médiévale et moderne*. Toulouse: Presses Universitaires du Mirail.

Biraben, Jean-Noël. 1975. *Les hommes et la peste en France et dans les pays européens et méditerranéens. I. La peste dans l'histoire*. Paris-La Haye: Mouton.

Bitsch, Irmgard, Trude Ehlert, and Xenja von Ertzdorff, eds. 1988. *Essen und Trinken in Mittlelalter und Neuzeit*. Sigmaringen: Thorbecke.

Black, Maggie. 1993. "Medieval Britain." In *A Taste of History: 10,000 Years of Food in Britain,* eds. Peter Brears, Maggie Black, Gill Corbishley, Jane

Renfrew, and Jennifer Stead, 95–135. London: English Heritage in association with British Museum Press.

Blanshei, S. R. 1976. "Perugia, 1260–1340: Conflict and Change in a Medieval Italian Urban Society." *Transactions of the American Philosophical Society* 66: 1–128.

Bloch, Marc. 1939–1940. *La société féodale*, vol. 2. Paris: Albin Michel.

Blockmans, W., and H. Dubois. 1997. "Le temps des crises (XIVe et XVe siècles)." In *Histoire des populations de l'Europe, I. Des origines aux prémices de la révolution démographique,* eds. J.-P. Bardet and J. Dupâquier, 185–217. Paris: Fayard.

Blofeld, John. 1985. *Chinese art of tea.* Boston: Shambhala.

Bolens, Lucie. 1993. "Al-Andalus: la vigne et l'olivier, un secteur de pointe (XIᵉ-XIIIᵉ siècles)." In *La production du vin et l'huile en Mediterranée,* 343–58. Athènes: École Française d'Athènes.

Braudel, Ferdinand. 1967. *Civilisation matérielle, économie et capitalisme: XVᵉ-XVIIIᵉ siècle,* vol. 1 [*Les Structures du quotidien: le possible et l'impossible*]. Paris: Armand Colin.

Braudel, Fernand. 1982. *Le strutture del quotidiano (Civiltà materiale, economia e capitalismo, 1).* Torino: Einaudi. (Orig. Paris: Armand Colin, 1979.)

Bray, D. 1999. "Sacral Elements of Irish Kingship." In *This Immense Panorama: Studies in Honour of Eric J. Sharpe,* 105–16. Sydney: The University of Sydney.

Britnell, Richard H. 1989. "England and Northern Italy in the Early Fourteenth Century: The Economic Contrasts." *Transactions of the Royal Historical Society,* 5th Series, 39: 167–83.

Britnell, Richard H. 1996. *The Commercialization of English Society, 1000–1500.* Cambridge: Cambridge University Press.

Brühl, Carlrichard. 1969. *Fodrum, gistum, servitium regis: Studien zu den wirtschaftlichen Grundlagen des Königtums im Frankenreich und in den fränkischen Nachfolgestaaten Deutschland, Frankreich und Italien vom 6. bis zur Mitte des 14. Jahrhunderts.* Köln: Bohlau.

Bruneton-Governatori, A. 1984. *Le pain de bois. Ethnohistoire de la châtaigne et du châtaignier.* Toulouse: Eché.

Bullough, David A. 1991. *Friends, Neighbours and Fellow-Drinkers: Aspects of Community and Conflict in the Early Medieval West.* Cambridge: Blackwell.

Bulst, N. 1997. "L'essor (Xᵉ–XIVᵉ siècles)." In *Histoire des populations de l'Europe, I. Des origines aux prémices de la révolution démographique,* eds. J.-P. Bardet and J. Dupâquier, 168–84. Paris: Fayard.

Campanini, Antonella. 2006. "La table sous contrôle: les banquets et l'excès alimentaire dans le cadre des lois somptuaires en Italie entre le Moyen Âge et la Renaissance." *Food and History* 4: 131–50.

Capatti, Alberto, and Massimo Montanari. 1999. *La cucina italiana. Storia di una cultura.* Roma-Bari: Laterza.

Capatti, Alberto, and Massimo Montanari. 2003. *Italian Cuisine: A Cultural History*. New York: Columbia University Press.

Carlin, Martha. 1998. "Fast Food and Urban Living Standards in Medieval England." In *Food and Eating in Medieval Europe*, eds. Martha Carlin and Joel T. Rosenthal, 27–51. London: The Hambledon Press.

Carlin, Martha, and Joel T. Rosenthal, eds. 1998. *Food and Eating in Medieval Europe*. London: The Hambledon Press.

Carpentier, E. 1962. "Autour de la peste noire: famines et épidémies dans l'histoire du XIVe siècle." *Annales ESC* 17: 1062–92.

Casagrande, Carla, and Silvana Vecchio. 2000. *I sette vizi capitali. Storia dei peccati nel Medioevo*. Torino: Einaudi.

Ceschi, D. 2003. "La Norcineria nella Lunigiana storica." In *Il lardo nell'alimentazione toscana dall'antichità ai nostri giorni*, ed. L. Galoppini. Modena: Aedes muratoriana.

Chang, K. C. 1977. *Food in Chinese Culture*. New Haven, CT: Yale University Press.

Chapelot, J., and R. Fossier. 1980. *Le village et la maison au Moyen Age*. Paris: Hachette.

Chasse (La) au Moyen Age. 1980. Actes du Colloque de Nice (22–24 juin 1979). Nice: Les Belles Lettres.

Chenis, C. 1991. *Fondamenti teorici dell'arte sacra. Magistero post-conciliare*. Roma: LAS.

Cherubini, Giovanni. 1981. "La civiltà del castagno in Italia alla fine del Medioevo." *Archeologia Medievale* 8: 247–80.

Cherubini, Giovanni. 1984. *L'Italia rurale del basso Medioevo*. Roma-Bari: Laterza.

Citter, Carlo, ed. 2002. "Castel di Pietra (Gavorrano–Gr): relazione preliminare della campagna 2001." *Archeologia Medievale* 29: 115–68.

Cohn, S. K. 2006. *Lust for Liberty: The Policy of Social Revolt in Medieval Europe, 1200–1425, Italy, France, and Flanders*. Cambridge, MA: Harvard University Press.

Colker, M. L. 1965. "Texts of Jocelyn of Canterbury which Relate to the History of Barking Abbey." *Studia Monastica* 7 (2): 383–460.

Comba, Rinaldo. 1978. *Il Medioevo*. Torino: Loescher.

Comba, Rinaldo. 1988. "Crisi del sistema curtense e sperimentazioni aziendali (secoli XI–XIII)." In *La Storia. I grandi problemi dal Medioevo all'Età Contemporanea*. I. *Il Medioevo*. 1, *I quadri generali,* eds. Nicola Tranfaglia and Massimo Firpo, 91–116. Torino: UTET.

Comet, Georges. 1992. *Le paysan et son outil. Essai d'histoire technique des céréales (France, VIIIe–XVe siècle)*. Rome: École française de Rome.

Connah, Graham. 1987. *African Civilizations: An Archaeological Perspective*. Cambridge: Cambridge University Press.

Constable, Olivia Remie. 1994. *Trade and Traders in Muslim Spain: The Commercial Realignment of the Iberian Peninsula, 900–1500*. Cambridge: Cambridge University Press.

Contamine, Philippe. 1985. "Les aménagement de l'espace privé." In *Histoire de la vie privée. De l'Europe féodale à la Renaissance,* eds. Philippe Ariès and Georges Duby, 421–501. Paris: Le Seuil.

Corradi, A. 1894. *Annali delle epidemie occorse in Italia dalle prime memorie fino al 1860.* Bologna: Forni.

Cortonesi, Alfio. 2004. "Autoconsumo y mercado: la alimentación rural y urbana en la baja Edad Media". In *Historia de la alimentación,* eds. Jean-Louis Flandrin and Massimo Montanari. Somonte-Cenero, Gijón: Trea.

Cortonesi, Alfio. 1995. *Ruralia. Economie e paesaggi del medioevo italiano.* Roma: Il Calamo.

Cortonesi, Alfio. 1999. "Avvicendamenti colturali e pratiche cerealicole nell'Italia tardo medievale." *Quaderni Medievali* 48: 6–34.

Cortonesi, Alfio. 2004. "Autoconsumo y mercado: la alimentación rural y urbana en la baja Edad Media." In *Historia de la alimentación,* eds. Jean-Louis Flandrin and Massimo Montanari. Somonte-Cenero, Gijón: Trea.

Cracco Ruggini, Lelia. 1995. *Economia e società nell'Italia annonaria. Rapporti tra agricoltura e commercio dal IV al VI secolo d. C.* Bari: Edipuglia.

Curschmann, Fritz. 1900. *Hungersnöte im Mittelalter. Ein Beitrag zur deutschen Wirtschaftsgeschichte des 8. bis 13. Jahrhunderts.* Leipzig.

Curtin, Philip D. 1984. *Cross-Cultural Trade in the World History.* Cambridge: Cambridge University Press.

Cuvillier, J.-P. 1974. "Barcelone, Gênes et le commerce du blé de Sicilie vers le milieu du XIIIe siècle." In *Atti del I Congresso Storico Liguria-Catalogna,* 161–70. Bordighera: Istituto internazionale di studi liguri.

D'Ambrosio, Angelo, and Mario Spedicato. 1998. *Cibo e clausura. Regimi alimentari e patrimoni monastici nel Mezzogiorno Moderno (sec. XVII–XIX).* Bari: Cacucci.

Decker, Michael. 2009. "Plants and Progress: Rethinking the Islamic Agricultural Revolution." *Journal of World History* 20 (2): 197–206.

De La Roncière, Charles-Marie. 1982. *Prix et salaires à Florence au XIVe siècle (1280–1380).* Roma: École Française de Rome.

De La Roncière, Charles Marie. 1985a. "L'approvisionnement des villes italiennes au Moyen Âge (XIVe–XVe siècles)." In *L'approvisionnement des villes de l'Europe occidentale au Moyen Âge et aux Temps modernes,* 33–51. Auch: Centre Culturel de l'abbaye de Flaran.

De La Roncière, Charles-Marie. 1985b. "La vie privée des notables toscans au seuil de la Renaissance." In *Histoire de la vie privée. De l'Europe féodale à la Renaissance,* eds. Philippe Ariès and Georges Duby, 163–309. Paris: Seuil.

Del Treppo, Mario. 1972. *I mercanti catalani e l'espansione della Corona d'Aragona.* Napoli: L'Arte tipografica.

Delumeau, Jean. 1983. *Le péché et la peur: la culpabilisation en Occident (XIIIe–XVIIIe siècles).* Paris: Fayard.

Derolez, A., ed. 1968. "Lamberti Audomarensis canonici Liber Floridus codex autographus Bibliothecae Universitatis Gandavensis." Ghent.

Desportes, Françoise. 1981. "Droit économique et police des métiers en France du Nord (milieu du XIIIe–début du XVe siècle)." *Revue du Nord* 63: 321–36.

Desportes, Françoise. 1987. *Le pain au Moyen Âge.* Paris: Olivier Orban.

Desportes, Françoise. 1996. "Les métiers de l'alimentation." In *Histoire de l'alimentation,* eds. Jean-Louis Flandrin and Massimo Montanari. Paris: Fayard.

Devroey, Jean-Pierre. 1986. "Réflexions sur l'économie des premiers temps carolingiens (768–877): grands domaines et action politique entre Seine et Rhin." *Francia. Forschungen zur Westeuropäischen Geschichte* 13: 475–88.

Devroey, Jean-Pierre. 2003. *Économie rurale et société dans l'Europe franque (VIe–IXe siècles).* Paris: Belin.

Devroey, Jean-Pierre. 2006. *Puissants et misérables. Système social et monde paysan dans l'Europe des Francs (VIe–IXe siècles).* Bruxelles: Académie royale de Belgique.

Dierkens, Alain, and Liliane Plouvier. 2008. *Festins mérovingiens.* Brussels: Timperman.

Dion, Roger. 1959. *Histoire de la vigne et du vin en France des origines au XIXe siècle.* Paris: Chez l'auteur.

Duby, Georges. 1962. *L'économie rurale et la vie des campagnes dans l'Occident médiéval (France, Angleterre, Empire, IX–XV siècles). Essai de synthèse et perspectives de recherches.* Paris: Aubier.

Duby, Georges. 1973. *Guerriers et paysans, VIIe–XIIe siècle. Premier essor de l'économie européenne.* Paris: Gallimard.

Duby, Georges, and Armand Wallon, eds. 1975. "La formation des campagnes françaises des origines au XIVe siècle." In *Histoire de la France rurale,* vol 1. Paris: Seuil.

Duby, Georges. 1985. "Convivialité." In *Histoire de la vie privée. De l'Europe féodale à la Renaissance,* eds. Philippe Ariès and Georges Duby. Paris: Seuil.

Dufourcq, Charles E. 1966. *L'Espagne Catalane et le Maghreb aux XIIIe et XIVe siècles.* Paris: Presses Universitaires de France.

Dufournet, Jean. 2005. *Jean Bodel: Le jeu de saint Nicolas.* Paris: Flammarion.

Dupâquier Jacques. 1997. "Les vicissitudes du peuplement (XVe-XVIIIe siècles)." In *Histoire des populations de l'Europe. I. Des origines aux prémices de la révolution démographique,* eds. J.-P. Bardet and J. Dupâquier, 239–61. Paris: Fayard.

Dyer, Charles. 1989. *Standards of living in the later Middle Ages. Social change in England, c. 1200–1520.* Cambridge: Cambridge University Press.

Effros, Bonnie. 2002. *Creating community with food and drink in Merovingian Gaul.* New York: Palgrave Macmillan.

Enright, Michael J. 1996. *Lady with a mead cup: Ritual, prophecy and lordship in the European warband from La Tène to the Viking Age.* Dublin: Four Courts Press.

Evans, John C. 1992. *Tea in China.* New York: Greenwood.

Fagan, B. 2000. *The Little Ice Age: How Climate Made History, 1300–1850.* New York: Basic Books.

Fasano, Michele, Laura Pasquini, and Giovanni Barba, eds. 2009. *Otranto, il mosaico, il viaggio di Seth.* Bologna: Sattva Films.

Faugeron, Fabien. 2006. "Nourrir la ville: l'exemple de la boucherie vénitienne à la fin du Moyen Âge." *Consommer en ville au Moyen Âge. Histoire urbaine* 16: 53–70.

Faugeron, Fabien. 2009. *Nourrir la ville: ravitaillement, marches et métiers de l'alimentation à Venise dans les derniers siècles du Moyen Âge,* Université de Paris IV-Sorbonne, Thèse de doctorat, École doctorale I, Paris.

Fenelli, Laura. 2006. *Il tau, il fuoco, il maiale: i canonici regolari di sant'Antonio Abate tra assistenza e devozione.* Spoleto: Fondazione CISAM.

Fichtenau, Heinrich. 1991. *Living in the Tenth Century: Mentalities and Social Orders.* Chicago: University of Chicago Press.

Finberg, H.P.R., ed. 1972. *The Agrarian History of England and Wales,* I. II. General ed. J. C. Thirsk. Cambridge: Cambridge University Press.

Firpo, Luigi, ed. 1972. *Medicina medievale.* Torino: UTET.

Fiumi, Enrico. 1956. "Sui rapporti economici tra città e contado nell'età comunale." *Archivio storico italiano* 114: 18–68.

Flandrin, Jean-Louis, and Odile Redon. 1981. "Les livres de cuisine italiens des XIVe et XVe siècles." *Archeologia Medievale* 8: 393–408.

Flandrin, Jean-Louis, and Massimo Montanari, eds. 1996. *Histoire de l'alimentation.* Paris: Fayard.

Flandrin, Jean-Louis, and Massimo Montanari. 1997. *Storia dell'alimentazione.* Roma-Bari: Laterza.

Flandrin, Jean-Louis, and Massimo Montanari. 1999. *Food: A Culinary History from Antiquity to the Present,* ed. Albert Sonnenfeld. New York: Columbia University Press.

Flandrin, Jean-Louis, and Massimo Montanari. 2004. *Historia de la alimentación.* Somonte-Cenero, Gijón: Trea.

Fossati, Severino, and Tiziano Mannoni. 1981. "Gli strumenti della cucina e della mensa." *Archeologia Medievale* 8: 409–19.

Franklin, Alfred. 1984. *Les rues et les cris de Paris au XIIIe siècle.* Paris. (1st ed., 1874.)

Freedman, Paul. 2008. *Out of the East: Spices and the Medieval Imagination.* New Haven, CT: Yale University Press.

Frugoni, Chiara. 1996. *Wiligelmo. Le sculture del duomo di Modena.* Modena: Panini.

Fumagalli, Vito. 1976. *Terra e società nell'Italia padana. I secoli IXe X.* Torino: Einaudi.

Furnivall, Frederick James, ed. [1868] 1969. *Early English Meals and Manners.* Detroit: Singing Tree Press.

Fussell, Betty. 1992. *The Story of Corn.* New York: North Point Press.

Galetti, Paola. 1997. *Abitare nel Medioevo. Forme e vicende dell'insediamento rurale nell'Italia altomedievale.* Firenze: Le Lettere.

Galetti, Paola. 2002. "Aspetti di cultura materiale nelle raffigurazioni del ciclo dei Mesi di Ferrara." In *Le formelle del Maestro dei Mesi di Ferrara. Storia, arte, cultura materiale. Problemi di conservazione e restauro,* 39–52. Ferrara: Museo della Cattedrale.

Galoppini, Laura. 1999. "Le commerce des pâtes alimentaires dans les Aduanas Sardas." *Médiévales* 36: 111–27.

Galoppini, Laura. 2003. "Il lardo nella Toscana del Medioevo: produzione e commercio." In *Il lardo nell'alimentazione toscana dall'antichità ai nostri giorni,* ed. L. Galoppini. Modena: Aedes muratoriana.

Galoppini, Laura. 2006. "Produzione e commercio dei formaggi nella Toscana del Medioevo." *Bollettino della Accademia degli Euteleti* 73: 427–28.

Ganshof, François-Louis. 1927. "La *tractoria.* Contribution à l'étude du droit de gîte." *Tijdschrift voor rechtsgeschiedenis/Revue d'histoire du droit* 8: 69–91.

García de Cortázar, J. A. 1988. *La sociedad rural en la España Medieval.* Madrid: Siglo XXI.

Garcìa Marsilla, J. V. 1993. *La jerarquìa de la mesa. Los sistemas alimentarios en la Valencia bajomedieval.* Valencia: Diputación Provincial.

Garnsey, Peter. 1988. *Famine and Food Supply in the Graeco-Roman World: Responses to Risk and Crisis.* Cambridge: Cambridge University Press.

Gaulin, Jean-Louis, and François Menant. 1998. "Crédit rural et endettement paysan dans l'Italie communale." In *Endettement paysan et crédit rural dans l'Europe médiévale et moderne,* ed. M. Berthe, 35–67. Toulouse: Presses Universitaires du Mirail.

Gautier, Alban. 2006a. *Le festin dans l'Angleterre anglo-saxonne, V^e–XIe siècles.* Rennes: Presses Universitaires de Rennes.

Gautier, Alban. 2006b. "Palais, itinéraires et fêtes alimentaires des rois anglo-saxons aux Xe et XIe siècles." *Food and History* 4 (1): 29–44.

Gautier, Alban. 2009. "Hospitality in pre-Viking Anglo-Saxon England." *Early Medieval Europe* 17 (1): 23–44.

Gautier, Alban. 2010. "Manger de la viande, signe extérieur de richesse? Le cas des îles Britanniques." In *Les élites et la richesse au haut Moyen Âge,* eds. J.-P. Devroey, L. Feller, and R. Le Jan, 285–303. Turnhout: Brepols.

Gauvard, Claude. 1992. "Cuisine et paix en France à la fin du Moyen Âge." In *La sociabilité à table. Commensalité et convivialité à travers les âges,* eds. Martin Aurell, Olivier Dumoulin, and FrançoiseThelamon, 325–34. Rouen: Publications de l'Université de Rouen.

Gelichi, Sauro. 1997. *Introduzione all'archeologia medievale. Storia e ricerca in Italia.* Roma: Carocci.

Gies, Joseph and Francis. 1979. *Life in a Medieval Castle.* New York: Harper and Row.

Ginatempo, Maria, and Lucia Sandri. 1990. *L'Italia delle città. Il popolamento urbano tra Medioevo e Rinascimento (secoli XIII–XVI).* Firenze: Le Lettere.

Goetz, Hans-Werner. 1995. "Social and Military Institutions." In *New Cambridge Medieval History,* vol. 2, ed. R. McKitterick. Cambridge: Cambridge University Press.

Grieco, Allen J. 1991. "The Social Politics of pre-Linnean Botanical Classification." *I Tatti Studies* 4: 131–49.

Grieco, Allen J. 1993. "Olive Tree Cultivation and the Alimentary Use of Olive Oil in Late Medieval Italy (ca. 1300–1500)." In *La production du vin et l'huile en Méditerranée,* 297–306. Athènes: École Française d'Athènes.

Grieco, Allen J. 1999. "Food and Social Classes in Late Medieval and Renaissance Italy." In *Food: A Culinary History,* eds. Jean-Louis Flandrin and Massimo Montanari, 302–12. New York: Columbia University Press.

Guerreau-Jalabert, Anita. 1992. "Les nourritures comme figures symboliques dans les romans arthuriens." In *La sociabilité à table. Commensalité et convivialité à travers les âges,* eds. Martin Aurell, Olivier Dumoulin, and Françoise Thelamon, 35–40. Rouen: Publications de l'Université de Rouen.

Hallam, H. E., ed. 1988. *The Agrarian History of England and Wales,* vol. 2. General ed. J. C. Thirsk. Cambridge: Cambridge University Press.

Hammond, P. W. 1993. *Food and Feast in Medieval England.* Stroud, UK: Alan Sutton.

Hellmuth, Leopold. 1984. *Gastfreundschaft und Gastrecht bei den Germanen.* Wien: Österreichische Akademie der Wissenschaften.

Hen, Yitzhak. 2006. "Food and Drink in Merovingian Gaul." In *Tätigkeitsfelder und Erfahrungshorizonte des ländlichen Menschen in der frühmittelalterlichen Grundherrschaft (bis ca. 1000). Festschrift für Dieter Hägermann zum 65. Geburtstag,* ed. B. Kasten, 99–110. Stuttgart: Franz Steiner Verlag.

Henisch, Bridget-Ann. 1976. *Fast and Feast: Food in Medieval Society.* University Park: Pennsylvania State University Press.

Herrer, Oliva, Rafael Hipólito Rafael, and Pere Benito Monclus, eds. 2007. *Crisis de subsistencia y crisis agrarias en la Edad Media.* Sevilla: Universidad de Sevilla.

Hibbert, A. P. 1965. "The Eeconomic Policy of Towns." In *The Cambridge Economic History of Europe. 3: Economic Organization and Politics in the Middle Ages.* Cambridge: Cambridge University Press.

Hilton, Rodney. 1973. *Bond Men Made free: Medieval Peasant Movements and the English Rising of 1381.* London: Viking Books.

Hilton, Rodney. 1983. *A Medieval Society. The West Midlands at the End of the Thirteenth Century.* Cambridge: Cambridge University Press.

Hocquet, Jean-Claude. 1978. *Le sel et la fortune de Venise, I. Production et monopole.* Villeneuve d'Ascq: Université de Lille III.

Hocquet, Jean-Claude, ed. 1987. *Le roi, le marchand et le sel. Actes de la table ronde "L'impôt du sel en Europe, XIIIe-XVIIIe siècle", Saline royale d'Arc-et-Senans, 23–25 sept. 1986.* Lille: Presses Universitaires de Lille.

Horn, W., and Born, E. 1979. *The Plan of St Gall: A Study of the Architecture and Economy of, and Life in a Paradigmatic Carolingian Monastery.* Berkeley: University of California Press.

Hourani, Albert. 1991. *Histoire des peuples arabes.* Paris: Seuil.

Hourani, George F. 1995. *Arab Seafaring: In the Indian Ocean in Ancient and Early Medieval Times.* Princeton, NJ: Princeton University Press.

Hübner, Hans-Jürgen. 1997. "Larghezza e strettezza. Hard-money-economy ed i ritmi dei mercati del credito e del grano a Venezia." In *Alimentazione e nutrizione, secc. XIII–XVIII,* 351–64. Prato: Istituto Internazionale di Storia Economica "F. Datini."

Ishige, Naomichi. 2001. *The History and Culture of Japanese Food.* London: Kegan Paul.

Jarman, A.O.H. 1988. *Aneirin: Y Gododdin. Britain's Oldest Heroic Poem.* Llandysul: Gomer Press.

Jordan, W. C. 1996. *The Great Famine in Northern Europe in the Early Fourteenth Century.* Princeton, NJ: Princeton University Press.

Kerr, Julie. 2002. "The Open Door: Hospitality and Honour in Twelfth/Early Thirteenth-century England." *History* 87: 322–35.

Kerr, Julie. 2006. "Food, Drink and Lodging: Hospitality in Twelfth-century England." *Haskins Society Journal* 18: 72–92.

Ketcham Wheaton, Barbara. 1983. *Savoring the Past: French Kitchen and Table from 1300 to 1789.* Philadelphia: University of Pennsylvania Press.

Kiple, Kenneth K. 2007. *A Movable Feast.* New York: Cambridge University Press.

Lafortune-Martel, Agathe. 1992. "De l'entremets culinaire aux pièces montées d'un menu de propagande." In *Du manuscript à la table: Essais sur la cuisine au moyen-âge et répertoire des manuscrits médiévaux contenant des recettes culinaires,* ed. Carole Lambert, 121–29. Montréal: Les Presses de l'Université de Montréal and Paris: Champion-Slatkine.

Lambert, Carole, ed. 1992. *Du manuscript à la table: Essais sur la cuisine au moyen-âge et répertoire des manuscrits médiévaux contenant des recettes culinaires.* Montréal: Les Presses de l'Université de Montréal and Paris: Champion-Slatkine.

Lambert, Carole. 2002. "Medieval France. The South." In *Regional Cuisines of Medieval Europe: A Book of Essays,* ed. Melitta Weiss Adamson. New York: Routledge.

Langdon, John. 1991. "Water-mills and Windmills in the West Midlands, 1086–1500." *Economic History Review* 44: 424–44.

Laurioux, Bruno. 2002. *Manger au Moyen Âge.* Paris: Hachette.

Laurioux, Bruno. 2005a. *Une histoire culinaire du Moyen Âge.* Paris: Champion.

Laurioux, Bruno. 2005b. "Les épices dans l'alimentation médiévale." In *Une histoire culinaire du Moyen Âge, 157–96*. Paris: Champion.

Laurioux, Bruno. 2005c. "Le goût médiéval est-il arabe?" In *Une histoire culinaire du Moyen Âge, 305–35*. Paris: Champion.

Le Goff, Jacques. 1969. *La civilisation de l'Occident médiéval*. Paris: Arthaud.

Le Goff, Jacques. 1992. "Saint Louis à table: entre commensalité royale et humilité alimentaire." In *La sociabilité à table. Commensalité et convivialité à travers les âges,* eds. Martin Aurell, Olivier Dumoulin, and FrançoiseThelamon, 133–44. Rouen: Publications de l'Université de Rouen.

Le Goff, Jacques. 1997. "Bulletins météorologiques au XIIIe siècle." In *Milieux naturels, espaces sociaux. Études offertes à Robert Delort, 55–70*. Paris: Publications de la Sorbonne.

Le Roy Ladurie, Emmanuel. 1967. *Histoire du climat depuis l'an mil*. Paris: Flammarion.

Le Roy Ladurie, Emmanuel. 1975. *Montaillou, village occitan de 1294 à 1324*. Paris: Gallimard.

Lévi-Strauss, Claude. 1990. *"The Origin of Table Manners."* In *Mythologiques,* vol. 3. Chicago: University of Chicago Press.

Lisini, Alessandro. 1911. *La forchetta da tavola*. Siena: Lazzeri.

Lizier, Augusto. 1895. *Osservazioni a proposito delle cause che possono aver dato origine alla Satira contro il Villano*. Treviso: Turazza.

Lobbedey, Uwe. 2003. "Carolingian Royal Palaces: The State of Research from an Architectural Historian's Viewpoint." In *Court Culture in the Early Middle Ages,* ed. Cubitt, 129–54. Turnhout: Brepols.

Lorcin, Marie-Thérèse. 1984. "Manger et boire dans les fabliaux: rites sociaux et hiérarchie des plaisirs." In *Manger et boire au Moyen Âge. Actes du colloque de Nice, 15-17 octobre 1982,* ed. D. Menjot, 1:227–37. Paris: Publications de la Faculté des lettres et sciences humaines de Nice.

Lucas, H. S. 1930. "The Great European Famine of 1315–1316 and 1317." *Speculum 5* (4): 343–77.

Magennis, Hugh. 1999. *Food, Drink and Feast in Anglo-Saxon and Germanic Literary Traditions*. Dublin: Four Courts Press.

Mandrou, Robert. 1961. "Théorie ou hypothèse de travail?" *Annales ESC* 16: 965–71.

Mane, Perrine. 1983. *Calendriers et techniques agricoles (France–Italie, XIIe–XIIIe siècles)*. Paris: Le Sycomore.

Mane, Perrine. 1994. "I recipienti da vino nell'iconografia italiana dei secoli XIV–XV." In *Dalla vite al vino. Fonti e problemi della vitivinicoltura italiana medievale,* eds. Jean-Louis Gaulin and Allen J. Grieco, 85–115. Bologna: Clueb.

Manger et boire au Moyen Âge. 1984. *Actes du Colloque de Nice (15–17 octobre 1982)*. Paris: Publications de la Faculté des Lettres et Sciences Humaines de Nice.

Mann, Charles C. 2005. *1491: New Revelations of the Americas before Columbus.* New York: Alfred A. Knopf.

Marassi, A. 1927. "Affreschi romanici di Castel Appiano." *Bollettino d'Arte del Ministero della Pubblica Istruzione 5* (7): 433–58.

Marìn, Manuela. 2000. "Beyond Taste." In *A Taste of Thyme: Culinary Cultures of the Middle East,* eds. Sami Zubaida and Richard Tapper. London: Tauris Parke.

Martin, Laura C. 2007. *Tea: The Drink That Changed the World.* Rutland, VT: Tuttle Publishing.

Mastrelli, Carlo Alberto. 2003. *Gnocchi e canederli.* Firenze: Istituto di Studi per l'Alto Adige.

Mazoyer, Marcel, and Laurence Roudart. 2002. *Histoire des agricultures du monde.* Paris: Seuil.

Mazumdar, Sucheta. 1998. *Sugar and Society in China: Peasants, Technology, and the World Market.* Cambridge, MA: Harvard University Press.

McCormick, Michael, 2001. *Origins of the European Economy. Communications and Commerce, A.D. 300–900.* Cambridge: Cambridge University Press.

McKitterick, Rosamond. 2008. *Charlemagne: The Formation of a European Identity.* Cambridge: Cambridge University Press.

Meggers, Betty J. 1954. "Environmental Limitations on the Development of Culture." *American Anthropologist 56* (5, pt. 1): 801–24.

Meggers, Betty J. 2001. "The Mystery of Marajoara: An Ecological Solution." *Amazoniana 16* (3–4): 421–40.

Menant, François. 2007. "Crisis de subsistencia y crisis agrarias en la Edad Media: algunas reflexiones previas." In *Crisis de subsistencia y crisis agrarias en la Edad Media,* eds. Hipólito Rafael, Oliva Herrer, and Pere Benito Monclus, 17–60. Sevilla: Universidad de Sevilla.

Mollat, Michel, ed. 1968. *Le rôle du sel dans l'histoire.* Paris: Presses Universitaires de France.

Mollat, Michel. [1978] 1992. *Les pauvres au Moyen Âge,* 2nd ed. Brussels: Complexe. (Orig. Paris: Hachette.)

Montanari, Massimo. 1979. *L'alimentazione contadina nell'alto Medioevo.* Napoli: Liguori.

Montanari, Massimo. 1984. *Campagne medievali. Strutture produttive, rapporti di lavoro, sistemi alimentari.* Torino: Einaudi.

Montanari, Massimo. 1985. "Gli animali e l'alimentazione umana." In *L'uomo di fronte al mondo animale nell'alto Medioevo,* I, 619–72. Spoleto: Centro italiano di studi sull'alto Medioevo. Montanari, Massimo. 1988. *Alimentazione e cultura nel Medioevo.* Roma-Bari: Laterza.

Montanari, Massimo. 1988a. *Der Gusto der Vielfalt–Vom Duft der Unterscheidung.* In *Austria/Europa. Zur 1. EU-Präsidentschaft Österreichs 1998,* ed. Wolfgang Schüssel, 152–57. Wien: Bundesministerium für Auswärtige Angelegenheiten,

Montanari, Massimo. 1989. *Convivio. Storia e cultura dei piaceri della tavola dall'Antichità al Medioevo*. Roma-Bari: Laterza.

Montanari, Massimo. 1993. *La fame e l'abbondanza. Storia dell'alimentazione in Europa*. Roma-Bari: Laterza.

Montanari, Massimo. 1994: *The Culture of Food*. Oxford: Blackwell.

Montanari, Massimo. 1995: *La faim et l'abondance. Histoire de l'alimentation en Europe*. Paris: Seuil.

Montanari, Massimo. 1995. "Maometto, Carlo Magno e lo storico dell'alimentazione." *Quaderni medievali* 40: 64–71.

Montanari, Massimo. 1997a. "Modelli alimentari e identità culturali." In *Storia dell'alimentazione*, eds. Jean-Louis Flandrin and Massimo Montanari, 245–49. Roma-Bari: Laterza.

Montanari, Massimo. 1997b. "Strutture di produzione e sistemi alimentari nell'alto Medioevo." In *Storia dell'alimentazione*, eds. Jean-Louis Flandrin and Massimo Montanari, 217–25. Roma-Bari: Laterza.

Montanari, Massimo. 2000. "Immagine del contadino e codici di comportamento alimentare." In *Per Vito Fumagalli. Terra, uomini, istituzioni medievali*, eds. Massimo Montanari and Augusto Vasina, 199–213. Bologna: Clueb.

Montanari, Massimo. [1999] 2003. "Alimentazione." In *Dizionario dell'Occidente medievale. Temi e percorsi*, eds. Jacques Le Goff and Schmitt, 17–28. Torino: Einaudi.

Montanari, Massimo. 2004. *Il cibo come cultura*. Roma-Bari: Laterza. (*Food Is Culture*. New York: Columbia University Press, 2006.)

Montanari, Massimo. 2005. "Continuidad y rupturas, incorporaciones, diversificaciones en la época medieval y la era moderna." In *Sabores del Mediterráneo. Aportaciones para promover un patrimonio alimentario común*, eds. J. Contreras, A. Riera Melis, and F. Xavier Medina, 122–30. Barcelona: IEMed.

Montanari, Massimo. 2008. *Il formaggio con le pere. La storia in un proverbio*. Roma-Bari: Laterza. 2010: *Cheese, pears and history in a proverb*. New York: Columbia University Press.

Montanari, Massimo, and Françoise Sabban, eds. 2004. *Atlante dell'alimentazione e della gastronomia*. Torino: UTET.

Motis Dolader, Miguel Angel. 1997. "L'alimentazione degli ebrei nel Medioevo." In *Storia dell'alimentazione*, eds. Jean-Louis Flandrin and Massimo Montanari, 282–300. Roma-Bari: Laterza.

Moulin, Léo. 1984. "La bière, une invention médiévale." In *Manger et boire au Moyen Âge. Actes du Colloque de Nice (15–17 octobre 1982)*, I, 13–31. Paris: Publications de la Faculté des Lettres et Sciences Humaines de Nice.

Moulin, Leo. [1975] 1993. *L'Europa a tavola*. Reprint, Milano: Mondadori.

Murari, Krishna. 1977. *The Chalukyas of Kalyani*. Delhi: Concept Publishing.

Mutgé, Josefina. 1987. *La ciudad de Barcelona durante el reinado de Alfonso el Benigno (1327–1336)*. Madrid: Consejo Superior de Investigaciones Científicas.

Nada Patrone, Anna Maria. 1981. *Il cibo del ricco ed il cibo del povero. Contributo alla storia qualitativa dell'alimentazione. L'area pedemontana negli ultimi secoli del Medio Evo.* Torino: Centro studi piemontesi.

Nascimbeni, G. 1992. "Le nostre tasse che vengono dal Medioevo." *Corriere della Sera* (July 17): 9.

Neveu, H. 1973. "L'alimentation du XIVe au XVIIIe siècle. Essai de mise au point." *Revue d'Histoire Economique et Sociale* 51.

Newhauser, Richard. 1993. *The treatise on vices and virtues in Latin and the vernacular.* (Typologie des Sources du Moyen Age, fasc. 68.) Turnhout: Brepols.

Nicholls, Jonathan. 1985. *The Matter of Courtesy. Medieval Courtesy Cooks and the Gawain Poet.* Woodbridge: Brewer.

Nicoud, Marilyn. 2007. *Les régimes de santé au Moyen Âge: naissance et diffusion d'une écriture médicale, XIIIe–XVe siècle.* Rome: Ecole française de Rome.

Oexle, Otto Gerhard. 1979. "Die mittelalterliche Gilden: ihre Selbstdeutung und ihr Beitrag zu Formung sozialer Strukturen." In *Soziale Ordnungen in Selbstverständnis des Mittelalters,* ed. A. Zimmermann, 203–26. Berlin: de Gruyter.

Olio e vino nell'alto Medioevo. 2007. Atti della LIV Settimana di studio. 2 volumes. Spoleto: Centro italiano di studi sull'alto Medioevo.

Oliveira Marques (de) A.H. 1978. *Introduçao à história da agricultura em Portugal. A questão cerealífera durante a Idade Média.* Lisboa: Edições Cosmos.

Palermo, Luciano. 1997. *Sviluppo economico e società preindustriali. Cicli, strutture e congiunture in Europa dal medioevo alla prima età moderna.* Roma: Viella.

Pasquali, Gianfranco. 2002. *L'azienda curtense e l'economia rurale dei secoli VI–XI.* In *Uomini e campagne nell'Italia medievale,* eds. Alfio Cortonesi, Gianfranco Pasquali, and Gabriella Piccinni, 3–71. Roma-Bari: Laterza.

Pasquali, Gianfranco. 2006. "Rapporti e patti di lavoro nelle campagne inglesi nei secoli X–XII." In *Contratti agrari e rapporti di lavoro nell'Europa medievale,* Alfio Cortonesi et al., 65–86. Atti del Convegno internazionale di studi (Montalcino, 20–22 settembre 2001). Bologna: Clueb.

Pastoureau, Michel. 2007. *L'ours. Histoire d'un roi déchu.* Paris: Seuil.

Pertusi, Agostino. 1983. "Civiltà della tavola a Bisanzio e a Venezia." In *Civiltà della tavola dal Medioevo al Rinascimento,* 3–13. Vicenza: Neri Pozza.

Pesez, Jean-Marie. 1984. *La maison médiévale (XIe–XIIIe). Matériaux pour l'histoire des cadres de vie dans l'Europe occidentale (1050–1250),* 109–34. Nice: Centre d'études médiévales.

Petrone, Petronio. 2007. *Curiosa historia della forchetta.* Napoli: Guida.

Peyer, Hans Conrad. 1950. *Zur Getreidepolitik oberitalienischer Städte im 13. Jahrhundert.* Wien.

Peyer, Hans Conrad. 1987. *Von der Gastfreundschaft zum Gasthaus. Studien zur Gastlichkeit im Mittelalter.* Hannover: Monumenta Germaniae Historica, Schriften Bd. 31.

Pilcher, Jeffrey. 1998. *Que vivan los tamales! Food and the Making of Mexican Identity.* Albuquerque: University of New Mexico Press.

Pini, Antonio Ivan. 1989. *Vite e vino nel Medioevo.* Bologna: Clueb.

Pinto, Giuliano. 1978. *Il Libro del Biadaiolo. Carestie e annona a Firenze dalla metà del'200 al 1348.* Firenze: Olschki.

Pinto, Giuliano. 1982. *La Toscana nel tardo Medioevo. Ambiente, economia rurale, società.* Firenze: Sansoni.

Pinto, Giuliano. 1996. "Dalla tarda antichità alla metà del XVI secolo." In *La popolazione italiana dal Medioevo a oggi,* eds. Lorenzo Del Panta, Massimo Livi Bacci, and Giuliano Pinto. Roma-Bari: Laterza.

Pinto, Giuliano. 2008. "Congiuntura economica, conflitti sociali, rivolte." In *Rivolte urbane e rivolte contadine nell'Europa del Trecento. Un confronto,* eds. Monique Bourin, Giovanni Cherubini, and Giuliano Pinto. Firenze: Firenze University Press.

Pinto, Giuliano, and Eugenio Sonnino. 2007. "L'Italie." In *Histoire des populations de l'Europe. I. Des origines aux prémices de la révolution démographique,* eds. J.-P. Bardet and J. Dupâquier, 485–508. Paris: Fayard.

Piponnier, Françoise. 1997. "Dal fuoco alla tavola: archeologia dell'attrezzatura alimentare alla fine del Medioevo." In *Storia dell'alimentazione,* eds. Jean-Louis Flandrin and Massimo Montanari, 408–16. Roma-Bari: Laterza.

Pirani, Emma. 1996. *Miniatura Romanica.* Milano: Fabbri.

Pirenne, Henri. 1951. "Le consommateur au Moyen Âge." *Histoire économique de l'Occident médiéval,* 532–34. Paris: Desclée.

Pomeranz, Kenneth, and Steven Topik. 1999. *The World That Trade Created.* Armonk, NY: M. E. Sharpe.

Postan, Michael. 1952. "The Trade of Medieval Europe: The North." In *Cambridge Economic History of Europe,* vol. 2: *Trade and Industry in the Middle Ages,* ch. 4. Cambridge: Cambridge University Press.

Postan, Michael. 1972. *The Medieval Economy and Society. An Economic History of Britain in the Middle Ages.* Harmondsworth, Middlesex: Penguin Books.

Pounds, N.J.G. 1989. *Heart and Home. A History of Material Culture.* Bloomington: Indiana University Press.

Pray Bober, Phyllis. 1999. *Art, Culture, and Cuisine: Ancient & Medieval Gastronomy.* Chicago: The University of Chicago Press.

Pucci Donati, Francesca. 2007. *Dieta, salute, calendari. Dal regime stagionale antico ai 'regimina mensium' medievali: origine di un genere nella letteratura medica occidentale.* Spoleto: Centro italiano di studi sull'alto Medioevo.

Pucci Donati, Francesca. 2008. "Codici di comportamento alimentare nella tradizione proverbiale italiana del Medioevo e della prima Età Moderna." *Studi Medievali* III s. 49 (2): 679–701.

Redon, Odile. 1984. "Les usages de la viande en Toscane au XIVe siècle." In *Manger et boire au Moyen Âge. Actes du Colloque de Nice (15–17 octobre 1982).* Paris: Publications de la Faculté des Lettres et Sciences Humaines de Nice, II.

Redon, Odile, Françoise Sabban, and Silvano Serventi. 1998. *The Medieval Kitchen: Recipes from France and Italy* Trans. Edward Schneider. Chicago: University of Chicago Press.

Reglero, Carlos. 2011. "Les disettes dans le royaume de Castille (entre 1250 et 1348)." In *Les disettes dans la conjoncture de 1300 en Méditerranée occidentale,* eds. Monique Bourin, John Drendel, and François Menant. Roma: École Française de Rome.

Renouard, Yves. 1959. "Le grand commerce des vins de Gascogne au Moyen Âge." *Revue Historique* 221: 261–304.

Reuter, Timothy. 1991. *Germany in the Early Middle Ages, c. 800–1056.* London: Longman.

Reynolds, Philip Lyndon. 1999. *Food and the Body: Some Peculiar Questions in High Medieval Theology.* Leiden: Brill.

Riera Melis, Antoni. 1997. "Società feudale e alimentazione (secoli XII–XIII)." In *Storia dell'alimentazione,* eds. Jean-Louis Flandrin and Massimo Montanari, 307–24. Roma-Bari: Laterza.

Riera Melis, Antoni. 2000. "Transmarina vel orientalis especies magno labore quaesita, multa precio empta. Especias y sociedad en el Mediterráneo noroccidental en el siglo XII." *Anuario de Estudios Medievales* 30 (2): 1015–90.

Riera Melis, Antoni. 2005. "Las alimentaciones cristianas en Occidente durante la Edad Media." In *La alimentación y la nutrición a través de la historia,* eds. Jordi Salas-Salvadó, Pilar García-Lorda, and José Maria Sánchez-Ripollés. Barcelona: Editorial Glosa.

Riera Melis, Antoni. 2007. "Crisis frumentarias y políticas municipales de abastecimiento en las ciudades catalanas durante la Baja Edad Media." In *Crisis de subsistencia y crisis agrarias en la Edad Media,* eds. H. R. Oliva Herrer and P. Benito Monclús. Sevilla: Universidad de Sevilla.

Riera Melis, Antoni, Maria Àngels Perez-Sampe, and Mercè Gras. 1997. "El pan en las ciudades catalanas (siglos XIV–XVIII)." *Alimentazione e nutrizione, secc. XIII–XVIII,* 285–300. Prato: Istituto Internazionale di Storia Economica "F. Datini."

Rigotti, Francesca. 1999. "Del vizio della gola e di altri vizi." *Intersezioni* 19 (2): 157–84.

Roden, Claudia. 1998. *The Book of Jewish Food.* New York: Alfred A. Knopf.

Rodinson, Maxime. 1949. "Recherches sur des documents arabes relatifs à la cuisine." *Revue des études islamiques* 17: 95–165.

Romano, Giovanni. 1991. *Studi sul paesaggio.* Torino: Einaudi.

Romano, Ruggiero. 1953. "A propos du commerce du blé dans la Méditerranée des XIVᵉ et XVᵉ siècles." In *Éventail de l'histoire vivante. Hommage à Lucien Febvre* 2:149–61. Paris: Armand Colin.

Roosevelt, Anna. C. 1991. *Moundbuilders of the Amazon.* San Diego, CA: Academic Press.

Rosenberger, Bernard. 1997. *La cucina araba e il suo apporto alla cucina europea.* In *Storia dell'alimentazione,* eds. Jean Louis Flandrin and Massimo Montanari, 266–81. Roma-Bari: Laterza.

Rösener, Werner. 1985. *Bauern im Mittelalter.* München: Beck.

Rouche, Michel. 1997. "Le haut Moyen Age." In *Histoire des populations de l'Europe. I. Des origines aux prémices de la révolution démographique,* eds. J.-P. Bardet and J. Dupâquier, 133–67. Paris: Fayard.

Russel, J. C. 1972. "Population in Europe, 500–1500." In *Fontana Economic History of Europe,* 1:25–70. Edinburgh: Collins.

Sabban, Françoise, and Silvano Serventi. 2000. *La pasta. Storia e cultura di un cibo universale.* Roma-Bari: Laterza. (*Pasta: The Story of a Universal Food.* New York: Columbia University Press, 2002.)

Salrach, Josep. M. 2009. *La fam al món. Passat i present.* Vic: Eumo Editorial.

Salvatico, Antonella. 2004. *Crisi reali e carestie indotte. La produzione cerealicola nelle castellanie sabaude del Piemonte occidentale tra la metà del Duecento e il 1348.* Alessandria: Edizioni dell'Orso.

Samaritani, Antonio, and Carla Di Francesco, eds. 1999. *Pomposa. Storia, Arte, Architettura.* Ferrara: Corbo.

Santich, Barbara. 1995. "The Evolution of Culinary Techniques in the Medieval Era." In *Food in the Middle Ages: A Book of Essays,* ed. Melitta Weiss Adamson, 61–81. New York: Garland Publishing.

Schafer, Edward. 1963. *The Golden Peaches of Samarkand: A Study of T'ang Exotics.* Berkeley: University of California Press.

Schmitz, H.-J. 1968. *Faktoren der Preisbildung für Getreide und Wein in der Zeit von 800 bis 1350.* Stuttgart: Fischer.

Schmitz, Philibert. 1942–56. *Histoire de l'Ordre de Saint Benoît.* Maredsous: Éditions de Maredsous.

Schofield, Ph. R. 1998. "L'endettement et le crédit dans la campagne anglaise au Moyen Âge." In *Endettement paysan et crédit rural dans l'Europe médiévale et moderne,* ed. M. Berthe, 69–97. Toulouse: Presses Universitaires du Mirail.

Schofield, Ph. R. 2007. "Respuestas a la carestía y al hambre en el mundo rural inglés en los siglos XIII y XIV." In *Crisis de subsistencia y crisis agrarias en la Edad Media,* eds. H. R. Oliva Herrer and P. Benito Monclus, 229–43. Sevilla: Universidad de Sevilla.

Schubert, E. 2006. *Essen und Trinken im Mittelalter.* Darmstadt: Primus Verlag.

Scully, Terence. 1995. *The Art of Cookery in the Middle Ages.* Woodbridge, UK: Boydell Press.

Sereni, Emilio. 1961. *Storia del paesaggio agrario italiano.* Roma-Bari: Laterza.

Shanzer, Danuta. 2001. "Bishops, Letters, Fast, Food, and Feast in Later Roman Gaul." In *Society and Culture in Late Antique Gaul. Revisiting the Sources,* eds. R. W. Mathisen and D. Shanzer, 217–36. Aldershot: Ashgate.

Sierck, Michael. 1995. *Festtag und Politik: Studien zur Tagenwahl karolingischer Herrscher.* Köln: Böhlau.

Simms, Katherine. 1978. "Guesting and Feasting in Gaelic Ireland." *Journal of the Royal Society of Antiquaries of Ireland* 108: 67–95.

Singer, Amy. 2002. *Constructing Ottoman Beneficence: An Imperial Soup Kitchen in Jerusalem*. Albany: State University of New York Press.

Smith, Brian K. 1990. "Eaters, Food, and Social Hierarchy in Ancient India: A Dietary Guide to a Revolution of Values." *Journal of the American Academy of Religion* 58 (2): 177–205.

Smith, J.M.H. 2005. *Europe after Rome. A New Cultural History 500–1000*. Oxford: Oxford University Press.

Sourdel, Dominique, and Janine Sourdel. 1983. *La civilization de l'Islam classique*. Paris: Arthaud.

Sterckx, Roel, ed. 2005. *Of Tripod and Palate. Food, Politics, and Religion in Traditional China*. New York: Palgrave Macmillan.

Stouff, Louis. 1969. "La viande. Ravitaillement et consommation à Carpentras au XVe siècle." *Annales ESC* 24: 1431–48.

Stouff, Louis. 1970. *Ravitaillement et alimentation en Provence aux XIVe et XVe siècles*. Paris: Mouton.

Stouff, Louis. 1994. "Grains et pain dans la Provence de la fin du Moyen Âge." In *Les céréales en Méditerranée*, 39–50. Paris: CNRS.

Stouff, Louis. 1996. *La table provençale. Boire et manger en Provence à la fin du Moyen Âge*. Avignon: Alain Barthélemy.

Stubbs, W. 1874. *Memorials of St Dunstan*. (Rolls Series, n. 63.) London: Longman.

Titow, J. 1960. "Evidence of Weather in the Account Rolls of the Bishopric of Winchester, 1209–1350." *The Economic History Review* 12: 360–407.

Tits-Dieuaide, M.-J. 1975. *La formation des prix céréaliers en Brabant et en Flandre au XVᶜ siècle*. Bruxelles: Editions de l'Université de Bruxelles.

Tits-Dieuaide, M.-J. 1984. "Le grain et le pain dans l'administration des villes de Brabant et de Flandre au Moyen Âge." In *L'initiative publique des communes en Belgique. Fondements historiques (Ancien Régime)*. Bruxelles: Crédit communale de Belgique.

Toubert, Pierre. 1983. "Il sistema curtense: la produzione e lo scambio interno in Italia nei secoli VIII, IX e X." In *Storia d'Italia. Annali*, VI. *Economia naturale, economia monetaria*, eds. Ruggiero Romano and Ugo Tucci, 5–63. Torino: Einaudi.

Unger, Richard W. 2004. *Beer in the Middle Ages and Renaissance*. Philadelphia: University of Pennsylvania Press.

Valenti, Mauro, ed. 1996. *Poggio Imperiale a Poggibonsi: dal villaggio di capanne al castello di pietra*. I, *Diagnostica archeologica e campagne di scavo 1991–1994*. Firenze: All'insegna del Giglio.

Van Uytven, Raymond. 1985. "L'approvisionnement des villes des anciens Pays-Bas au Moyen Âge." In *L'approvisionnement des villes de l'Europe occidentale au Moyen Âge et aux Temps modernes*, 75–116. Auch: Centre Culturel de l'abbaye de Flaran.

Van Werveke, H. 1959. "La famine de l'an 1316 en Flandre et dans les régions voisines." *Revue du Nord* 41: 5–14.

Van Werveke, H. 1967. "De middeleeuwse hongersnood." *Mededelingen van de Koninklijke Vlaamse Academie van België* 29 (3).

Verhulst, Adriaan. 2002. *The Carolingian Economy.* Cambridge: Cambridge University Press.

Vogüé, Adalbert de. 1964. "Travail et alimentation dans les règles de saint Benoît et du Maître." *Revue bénédictine* 74: 242–51.

Volpe, Alessandro. 1999. "Pittura a Pomposa." In *Pomposa. Storia, Arte, Architettura,* eds. Antonio Samaritani and Carla Di Francesco, 95–149. Ferrara: Corbo.

Watson, Andrew. 1983. *Agricultural Innovation in the Early Islamic World.* Cambridge: Cambridge University Press.

Weatherford, Jack. 2004. *Genghis Khan and the Making of the Modern World.* New York: Three Rivers Press.

Weber, Alan S. 1998. "Queu du Roi, Roi des Queux: Taillevent and the Profession of Medieval Cooking." In *Food and Eating in Medieval Europe,* eds. Martha Carlin and Joel T. Rosenthal. London: The Hambledon Press.

Weiss, Stefan. 2002. *Die Versorgung des päpstlichen Hofes in Avignon mit Lebensmitteln (1316–1378): Studien zur Sozial- und Wirtschaftsgeschichte eines mittelalterlichen Hofes.* Berlin: Akademie-Verlag.

Wickham, Chris. 1998. "Economia altomedievale." In *Storia medievale,* 203–26. Roma: Donzelli.

Willmes, Peter. 1976. *Der Herrscher-'Adventus' im Kloster des Frühmittelalters.* Münich: Wilhelm Fink.

Wilson, C. Anne, ed. 1991. "Ritual, Form, and Colour in the Medieval Food Tradition." In *The Appetite and the Eye: Visual Aspects of Food and its Presentation within Their Historic Context.* Edinburgh: Edinburgh University Press.

Winterbottom, M., and R. M. Thomson. 2002. *William of Mamlesbury, Saints' Lives: Lives of SS. Wulfstan, Dunstan, Patrick, Benign and Indract.* Oxford: Oxford University Press.

Wolff, Philippe. 1959. "Un grand commerce médiéval: les céréales dans le bassin de la Méditerranée occidentale." In *VI Congreso de Historia de la Corona de Aragón,* 147–64. Madrid: Arges.

Wolff, Philippe. 1985. "L'approvisionnement des villes françaises au Moyen Âge." In *L'approvisionnement des villes de l'Europe occidentale au Moyen Âge et aux Temps modernes.* Auch: Centre Culturel de l'abbaye de Flaran.

Woolgar, C. M. 1999. *The Great Household in Late Medieval England.* New Haven, CT: Yale University Press.

Wright, Clifford A. 1999. *A Mediterranean Feast.* New York: William Morrow.

Zaouali, Lilia. 2004. *L'Islam a tavola. Dal Medioevo a oggi.* Roma-Bari: Laterza. (*Medieval Cuisine of the Islamic World.* Berkeley: University of California Press, 2007.)

Zulaica Palacios, F. 1994. *Fluctuaciones económicas en un periodo de crisis. Aragón en la Baja Edad Media (1300–1430).* Zaragoza: Institución Fernando el Católico.

Zylbergeld, Léon. 1973. "Le prix des céréales et du pain à Liège dans la pre-
mière moitié du XIIIe siècle." *Revue belge de philologie et d'histoire* 51: 271–
98, 761–85.

Zylbergeld, Léon. 1982. "Contribution à l'étude des ordonnances du pain du XIIIe
siècle: l'exemple de la Brodtaxe de Lübeck (1255)." *Revue belge de philologie
et d'histoire* 60: 263–304.

Zylbergeld, Léon. 1991. "Les régulations du marché du pain au XIIIe siècle en Occident et l'*Assize of Bread* de 1266–1267 pour l'Angleterre." In *Villes et campagnes au Moyen Âge. Mélanges Georges Despy,* eds. Jean-Marie Duvosquel
and Alain Dierkens, 791–814. Liège: Éditions du Perron.

NOTES ON CONTRIBUTORS

Bruno Andreolli is full professor of medieval history at the University of Bologna, Italy. His publications include *Uomini nel Medioevo. Studi sulla società lucchese dei secoli VIII–XI* (1983); *Signori e contadini nelle terre dei Pico. Potere e società rurale a Mirandola tra Medioevo ed Età moderna* (1988); and *Contadini su terre di signori. Studi sulla contrattualistica agraria dell'Italia medievale* (1999). With M. Montanari he wrote *L'azienda curtense in Italia. Proprietà della terra e lavoro contadino nei secoli VIII–XI* (1983) and edited *Il bosco nel Medioevo* (1988). With G. L. Tusini he published the volume *Memorie di un cuoco di casa Pico. Banchetti, cerimoniali e ospitalità di una corte al suo tramonto* (2002).

Pere Benito has worked as a researcher at the National Research Counsil, University of Barcelona, and the University of Paris I, Panthéon-Sorbonne. He is currently a Ramon and Cajal Researcher at the Univeristy of Lleida, where he directs two projects (financed by the Spanish Ministry of Science and Innovation and the European Commission) on the study of famine and starvation during the medieval period, and teaches in this area of specialty. He is the author of *Senyoria de la terra i tinença pagesa al comtat de Barcelona, segles XI–XIII* (2003) and coeditor of *Crisis de subsistencia y crisis agrarias en la Edad Media* (2007).

Alfio Cortonesi is full professor of medieval history at the University of Tuscia, Viterbo, Italy. He conducts research on the economic and social history of medieval Europe, with particular reference to the history of the countryside and rural work. His publications include *Uomini e campagne nell'Italia medievale* (2002, with G. Pasquali and G. Piccinni); *Medioevo delle campagne. Rapporti di lavoro, politica agraria, protesta contadina* (2008, with G. Piccinni).

Jean-Pierre Devroey is full professor of medieval history at the Université Libre de Bruxelles, and, since 2000, a member of the Belgian Royal Academy. His current research focuses on the economy and society of medieval western Europe, as well as the history of food and food systems, vineyards, and wine to the present day. An extensive survey on the rural economy and society in Europe from the sixth to the ninth centuries led to the publication of two books: *Économie rurale et société dans l'Europe franque* (2003) and *Puissants et misérables. Système social et monde paysan dans l'Europe des Francs* (2006). He also wrote the chapter "Economy" in the *Short Oxford History of Europe: The Early Middle Ages* (2001), edited by R. McKitterick.

Alban Gautier teaches medieval history at the Université du Littoral Côte d'Opale, Boulogne-sur-Mer, France, and his current research concerns the history and culture of post-Roman Christian societies in northern and northwest Europe. His doctoral thesis on feasting in Anglo-Saxon England later became a book (*Le festin dans l'Angleterre anglo-saxonne, Ve–XIe siècle*, 2006). He also published a handbook on medieval food history (*Alimentations médiévales*, 2009) and a "biography" of King Arthur (*Arthur*, 2007).

Grieco, Allen J. is a Senior Research Associate at Villa I Tatti. Dr. Grieco has co-edited several collective volumes which include: *Food Excesses and Constraints in Europe*, special issue of *Food & History* (2006), *Dalla vite al vino. Fonti e problemi della vitivinicoltura italiana nel medioevo* (Bologna, 1994) and *Le Monde végétal (XIIe–XVIIe siècles): savoirs et usages sociaux* (Vincennes, 1993). He has also published a short volume entitled *The Meal* (London and New York, 1992). Currently, he is co-editor-in-chief of *Food & History* (Turnhout, Brepols) and is also in charge of a bibliographic project on the history of food in Europe (http://www.foodbibliography.eu/index_en.asp) funded by the Mellon Foundation and the Bibliothèque Nationale de France. He has taught at Harvard, Florence, and Bologna and created an English-language graduate program at the Università delle Scienze Gastronomiche.

Massimo Montanari is full professor of medieval history at the University of Bologna, Italy. He has devoted his research to the history of agriculture, rural society, and productive systems. His most successful studies are those about food history, including in such wide-ranging areas as economics, culture, and institutions. In 2001 he was among the promoters of the European Institute for Food History and Cultures (IEHCA, Tours, France). He is the founder and director of the Master on Food History and Culture, instituted in 2002 at Bologna University and now held in collaboration with the universities of Tours, Barcelona, and Bruxelles. His main publications (several of which were translated into several languages): *L'alimentazione contadina nell'alto Medioevo* (1979); *Campagne medievali* (1984); *Alimentazione e cultura nel Medioevo* (1988); *La fame e l'abbondanza. Storia dell'alimentazione in Europa* (1993); *La cucina italiana, storia di una cultura* (with A. Capatti, 1999); *Il cibo come cultura* (2004); *Il formaggio con le pere. La storia in un proverbio* (2008); *Il riposo della polpetta e altre storie intorno al cibo* (2009); and *L'identità italiana in cucina* (2010). He edited *Storia dell'alimentazione* (1997, with J.-L. Flandrin); *Il mondo in cucina. Storia, identità, scambi* (2002); and *Atlante della gastronomia e dell'alimentazione* (2004, with F. Sabban).

Fabio Parasecoli is associate professor of food studies at the New School in New York City. His research focuses on the intersections among food, media, and politics. His current projects focus on the history of Italian food and on the sociopolitical aspects of geographical indications. He is program advisor at Gustolab, a center for food and culture in Rome, and collaborates with other institutions such as the Universitat Oberta de Catalunya in Barcelona (Spain) and the University of Gastronomic Sciences in Pollenzo (Italy). His recent publications include *Food Culture in Italy* (2004), the introduction to *Culinary Cultures in Europe* (2005), and *Bite Me! Food in Popular Culture* (2008).

Gabriella Piccinni is full professor of medieval history at the University of Siena, Italy. Her research focuses on the history of the Italian society of the Middle Ages. Her recent publications include *Medioevo delle campagne* (2006, with A. Cortonesi); *Mezzadria e potere politico* (2007); *Fedeltà ghibellina, affari guelfi* (2008); *Sede pontificia contro Bonsignori di Siena. Inchiesta intorno ad un fallimento bancario* (2009); *Le calamità ambientali nel tardo medioevo europeo*

(2010, with M. Matheus, G. Pinto, and G. M. Varanini); and *Miti di città* (2010, with M. Bettini, M. Boldrini, and O. Calabrese).

Giuliano Pinto is full professor of medieval history at the University of Florence, Italy. Since 1997 he has been director of the *Archivio storico italiano*, the oldest history magazine printed in Italy, primarily interested in the economic and social history of the Italian Middle Ages. His books include *Il Libro del Biadaiolo. Carestie e annona a Firenze dalla metà del '200 al 1348* (1978); *La Toscana nel tardo Medioevo. Ambiente, economia rurale, società* (1982); *Città e spazi economici nell'Italia comunale* (1996); *Campagne e paesaggi toscani del Medioevo* (2002); and *Il lavoro, la povertà, l'assistenza. Ricerche sulla società medievale* (2008).

Melitta Weiss Adamson is full professor of German and comparative literature at the University of Western Ontario, Canada, and holds a cross-appointment with the Department of History of Medicine. From 2006 to 2011 she served as chair of the Department of Modern Languages and Literatures. Her areas of specialization are medieval preventive medicine and cookery. In addition to numerous articles on the subject, she published the books *Medieval Dietetics* (1995), *Food in the Middle Ages* (1995), *Daz buoch von guoter spise* (2000), *Regional Cuisines of Medieval Europe* (2002), *Food in Medieval Times* (2004), and with Francine Segan the two-volume encyclopedia *Entertaining from Ancient Rome to the Super Bowl* (2008).

INDEX

www.ingramcontent.com/pod-product-compliance
Lightning Source LLC
Chambersburg PA
CBHW081432270326
41932CB00019B/3177